To Dawn

# A
# PILGRIM'S
# SONG

Bless you!

Love,

Rick

Mary Varick and her Theology of Suffering

# A
# PILGRIM'S
# SONG

## RICHARD FRITZKY

TATE PUBLISHING
AND ENTERPRISES, LLC

Published by Tate Publishing & Enterprises, LLC
127 E. Trade Center Terrace | Mustang, Oklahoma 73064 USA
1.888.361.9473 | www.tatepublishing.com

Tate Publishing is committed to excellence in the publishing industry. The company reflects the philosophy established by the founders, based on Psalm 68:11,
*"The Lord gave the word and great was the company of those who published it."*

Book design copyright © 2015 by Tate Publishing, LLC. All rights reserved.
*Cover design by Nino Carlo Suico*
*Interior design by Angelo Moralde*

Published in the United States of America

ISBN: 978-1-63306-248-1
Biography & Autobiography / Religious
15.02.25

I dedicate this book, first and foremost, to the memory of Mary Varick, who is the alpha and omega of this effort, and also to the following pilgrims who have left us and who were loved by her.

To her husband, Bill Varick, the great love of her life, who once drove the bus and was her rock and her shield; to Jerry Sheehan, another love, who devoted himself to her and found the way for her; to her ever-faithful mom and dad, Agnes and James Cassidy; to her beloved daughter Billie and son-in-law Don Adriance; to her son-in-law Joe and granddaughter Debbie; to her brothers Jim, Joe, Bud, Father Frank "Skip," and Father Jack Cassidy; to her sisters-in-law Helen and Anne Cassidy; and to her sister Rose and brother-in-law Frank Fritzky (my mom and dad)

This tribute could go on for pages, and I have already been criticized for going as far as I have with this list, but the list that follows is both of Mary and myself, and I cannot close without recognizing and celebrating their names for oh what stories are there to be told of them.

To Flossie Oates, who loved and helped carry us all and to Hank Colling, who held on to her spirit and shared her with us in ways both common and uncommon.

To Eileen Kiely and Paul Russell and Neil Gulliksen and Anne Gerhardt and Connie and Howie Daniels and Fred Vanderhoof and Mary Hafmeister and Carol Fitzgerald and Jeanette and Cecile and Yvonne and Ron Pewsey and Eric Gosling and Bob Fritzky and Jack Duffy and Jim and Claire and David Cassidy and Helen Fritzky and Sis and Bill Burlington and Buster and Dixie Evans and the Millers and John and Anna Fritzky and

Miriam and Father Rinfret and Connie LoPresti and Father Matt Pisaniello and Straight Ed and Ed the Head and dozens upon dozens upon dozens more, pilgrims all.

To the following who remain forever in Mary's embrace on earth today. To Jim Varick and his Mary and to Mary and Bruno Pisaniello and to her daughter Barbara and to Mary Colling and to John Normandin and Bishop Peter Sutton and Sandi Gautreau and Rose Ronda and Dot Cassidy and Larry Crawford and Bob Monahan and to Father Don Arel and to the grandchildren and great-grandchildren.

To the keepers of her flame, Joan Murray and Maryanne Adriance and Mike and Amy Lenehan and Cathy Buchanan and Monsignor Paul Bochicchio, Father Kevin Carter, and Father Frank Fano.

To the countless others who devoted themselves to the First Saturday Club both in days gone by and today.

To all remembered by or prayed for by you.

All were welcome at Mary Varick's table and so too are they here. They are all part of Mary Varick's family and so too of this tribute.

# Contents

# Foreword

The following pages are a "labor of love" that capture, in a very meaningful way, a woman whose entire life and ministry were a "labor of love." Rich Fritzky powerfully captures his aunt Mary Varick, a woman who many of us knew and loved. Through research, interviews, and correspondence from great figures like Blessed Mother Teresa of Calcutta, Bishop Peter Sutton, and Father Jacques Rinfret, we experience vivid and inspiring memories. Our author paints a striking portrait of a woman deeply in love with God and "God's inner circle" and her suffering and loving disabled, whom she served with a reckless abandon.

The term *ministry* often applies to an official or ordained in service to God's people, but since the Second Vatican Council, we have seen the recognition of many ministries that have enriched not only the Church but also humanity at large. Mary was certainly a minister of God's love to many. From her deep and loving concern for others and her ability to recognize and affirm the human dignity of every person she met and especially of those who were part of "God's inner circle," she became a source of great inspiration to all whose paths she crossed.

I first met Mary when I was assigned for apostolic work and later as a transitional deacon at St. Lucy's parish in Newark, New Jersey. Mary lived in the Colonnade Apartments, not far from the church, and would often come to Mass at St. Lucy's. From the moment I met her, the bond of friendship was forged. We sponsored one of her First Saturday Club Masses and luncheons at St. Lucy's and in every parish at which I served as a priest: Our

Lady of Mercy, Holy Rosary, both in Jersey City; Our Lady of Mt. Virgin, Garfield; and currently, Holy Family, Nutley.

I accompanied Mary and the First Saturday family, as a chaplain, to Russia, Rome, Assisi, Lourdes, and the Holy Land, as well as, for the past forty-four years, to Canada, where we'd regularly visit Saint Joseph's Oratory in Montreal, Our Lady of The Cape in Trois-Rivieres, and Sainte-Anne-de-Beaupre outside of Quebec City. On these pilgrimages, it has been a joy to involve young people from all of the above named parishes as well as students from Roselle Catholic High School and Seton Hall University, where I once served as a campus minister, in the ministry of serving and learning from their brothers and sisters in "God's inner circle."

It was my privilege to visit Mary and learn more from this wonderful mentor on the day before she went home to the Lord on June 27, 1989, and to preach at her funeral Mass at St. Lucy's in Newark, as well as at the sixtieth anniversary of her cure at Sainte-Anne-de-Beaupre in Canada on July 17, 2011.

May these pages open your heart to discover a remarkable servant of God whose life and courageous faith will, hopefully, lead you to embrace the great and sustaining love of God.

Monsignor Paul L. Bochicchio

# Preface

My Aunt Mary!

There was no one quite like her. A woman of faith, she took risks and smiled when the storm clouds gathered.

In my childhood, I once thought that all children, everywhere, had to have an Aunt Mary. Why not? It just seemed to be one of those "natural order of the universe" deals. After all, didn't every child need a mom for the love and affection, a dad for the discipline and the structure, and an Aunt Mary for the truth and the wisdom?

Or an Aunt Mary to, at least, tell you the truth and reveal those hidden secrets about your mom and dad and your world, the ones that better humanize and clarify!

Certainly, all children should have had an Aunt Mary.

Why not?

But as one year gave way to the next and the next, I came to learn that, beyond my siblings and cousins, no one ever had an Aunt Mary who was anything quite like ours.

And I do mean no one.

For she, indeed, swayed to the beat of a different drummer and lively stepped to the music she heard, and though disabled and broken in so many ways, she lived to do extraordinary things in extraordinary ways for a God she deeply loved.

She was not perfect, but she did many perfect things. And she was most certainly larger than life.

Committed to a wheel chair, she bore the brightest smile and spent her whole life in the fast lane, bringing life and belonging and faith and purpose to the ever-expanding community of disabled that she formed and served or what she called "God's inner circle."

This is her story, not by way of strict biography, although the key components of biography will be well addressed, but rather by way of commentary, reflection, and even prayer.

We are, you see, much more interested in her soul and her spirit than in the fine details of pure biography.

Yes, it is the story of Mary Varick or Mary Cassidy Varick or Mary Varick (Sheehan) or just Mary or Mom or Grandma or Aunt Mary or the "leader of the band" of the Our Lady of Fatima First Saturday Club family. As time and tide warrant, she will be referenced as anyone of the above. That works, of course, because she was all of the above and ever so much more.

I know it sounds gratuitous, but I wish that you could have had her as your aunt as well. For everyone would have done well to have had her in their lives. That would have been a real good thing for our all-too-broken world, because she was a rainmaker of peace and goodwill, who loved her God and who strove, day-by-day, to know Him ever more intimately.

What is most important is that she had this extraordinary capacity to bring people home to God as well. That was her over-arching mission. Her life's calling!

She was oh-so intimate with God.

In bringing people to God, she bore no magic bullet, she was never pompous or overbearing, she was neither proud nor preachy nor over the top, she did not come down from on high, and she respected all for who they were right where they were and as they were. But naturally, freely, spontaneously, she could just get to people and move the mountains before them and the baggage that may have been weighing them down.

Bearing witness just came naturally to her.

And so did freeing people!

She touched souls and took them higher. With a devotion to Mary, the Mother of God, and Saint Anne, her Mother, that was unparalleled, each became, for her, a vibrant portal to the life and love of Jesus Christ. The overarching objective for Mary Varick forever remained to freely and easily help people make their way homeward to the embrace of God's peace and love.

So while not your aunt, it is our belief and hope that she can still be a touchstone and light in your life. And why not! Because what she did for good and grace most assuredly lives on and will be brightly affirmed here. Like each and every act of love ever extended, what she fashioned is still out there. It is my hope that her peace and the wonder fashioned by her mission, in memory and words and story, might still rain down upon you and others and make a difference in your lives today, just as it did, very powerfully, in the worlds of those who knew and followed her in her lifetime.

Her life was and remains a gift outright that can and should well be embraced by all, and so this work is tenderly offered as a gift of remembrance—*A Pilgrim's Song*.

Born Mary Cassidy, she came into the world on November 30 in 1914 in Margaret Hague Maternity Hospital in Jersey City, New Jersey, the poor man's New York City, which lies on the western side of the mighty Hudson River. And for the record, all claims to the contrary, Jersey City is the rightful home of the Statue of Liberty.

It belonged to Mary and her siblings and her neighbors.

Why, you could, through a maze of low-lying apartment and industrial buildings, see Lady Liberty right from the home where Mary grew up.

She came into life as "the war to end all wars" was in full throttle and President Woodrow Wilson was mapping out his Fourteen Points and plans for a League of Nations which he promised would assure peace among all nations forevermore. She came into life just as young Americans, in the hundreds of thousands, were about to go "over there, over there" to die for some vague illusion, in a war that made no sense whatsoever.

It is interesting that she entered the world at that time when world leaders would rather dare than think—at a time when the utter madness of World War One raged, for she, a peaceful warrior, was to be a harbinger of the very antithesis of war.

She would come to be the founder of an organization that offered as its primary mission—prayers for peace.

She was the third of the seven children to be born to James and Agnes Cassidy. As it was, James and Joseph preceded her, and she was to be followed by Rose, my sweet mom, Edward "Buddy," Francis "Skip," and John "Jack." Among the ten thousand or so semi-impoverished Irish families that dominated the urban heights of the Lafayette section of Jersey City at the time, her family subsisted at somewhere just above the poverty level as most of the Irish then did.

They were a close knit and proud and faithful family that didn't have a pride, so big, that it precluded them from accepting Mayor Frank "I Am the Law" Hague's free Thanksgiving and Christmas turkeys. As it was, there were two forces in play that were driving the sociological ascendancy of the Irish at the time. The first was politics, and the second was the organization of the American working man. The one was the power of office, and the other was the power of unionization.

All across the Northeast, Irish mayors were being elected and changing paradigms, and the fact that they were characters and rogues and largely corrupt only rendered them all the more charming and interesting.

Only the Irish!

In my Nana's or Agnes' later years (Mary's mom), I can see myself, with all the wisdom of the typical college student who thought he knew everything but actually knew very little, reproaching her for her lasting affection for Frank Hague and John V. Kenny, the crème de la crème of bosses who, for so long, ruled Jersey City with an iron fist. I'd say, "But, Nan, they were brutal crooks," and she'd say, "That may be true, but they weren't like the rest of them. For every three dollars they stole, they, at least, gave two dollars back to us."

By that accounting, my Nana's accounting, Hague then had to give away some twenty million dollars to people like her over the years for never having made more than nine thousand dollars per year as a public official, he retired with a fortune of some ten million dollars.

So there it was, the paradox, the irony, the rationalization of my almost-saintly grandmother, Mary's mother, who could no more deceive or cheat a living soul than have her teeth fall out, defending men who were most certainly among the greatest deceivers and cheaters in American political history. As to that other force, the unionization of the American working man, it came home directly to Mary for her dad, James or "Jim," the kindest man on earth, was in the thick of that fight, as he was a tenement-storming organizer for the Railroad Workers of America.

The Cassidys of Jersey City, like their Irish ancestors who built the intercontinental railroad that Abraham Lincoln remarkably set in motion in the midst of the Civil War, were a railroad family through and through.

But those two great forces, forces that would soon be dramatically compounded by the agony of the Great Depression that came into play, forces that so impacted my maternal family, were but ex-factors in the big picture. They affected for sure. How could they not? But they did not effect. What effected was the predominant driving force within the heart of the heart of that family, and that was their faith.

If there was ever a family that could truly live on faith alone, it was this bunch.

Two parents and seven incredibly decent children. Two of whom would become priests. And among the seven was Mary, my mom's sister and lifelong confidante! There's this picture of my own mom that never fades—there she is, sitting on the steps to the second floor by the desk that housed that old black rotary phone, talking somewhere around midnight to Mary. Night after night, that picture would be recreated, night after night, again and again and again, during the course of Mary and Rose's lifetime together.

Each of these seven Cassidys are, of course, worthy of their own stories, but this one is Mary's, who grew up Irish Catholic and looked to God and Jesus of Nazareth in all things and thanked Him, beyond measure, for the little that was hers—the little materially, that is.

For as to those spiritual, loving intangibles, she had it all and that's what she lived on when the cupboard was bare. And all of life, in her youth, somehow revolved around that wonderful old gothic or mini Notre Dame that was on the corner of their *Pacific* Avenue block, All Saints Church. Interesting that one who forever prayed for peace grew up on a street named after peace! It was All Saints Grammar School and All Saints Commercial and the good Sisters of Charity from Convent Station and the parish priests housed at All Saints Rectory who engaged Mary daily.

And I mean daily, as no child of Agnes Cassidy ever missed a day of school. It was perfect attendance medals for all. Year after year! The legend even suggests that she went so far as to send them to school with the chicken pox. All it took was a lot of calamine lotion and a shove out the door.

Now, as to the power of the stock that Mary came from, it also helps to understand that her mom ran away from home in Philadelphia when she was but sixteen years old. Yes, she ran away from an abusive father and had the moxie and courage to take her eleven-year-old younger sister, Mary, with her. Through the grace of God, she then ran into the arms of James Cassidy, the railroad man, in Jersey City. She was only seventeen when they were wed, and they eventually came to live at 243 Pacific Avenue in the Lafayette section of Jersey City, a quaint, brick-faced, classic, three-story walk-up.

It was a long thin house with great character and a small back-yard that was embraced and surrounded by teeming shores of row houses. It had the tiniest of kitchens and a dining room that was barely big enough to fit a table and china closet in, but it lives in my memory, as a slice of heaven, as it had this earthy warmth and coziness. In the early to mid-twentieth century, its greatest asset, however, lied in the fact that it was, most importantly and for-tuitously, just a stroll down the corner to All Saints Church. This allowed Agnes and Jim to attend mass daily in the wee hours before the day's demands would crash down upon them. And this daily act of devotion had more to do with how their children were raised and what Mary would forever carry throughout her life than anything else that Agnes and Jim ever did.

Mary would be challenged and challenged, bitterly at times, by the polio that struck her in 1916 at the toddling age of sixteen months during the great polio epidemic and by ever so much more over the years. While she doubted, in her youth and in the wake of her polio, that anything about her life could ever be nor-mal, life turned upside down when she met the handsome and endearing Bill Varick, who was eight years her senior, at Crater Lake. Bill vacationed in the cabin right next door to the green-and-white clapboard cabin that Mary's dad, brothers, and friends managed to build there despite the depression.

Crater Lake was a great and naturally beautiful haven and escape in the Blue Mountains of northwestern New Jersey, a heaven on earth, and it is somehow fitting that its sweet summer breezes and cool waters and blazing sunsets conspired to bring

Bill and Mary together by the old red swing on the porch of the Cassidy's *Glocca Morra*.

While they fell in love, they put the question of whether or not they belonged together into God's hands and made a novena to the Sacred Heart of Jesus in the fall of 1936 to reflect upon the same. Can you imagine that? For who among us invites God to so freely weigh in on such matters of the heart today? It is enough for us to know that Mary Cassidy and Bill Varick most certainly did.

On the last night of that novena, while sitting at the dining room table at 243 Pacific Avenue, they received their answer, as God speaks in the most ordinary of ways. Mary's mom approached them and said that she had been noticing how much time they had been spending together and, as such, she had a gift for the two of them.

It just happened to be a framed picture of the Sacred Heart, a gift that answered all questions and eliminated all doubts for Bill and Mary. They were wed on June 4, 1937, appropriately upon the Feast of the Sacred Heart, and they proceeded, in time, to live in the row house immediately next door to her mom and dad at 241 Pacific Avenue, which allowed Agnes to assist Mary in raising the four children that she and Bill brought into the world. Billie, Jimmy, Barbara, and Mary, all of whom, of course, will live large in this—their mom's—story.

Indeed, to contact each other, all Agnes or Mary needed to do was to simply knock on the wall.

But the defining moment in Mary's life was a by-product of a vile bone cancer that invaded her body at the age of thirty-six. Deemed by her doctor to be terminal, he told Bill that she had no more than six months to live, yet in desperation, he still proceeded to radiate her twice a week, when radiation was but experimental.

Her dying "make a wish" was to visit the Basilica of Sainte-Anne-de-Beaupre, the Lourdes of North America, which was just north of Quebec City in the province of Quebec, Canada on the banks of the mighty Saint Lawrence River. Through personal prayer and long reflection, she had grown particularly close and devoted to Blessed Mary, the Mother of Jesus, and Mary's own Mother, Good Saint Anne. So visiting Sainte-Anne's was all that she wished for, just to see this place that her dad had told her about long ago, as he massaged her legs in the early-morning hours to prevent atrophy, when she was a child.

Her doctor considered the mere idea of such a journey to be insane and strongly advised against it, as he believed that the travel would be far too much for Mary to bear, given the state of her cancer. Bill, then a bus driver for Public Service, and Buddy, her younger brother and a railroad man, despite the admonitions of the doctor, made ready anyway.

Because Mary, as you will come to realize, was one particularly persuasive woman!

They took off in the heat of July of 1951. To Quebec and Sainte-Anne-de-Beaupre, they traveled north in a borrowed vehicle, with an extremely sick Mary, who had been largely relegated to bed. So she lied in a rough-hewn car bed that they had fashioned across the backseat. Very sick, but very elated, she was.

It was all so out of the box, for this wasn't a great tourist destination or marvelous city or beach or even her own beloved Crater Lake that she longed for, but Sainte-Anne-de-Beaupre, a basilica that sat on the banks of the Saint Lawrence in northern Quebec, a place devoted to Mary, the mother of Jesus, and to her mother, Good Saint Anne.

In her sights, for whatever reason, there was simply this long, lingering desire to gather with Saint Anne. It was an idea that had been planted in her mind by her dad when she was a mere child, an idea that had for so long lingered within. "How wonderful it would be to visit there together someday," they would both say, but it was not to be. And so, riddled with a deadly cancer, she said, "Now!"

The three wary travelers made it, after an exhausting three days. Mary was so sick that they had to get her out of the car repeatedly to allow her to lie on the green grass or weeds on the side of the road just to breathe the fresh air. The stifling combination of a late-stage cancer and July's oppressive heat and no air-conditioning conspired against the three of them, but they soldiered on. As it was, Buddy believed that they should have and urged them to turn back after the first day of travel, as the punishment Mary was taking was just too much.

But she insisted and they made it, and Mary, sick as she was on the way up, went on to spend what proved to be a few wonderful days in the loving embrace of the Mother of the Mother of God.

Finally fulfilled!

There at Sainte-Anne's, that "heaven on a hillside," the cancer notwithstanding, all was, for a moment in time, made right with the world and with Mary's way of being in it. And then on July 17, while praying before the statue of Saint Anne, the spectacular one by the main altar, carved from a single piece of oak, she found herself inexplicably rising from her wheelchair and then tearfully kneeling beneath it.

All the while, she had been praying not for a cure or an end to her disabilities, but rather and only for the hope of watching her children grow. Shaken and moved by what transpired, she well knew that something mysterious and profound had happened, but the ramifications of its ends remained wholly unknown.

The earth had, indeed, moved and she with it, but there was only wonder and mystery and the manifestation of grace in the moment. The wax on the candle she had been holding for the closing procession had, unbeknownst to her, melted and enveloped her hand—and long unable to transport herself, she had been unwittingly transported to the foot of the cross. She was kneeling and an unfamiliar and profound rush ran through her body.

While she knew something had happened, she knew not what. She clearly remained the same crippled victim of polio. After all, she had just prayed to remain disabled. What she always described as "her coveted place at the foot of the cross" had been secured.

On the return journey, however, back to work and to struggle and to the lonely and desperate inevitability of terminal cancer, Mary grew more active, more animated, and more alive.

No longer resigned to the bed in the backseat, she needed to sit up and enjoy the ride.

Enjoying herself, she laughed heartily at the frustration of Bill and Bud, when their tired and beat-up vehicle broke down! It was as if she had found a new source of energy, a new spark, a wholly new and unexpected vitality. Now, neither Bill's nor Bud's nor even Mary's mind wandered then to thoughts of the miraculous. Bill and Bud just thanked God that Mary had this wildly appreciated and wholly unanticipated gift of feeling good for a change—simply feeling good—for a few precious days.

That might well have been miracle enough!

No one could mistake the fact that she had come home renewed. Much more than renewed, her doctor was amazed, upon her next visit, shortly after her return, to discover that there was suddenly and impossibly no sign of the bone cancer that had been ravaging and destroying.

No sign whatsoever!

The killer in her had been slain.

Mary did not go to Canada or to the altar of Sainte-Anne-de-Beaupre for a miracle. Miracles hadn't even been in her vocabulary. She had gone for peace and resolution and understanding and grace, the grace with which to accept her own death and the grace with which to steel her husband and her children for her passing.

But then again, she did let Saint Anne know that it would be nice to, at least, hold the cancer at bay for a time, so she could watch her children grow some. She would gladly pay the price of piling on the suffering for some more time. Just to be with them as they grew. Yes, she longed for and prayed for more time only, more time—in the grip of a familiar suffering. She did not ask for a cure.

She expressed feelings only, without placing demands or harboring expectations.

But a miracle was precisely what she got.

A miracle was exactly what she got!

Now, no one sees themselves as being worthy of a miracle. Few even believe in the possibility. And some will, in the grasp of the doubt and fear that clouds their own living, never accept the reality or truth of a story like this, the story of Mary's miracle, of Mary's encounter with something that had been an impossibility up until the moment before it happened.

A miracle, after all, is a miracle, something that is—as it was written in the *Archives of Sainte-Anne-de-Beaupre*—beyond medical explanation.

There is no rationalizing a miracle and Mary's profoundly spoke for itself.

The cancer was gone!

Of course, she didn't need anyone's affirmation or approval. She just knew what lied ahead. And she determined to bear witness to what she knew, to the fact that she was, through the grace and intervention of her beloved Saint Anne, born again. Life was literally breathed back into her by a loving God and absolutely nothing would ever be the same.

So she would give all the days to come, somehow and someway, to service and to goodness and to God.

Thirty-seven when she was cured at Sainte-Anne's, she lived almost thirty-eight more years and died, with buoyant courage and expectation, in the company of her family and my mom and dad. Mother Teresa too had come to visit her just days before, upon learning how sick Mary was from her son Jim who had been invited to a private mass that was said by Archbishop McCarrick, then of the Newark Archdiocese, at the Contemplative House of her Missionaries of Charity in Plainfield, New Jersey.

On June 27, 1989, Mary, after a lifetime of joyful suffering, went home to God. As Mother Teresa told Mary's children, it was her "homegoing to Jesus."

It is the thirty-eight years that followed the cure and what she put in motion because of that cure that draw our attention, as well as the years that have followed her "homegoing."

Mary went on to spend the rest of her life organizing pilgrimages and eventually leading the Our Lady of Fatima First Saturday Club that worked to gather the suffering disabled from institutions, hospitals, developmental homes, homes for the blind, etc., together, at least once a month, to enjoy mass, pray the rosary, break bread together, and celebrate some. She organized a wide network of volunteers from throughout northern New Jersey parishes and got the parishes themselves to commit to hosting her club which grew and grew and grew.

In the summer of 1952, following her miracle, she organized her first pilgrimage with other disabled friends to the great shrines of Quebec, Saint Joseph's in Montreal, and, of course, her beloved Sainte-Anne's in Beaupre. May and Andy Gnapp were among the very first of Mary's pilgrims, and it was May, in the midst of the second pilgrimage in 1953, who spoke to Mary of Our Lady of the Cape in Three Rivers, which was geographically located right between Sainte-Anne's and Saint Joseph's. They stopped by on the way home and were invited to spend the night at the Pilgrim's House by a delighted Father Reneau, and it forever became part of the itinerary.

At first, they traveled in caravans of old automobiles, and then they went in trains of Pullman train cars and for some years by plane, but largely by bus. Some years, there were as many as four separate pilgrimages. But Mary didn't stop there, as she fundraised and begged, borrowed, and nigh on stole to take her legions of the disabled to Fatima and Lourdes and Rome and the Holy Land and Guadalupe and even Russia, in the heart of the Cold War, to pray the rosary at what was then Leningrad and now Saint Petersburg.

Who else but Mary could have gotten the politburo to allow this act of defiance in a land where even God Himself had been exiled?

Mary was always in trouble and flat broke and materially destitute, but always wildly happy and entirely devoid of fear. Temporal realities were never allowed to interfere with her endless spiritual missions.

She truly lived and acted on faith alone.

Dozens upon dozens of priests, religious, and bishops rallied to her cause over the years, and she walked in the company of spiritual luminaries like Bishop Sheen and her dear friend, Mother Teresa, the kindred spirit, who shortly before Mary died, said, "Mary, you are going home to God. Now when you get there, you tell him how much we love him—you put in a good word for me." To which Mary softly responded, "There is no need."

Two of Mary's younger brothers, in Agnes and Jim's faithful family, became priests, and they, Fathers John and Francis Cassidy, often walked with Mary in the early days. But prominent among the other priests who long served by her side were the Father Hornaks, also brothers from parishes in Jersey City and Gutenberg, New Jersey, in the formative days, Father Eugene Lefebvre, C.Ss.R. from Sainte-Anne's, and Father Jacques Rinfret from Our Lady of the Cape. Father Rob Garafolo came along later in the fifties, and later still, there were Father Don Arel, another member of the Oblates of Mary Immaculate, Bishop Stanton, and Bishop Peter Sutton, and for forty-four years now, there has been Monsignor Paul Bochicchio, recently the pastor of Holy Family in Nutley, who first joined arms with Mary when a deacon in the late sixties. Father Kevin Carter, today's pastor of Saint Margaret's in Little Ferry, also has had a more than thirty-six-year association with the First Saturday Club family that began when he was a young volunteer and friend of Michael Adriance, Mary's grandson.

Monsignor Paul and Father Kevin remain dedicated to Mary's ministry today in 2014, as does the recently ordained Father Frank Fano, who also has enjoyed a more than twenty-five-year association with the First Saturday Club's Canadian pilgrimages. His journey with the First Saturday family began when he was a bright, young altar boy.

The longevity of the associations with all three of these wonderful priests who continue to work with Mary's ministry, twenty-five years after her passing, speaks loudly and magnificently. As Father John Cassidy said so long ago, "When Mary got to you, you were gotten."

There were two components or purposes that Mary wanted to serve.

The first was spiritual. She wanted to help clean up the garbage and trash that people, who were hurting and on the edge, were carrying and cut through the heart of their brokenness to bring them closer to God. She wanted them to see, as she saw, to understand, as she understood, to recognize, as she long recognized that debilitation and brokenness and pain and suffering, in the end, only brought them closer to God.

They were, as she so often said, "God's inner circle."

The second was social. She opened the doors of the institutions where they were confined and, in so doing, opened the door to relationship and "friendship." She wanted to let them breathe

the free air every now and then and to be embraced by a community of love of their own making.

She wanted to build a mighty family and she did.

That's, indeed, what she did—she built a community of love that served her warriors in "God's inner circle." To Lourdes and Rome, she took sixty-seven people in wheel chairs on one trip alone in 1967. While the first pilgrimage to Canada was in the summer of 1952, the first gathering of her club was on a First Saturday in March of 1960.

It continues to this very day, as only one summer has been without a pilgrimage and only a few First Saturdays have ever been missed when severe weather or the oddest of circumstances precluded. While the first pilgrimage, in a then caravan of cars, was so quickly organized, the organization of the club followed some nine years later at the urging of Bill, who put the bug in Mary's ear about Our Lady of Fatima's call to devotion on First Saturdays.

He also envisioned the importance of building a family, a living and breathing and tangible community of support for her "inner circle," which they, indeed, became over time.

Almost twenty-five years after her passing, this legacy endures. Some are autistic and some are victimized by ALS or cerebral palsy and some by multiple sclerosis or muscular dystrophy and some lost their legs and some are quads and they are all hers, all Mary's still.

To this very day, they remain hers.

A dear friend, Hank Colling, passed away, in great peace, on Christmas Eve of 2012 in Williamsport, Pennsylvania. For forty-seven years, he suffered as a quadriplegic, after his life was forever turned upside down by a horrific fall from a roof when he was only twenty-three. It was he who told me over dinner at a cafeteria at Our Lady of the Cape a few years ago that Mary's story, this story, the full story needed to be written and that it fell to me to write it.

It was my task, he said, because I uniquely and singly bridged the world of both the volunteer and the disabled in the First Saturday family.

As a child, I, like many in my family, was drafted into Aunt Mary's army. There was no need to volunteer for you were volunteered, freely given up by your mom to Aunt Mary. I believe that I first went to Canada when I was fifteen in 1965, and I went fairly regularly every summer, at least on one of the trips, as there were multiple trips in the old days. I would, along with others, go to carry and push the chairs, to lift the disabled, to wash, to feed, to nurture, and to befriend.

I went regularly until the age of twenty-seven or so, when the pace of life and commitments and an eventually growing family took me out.

I look back upon it now and wonder how I ever let myself get pulled away, for every memory I have is sacrosanct. They were always engaging, wonderful experiences. With Aunt Mary, in Canada, as I ran around like a proverbial chicken with its head cut off, I was healed. Each time, healed. Blessed, holier, happier, life always became brighter there. There was always something about the disabled who you got close to or about the family and friends journeying with you that was special. Somehow in Canada, it was easy to let go of the baggage and oh-so easy to fall in love with a network of people forever.

I also was touched by the priests and so enjoyed the company. I have such fond memories of scurrying around with Jim Varick, Mary's son, and with magnificent priests like Father Bob Antzack and Father Don Arel. As to today's team, I am in love with them all.

In reaching out to God, through the great and loving portals of His Mother and His Mother's Mother, oh what wonders became yours.

With my Aunt Mary in Canada, I was lifted up. Always!

But I long went on sabbatical and did not return until the summer of 2007, fully thirty years later. As to why, it is enough to know that I married *up*—as we Irish say—my beautiful Maggie, became the loving father of twelve children, and lived in fourth gear or overdrive.

I did, after all, just say twelve children, so Canada somehow became but a fond and fading memory. Twelve children, needless to say, demand fourth gear and overdrive. To have twelve is to live a life uncommon. And God bless my Maggie, who alone in the world could actually make it seem normal.

I returned because Aunt Mary started calling me. Yes, Aunt Mary called me out first, but she was soon followed by my sister Joan, who together with my cousin Mary Anne Adriance, Mary's granddaughter, continue to organize the pilgrimages today.

After my bout with neisseria meningitidis in the fall of 2005 reduced me to physical rubble, after the coma, after the feverish deliriums, after the quadruple amputations, I found Aunt Mary in rehab at the Kessler Institute for Rehabilitation in West Orange, New Jersey. It happened on a bright Saturday morning in the gym as a brilliant sun radiated through the large windows. In the back of my head, the words *It was only on-the-job training* kept rising up. *It was only on-the-job training. Just on-the-job training, man!*

It was one of those "knockdown and say what" moments, as conscious me found himself confronting an extraordinary fact. *For there, with Aunt Mary, all those summers, long ago in Canada, I was being steeled, being made ready, for what I would become.* There I was, legless, atrophied, fingerless, and very, very broken and the voice within kept telling me, *You know the drill, man. You do.*

*What you experienced way back then was only on-the-job training. You know what this demands. You are called.*

I had taken a place among the "inner circle," so designated long, long ago by my Aunt Mary.

The thought that I had been in "on-the-job training," for what I would become thirty to forty years later, stunned me! Largely because it was true! Connie and Cecelia and Freddie and Ron and Anne and Howie and Flossie and Hank—they had all steeled me years ago, simply by sharing their loving, disabled humanity with me.

In having lived in their hearts, I knew what my new life demanded.

A bolt of lightning out of the blue, it threw me, and there I found myself once more, in rich four-color memory, sitting on the bottom of Aunt Mary's bed, just as I so often did, in the wee hours, after the troops had been settled. There we'd be at the Auberge at Sainte-Anne's or at the Madonna House or the Pilgrim's House at the Cape listening to Aunt Mary's stories or parables.

That room was always crowded and filled with laughter, for Aunt Mary believed that it was important to both pray hard and to play hard. Post midnight, we played, as Aunt Mary held court. Not because she pushed herself on people, but rather because people pushed themselves on her.

Everyone on every trip wanted a slice of her, for to be in her company was to be in the company of grace.

It was in those sessions where I well remember her voicing theories about the meaning of suffering. It was there when I first heard, my aunt, who suffered from just about every ailment known to human kind, say that pain must be given away to God, freely given away, for when so given, grace could be fashioned, a healing grace to be showered upon others.

What a wonder!

There was a power in suffering, and she suggested that the disabled and those in pain were given that power as a gift, which in the end would only free them from the cares of the world and bring them closer to their God.

Yes, give the pain away, she told me, and unlock its redemptive powers. Give it to God and free yourself and so transform the unbearable into the bearable. I have upfront and personal and profound memories of Aunt Mary preaching this gospel, one that she would articulate with unimagined wonder when reflecting upon the Stations of the Cross.

All of this gave way to her ever-evolving, profound theology of suffering.

And there, at Kessler, having lived when only dying was expected, there in the throes of a harsh and bitter and difficult and very painful recovery, there chalking off another day on what would be a 441-day journey before I earned home, there on the evening of the very morning that "on-the-job training" echoed in me, my friends Hank and Mary Colling arrived. Hank, ever Mary's apostle, was there, through the grace of God that night, to remind me of what Aunt Mary had long ago taught me and to fire up the embers that were still burning deep within.

I have no doubt that Aunt Mary, then in her seventeenth year with God, conspired with Hank Colling, my old and special friend, that day. For he was the affirmation and the exclamation point! He came, after all, on the very day that the memories of my beautiful aunt and having been on "on-the-job training" and the power of her theology of suffering burned in me.

Wow! It was a day that left no doubt and that profoundly moved, purposefully moved, a very broken, but not-dead-yet me.

Hank looked me in the eyes and reached into the heart of what was then unbelievable suffering, and said, "You must give it to God, Rich. You must give your pain away. Give it away and the grace of God will carry both you and others forward." That is exactly what my dear, long-suffering, quadriplegic friend said to me.

And he was right, just as Aunt Mary had been right. And so it is! Living testament to chronic pain that I am, I give it to God always. I do and what is intolerable is made tolerable.

I have faith and so it is, every time.

Every time, as Hank reminded me what Aunt Mary taught me! Every single time!

I live as Aunt Mary would have me live.

I do not ask for cures. I do not even ask God to take the pain away. I ask only that He be with me in the pain. And He is and I prevail. Again and again, I prevail, because God is with me.

And so, as one who has been upgraded to her "inner circle" today, I like to think that my Aunt Mary would be proud of me.

And so, I have here listened to Hank, once again. For like him, I too believe that it has fallen to me to try to do some justice, in words and in stories and in reflection, to what Mary Varick and her First Saturday Club have given to this world over the years.

Rich in faith and filled with the presence of God, there's a genuine magic in what she built and in the life and the love and the joy and the peace that countless people, through her intercession in their lives, enjoyed—simply because Mary Varick did not sit back when God called, but rather paid her own miracle forward.

As to the legions of the suffering and disabled who followed her lead over the years, there have been no further miracles—not one—but they did not go for miracles. They went for life. They went because they longed to become intimate with their God. They went to know him and to love Him and to share Him and His abundant love with everyone in their lives.

And that was found, and continues to be found, in rich and startling abundance.

This is the story of the wonder and magic that one human being who sought to bring people closer to their God can fashion.

It is the story of Mary Varick and what is now sixty-three years of pilgrimages to the great shrines of Quebec. It also is the story of fifty-four consecutive years of gathering on the First Saturday of each month to join with Our Blessed Mother in praying for peace on earth. In 2015, the Our Lady of Fatima First Saturday Club will gratefully celebrate its 650th consecutive session. Like the first time, Mass will be said and the rosary will be prayed, and a community of love will break bread together and love one another and explore ways to better serve.

The great good that it fashioned only ascended and expanded as the years passed.

A compelling sojourn into the heart and soul of Mary Varick, it just might fire up those embers burning inside you as well and take you to higher ground.

Which is, after all, why we write—and what is more, it is why we write from a place of wonder and great love and genuine passion. In this work, the author is not so much lost in a search to understand, but rather in a search as to how best to bear witness to what a life has meant, a life to be celebrated. For Mary Varick made a difference, an extraordinary difference, and the gifts she gave and the grace she fashioned may still be freely given.

## Placeholders

- She was not perfect, but she did many perfect things.

- For as to those spiritual, loving intangibles, she had it all and that's what she lived on when the cupboard was bare. And all of life somehow revolved around that wonderful old gothic or mini Notre Dame that was on the corner of their block, All Saints Church. It was All Saints Grammar School and All Saints Commercial and the sisters and priests housed there who engaged Mary daily.

- The earth had, indeed, moved and she with it, but there was only wonder and mystery and the manifestation of grace in the moment. The wax on the candle she had been holding for the closing procession had, unbeknownst to her, melted and enveloped her hand—and long unable to transport herself, she had been unwittingly transported to the foot of the cross. She was kneeling, and an unfamiliar rush ran through her body.

- What she always described as "her coveted place at the foot of the cross" had been secured.

- Now, no one sees themselves as being worthy of a miracle. Few even believe in the possibility. And some will, in the grasp of the doubt and fear that clouds their own living, never accept the reality or truth of a story like this, the story of Mary's miracle, of Mary's encounter with something that had been an impossibility up until the moment before it happened.

- Who else but Mary could have gotten the politburo to allow this act of defiance in a land where God Himself had been exiled?

- Mary was always in trouble and flat broke and materially desperate, but always wildly happy and entirely devoid of fear. Temporal realities were never allowed to interfere with her endless spiritual missions.

- It was one of those "knockdown and say what" moments, as conscious me found himself confronting an extraordinary fact. *For there, with Aunt Mary, all those summers, long ago in Canada, I was being steeled, being made ready, for what I would become.* There I was, legless, atrophied, fingerless, and very, very broken and the voice within kept telling me, *You know the drill, man. You do.*

- There was a power in suffering, and she suggested that the disabled and those in pain were given that power as a gift, which in the end would only free them from the cares of the world and bring them closer to their God.

- I do not ask for cures. I do not even ask God to take the pain away. I ask only that He be with me in the pain. And He is and I prevail. Again and again, I prevail, because my God is with me.

# Author's Note

So much, by way of approach and intent in this story, Mary Varick's story, came together, because people who loved and admired her so were ready and willing to share their memories and reflections and to lend their voices. Through their help, spiritually and otherwise, we will come to do both Mary Varick and her loving contributions and saintly service to countless others a measure of justice.

Yet much of it will remain untold, as lives are complex and complicated things and really big lives like these are even trickier still. Adventure is easy while holiness is not.

In these pages, however, we will still be pleased to present a reasonable account of her life's devotion and, especially, of her ministries, ministries that continue to make a difference for people today.

Please understand that it is her life's work or ministry and her service to others that has preoccupied us in this work and not the extraneous details of the life lived. While that is explored to some degree, it is not our primary concern. We are, first and foremost, after the impact and the effect.

It is altogether fitting to present Mary Varick to you and, yes, even to honor her. You will be introduced to a woman who ultimately and above all else wanted, in a life replete with great challenges and horrific suffering, to honor her God and to serve Him with great love.

What we have written is for those interested in the extraordinary gifts of a remarkable woman who made her devotion to the Eucharist the very cornerstone of her life…and for those interested in the disabled who she deemed "God's inner circle" and in a rich theology of suffering that she both developed and espoused…and for those interested in her pilgrimage journeys or the "communion of saints" that she forged through her Our Lady of Fatima First Saturday Club family…and for those interested in a profound story of healing and grace and peace and love or what were the driving components or gifts or forces in her life… and even for those who want to understand why there is wonder and magic to be found at places like Sainte-Anne-de-Beaupre and Our Lady of the Cape and Saint Joseph's Oratory, the great shrines of the province of Quebec, Canada, that became second homes to Mary's children.

The refined and definitive articulation of her theology of suffering is, to me, without question, one of her greatest legacies, and, as such, it will be both explored and highlighted, again and again, throughout this work.

It is worthy of redundancy.

—Rich Fritzky

# 1

# The Heart of a Pilgrim's Journey

Mary Varick bore no title of distinction, and she never appeared on the nightly news. She was always broke, and she was without any worldly power whatsoever. But she had that thing called charisma and that she had in abundance, and she loved her God as only the saints and poets and sages sometimes do. And, yes, she was a leader in that she moved people and helped bring them closer to home or to their God. And she was a healer in that she drew so many disabled people into her company and invited them to open their eyes and to see just how special and blessed they truly were.

In the weakness and frailty and impotence that others generally and usually saw, she rather saw extraordinary strength and rare courage and rich possibility.

She turned both perspectives and lives upside down and inside out. For where others saw darkness, she always saw the light.

The Our Lady of Fatima First Saturday Club that she formed in 1960 for both the disabled and the enabled alike, who would volunteer and embrace those less fortunate, became a source of light and life for so many people who had formerly been abandoned or left to decay in nursing homes and long-term care facilities or homes for the blind. It became a source of light and life for victims of cerebral palsy and multiple sclerosis and quadriplegics and paraplegics and the blind and the infirm. To her, they came and left the darkness that often surrounded them behind in order to join together on First Saturdays for mass and a shared rosary and a meal and camaraderie and belonging and value and meaning.

Yes, what she offered them and all she did was firmly rooted in Catholicism and she was Catholic to the bone, but all comers were welcome and people of many faiths participated and immersed themselves in the power and promise of both Mary's sociology and theology, a belief system that affirmed their unique closeness to God and their anointed places at the foot of the cross.

An anointed place at the foot of the cross—that is, where she saw all of her disabled.

Hers was a theology that invited all to sacrifice and to give and to become the literal instruments of grace. She helped people to appreciate just how greatly loved they were, and she taught them to seize the power that they possessed to extend that profound love, a force that could never be bound by physical ailment or deformity.

She also raised money to take them on annual pilgrimages to the great and spectacular shrines of Quebec and eventually to Fatima and Lourdes and to Rome and the Holy Land and elsewhere. But above all else, in doing all these things, she fashioned a community of love that has continued to perform its magic for more than sixty years.

Hers was a remarkable journey.

In chapters 2 and 3, we will bore into the life of Mary, but here in chapter 1, we will see the world she fashioned through the eyes of just two of her children, through the great shrines of Quebec that became her second homes and her touchstones, and through a handful of her fellow warriors and sojourners for the Lord.

I was struck again this year, as I long have been, by the sheer beauty of the people on the First Saturday Club's Canadian pilgrimage—from the simple faith of an eighty-four-year-old Brother Luke and a broken, but determined Sister Anna to the extraordinary love and goodness there to be found radiating from a young seventeen-year-old girl from Colts Neck and a seventeen-year-old boy from Nutley.

There is a raw power in simply being embraced by people of faith, who are determined to be of service.

Often, those who come to serve and give to the disabled are themselves broken in places that are not so obvious and in need of as much healing and grace as the most afflicted among them.

We break in different ways.

On the pilgrimage, both the disabled and enabled are invited to grow and to enjoy and to love one another. Both are invited to heal and to be empowered. It is as simple as that, and invariably, each and every time, psyches and hearts and souls with holes in them often begin to mend.

All through the power of love which is somehow, always and everywhere, each and every time, there in rich abundance.

As a veteran who has a broken forty-nine-year history with the Our Lady of Fatima First Saturday Club family, I can honestly and freely report that there is a kind of wonder in every journey together as we travel to the old places—cathedrals, basilicas, chapels, fields, riversides, cities—the places that Aunt Mary first introduced me to in my youth.

Let's consider that wonder to be a tangible gift, the same gift that was given to my companions and I, both in 1965, my first pilgrimage, and today in 2014, the same gift that keeps on giving across the wide span of more than half a century. The same gift—all around and enveloping me—every time—a gift, to be sure, that ever ascends and compounds and expands—touching hearts and souls and changing lives for more than sixty-three years now!

The journey—the pilgrimage—never disappoints.

The gift, mysterious and wonderful, is always freely given.

So, yes, my friend Hank Colling may have pushed me into this project, but it was my heart that answered.

As I try to wrap my mind around more than sixty-three years of pilgrimages to the great and magnificent shrines of Quebec and conjure up the images of so many beautiful people, more, naturally, who have gone home to God than remain here with us, I hear Walt Whitman's resounding voice.

I hear his eloquent reminder that, "Nothing ever collapses." It was his cry that in the extraordinary genius of God's creation, spirit ever and always and only expands and enlarges.

Just like energy, our spirits expand and explode into the all of our tomorrows.

"Nothing collapses," Walt Whitman resoundingly and joyously proclaimed.

Reminding us, assuring us, as so many of us need to be reminded, that those who have gone home to God so richly and steadfastly continue to abide in our hearts and souls today and in the wonder of a creation that our poor powers of imagination cannot even begin to fully comprehend, much less appreciate.

Interestingly, I was recently taken by a recording of the acclaimed Ram Dass, who, like me, is a great believer in life and in the power of the human spirit. It was a lecture on dying and about our need to embrace death with open hearts as it is just another of life's sacred processes and a portal through which the spirit ascends.

He was decrying the aspect of our culture that insists upon defying death at all costs, as if it is something to be feared. You won't meet Claude Bare until chapter 8, but clearly he was victimized by this insistence upon defying death. Ram Dass rather implores us to welcome death when it comes just as one welcomes an old friend. He argued that this is exactly what it is—a friend that brings us to our God—a friend that brings us home where the all of our life will be manifested.

The most powerful argument he made in the lecture was when he very passionately spoke of being asked by an academic colleague at Harvard if he really knew if there was an afterlife. The operative term for him was the word *know* as his response was that, "It is not for me to know. It is!

"It is! Whether or not I know it, it is," he said.

As sure as they were, in that moment, speaking with one another, it—a heaven—was, he said, and he might just as well have been asked if they or the earth existed.

To him, it was neither about belief nor knowledge nor faith.

Life simply does not end. The spirit is unconquerable and it endures.

To suggest otherwise is absurd.

Ram Dass and I may walk in different worlds, but here our paths most powerfully converged.

For here, his path converged with that of the Son of Man, Jesus Christ, who took on our humanity so that He could, in suffering and sacrifice, sustain us with the "life-giving waters" of eternal life. And so too, the beautiful lives of Ram Dass and Mary Varick also converged.

Mary Varick and her life's force and great passions were very well known to him.

Each year, I look forward to the First Saturday Club's annual pilgrimage to Canada. One passes and I wait, almost childlike, expectantly and excitedly for the next to begin.

No matter the pain within or the latest physical battles, no matter how broken, I am there, both because I can give to it and because there is so much to receive from it.

The pilgrimage and purpose and exploding spirits and life-giving waters are all of one to me.

Because *nothing ever collapses!*

It only expands!

As to where and what we visit on this pilgrimage, there are no surprises.

There are never any surprises. All the haunts are readily and pointedly familiar, and yet the anticipation is as great as if they had never before been seen. Why that is, is simple. Because these just happen to be places that level playing fields and focus one upon the faithful essentials of life.

They are places that heal and redeem and renew.

They are places that speak to us of home.

Especially Sainte-Anne-de-Beaupre and Cap de la Madeleine. And while many have found physical miracles in their embrace, the miracles for me and my companions are always of the heart and of the spirit.

So while I wait with childlike enthusiasm for what I already know so well, we begin our look back in an effort to better understand just what Mary Varick and her First Saturday Club pilgrimages have wrought over the years.

We want, as Henry David Thoreau would have written, "to suck the marrow out of all of this."

We'll start with a couple of well-worn images of mine and with some initial memories that were shared by my cousins Jim Varick and Mary Pisaniello, Mary Varick's only son and her youngest daughter, her second and fourth born, who religiously participated in all of the early pilgrimages. They were long adults (I use the term loosely, I assure you), before they first missed even one journey to Canada and their imprint upon them, even now, is forever imbedded and manifested.

It was just a few years ago on the 2008 pilgrimage of the First Saturday Club when something very strange and interesting occurred, and I was blessed to have a bird's eye view of it.

It was a simply gorgeous, not-a-cloud-in-the-sky, beckoning, and beaming day. It was a "blue skies up above and everyone is in love" kind of day. Standing in front of the inn in Beaupre, I was looking directly across the basilica grounds, beyond the wonderful new fountain and outdoor statue of a welcoming Saint Anne, into the eye of the spectacular basilica itself that was, in that moment, wrapped in a brilliant radiating blue from above.

That is, by the way, a sight that never gets old, a sight that is always somewhere just beyond spectacular.

On days like that, in the embrace of that basilica, you are just lifted on high.

In all honesty, there truly are no words to describe the marvel of the beauty that basilica takes on when it is wrapped in all the glory and bounty of nature. It is a grand and moving spectacle that is difficult to describe to one who has never seen it. Even our pointed choice of the word *spectacular* doesn't quite cut it!

A monumental gray edifice that oozes holiness, with twin steeples that ascend upward to the heavens, shrouded in billowing white clouds and the brightest blue, is radiated by beams of shimmering light that pour down from the sun's noon-ward height. That is what I saw, a picture, however often it is seen, that never ceases to stagger.

But I was struck by something odd, as my eyes were drawn to a distant yellow blur on the stone steps of the basilica.

It took me awhile to focus as my mind played tricks with itself.

For while it was as if I could reach out and touch the basilica itself, the distance made it a bit tough to identify the people beside it. But the grace of the movement of the yellow blur was telling and familiar. "Am I seeing what I think I see?" I asked myself, adding a "No, that can't possibly be."

That was quickly followed by an "I can't believe it, but I'm almost certain that the blur in yellow is my cousin Mary!"

"What on earth is she doing sweeping (as she appeared to be) the steps of the basilica?"

Now mind you, we are talking about some prodigious and formidable and downright massive steps, two distinct sets of magnificently rising steps that jump some forty feet from the ground up to the promenade that leads to the front doors of the basilica. And there was our Mary Varick Pisaniello, young Mary, filling what appeared to be a little dust pan, over and over again, step by lonely step, and dumping it into a garbage barrel.

To see those steps, you'd swear that it would take a regiment of the Fifth Army to sweep them all, but there, no doubt, was my cousin, bravely taking on that veritable mountainside of steps.

Alone!

In subdued awe, I watched her sweeping dance in what was a sun-speckled shimmering yellow, a yellow that was so perfectly offset by the rich greens and blues of the day and by the somber gray of the basilica itself in the background. I watched as she plodded on busily, rushing so as to overtake or beat back the inexorable movement of the sun, in the apparent hope of saving a piece of that glorious day for herself.

With a *brush–brush* here and a *brush–brush* there, she progressed, as the music from the *Wizard of Oz* reverberated in my head. Satisfied only after a good while, she finally pulled the barrel down the wheelchair ramp and disappeared into the base of the basilica.

Now my confinement to a wheelchair precluded any offer of assistance on my part anyway. But in all honesty, I would never have offered to help had I the ability, for the scene was just too incongruous and too mesmerizing. It was a show that deserved an audience, a show that was worthy of an audience and I just happened to be it.

She needed me.

Someone just had to be there to appreciate and chronicle her labors and that pretty yellow dress in that rich summer's sun and the fact that the whole scene was just so completely out of sync.

Yes, someone had to bear witness.

I needed to take it in and to pass on the memory of it to others, so as to make it the stuff of legend, as it so deserved to be.

In mild amusement, of course, I approached her upon her return to ask that one simple question. "Why?"

Just, "Why?"

Why on earth?

It was, as it turned out, a pure and simple mission of reverence. Disheartened by the trash—by the cigarette butts and candy wrappers and dropped ice cream cones and such—by the refuse she saw on the steps the evening before, she was shocked to find the same mess still there as she went to visit a Redemptorist priest and friend the next morning, so she detoured to the volunteers desk in the basement of the basilica to point out the problem and to respectfully request that it be attended to.

She was assured that it would be, but upon her return from her visit, she was dismayed and disheartened to find that nothing had yet been done. Shocked to then hear that they weren't certain when it could be attended to, she, rather than appeal or complain again, simply asked for the tools of the maintenance trade and sprung into action herself.

To her, it was an act of prayer and service.

It was, after all, her own Sainte-Anne-de-Beaupre.

It was, after all, one of the second homes of her childhood.

She swept the steps because it was sacred ground, holy ground.

And sure it belonged to the masses, but it also was uniquely hers.

She did so then, she told me, because it was a holy place and because Our Lady and Saint Anne deserved better from all of us. To Mary Pisaniello, Mary Varick's baby, revering the basilica was ultimately the responsibility of all of the faithful.

This, after all, was her mom's "heaven on a hillside," a special place to all of us, but most especially to a Mary Varick Pisaniello, who, after all, grew up on those very steps.

On July 17, 1951, sixty-three years ago now, it was where her mom's deadly bone cancer was sent back to the abyss from where it had come, and so, it was, first and foremost, a place of miracles.

A place of miracles and wonder!

To me, the Basilica of Sainte-Anne-de-Beaupre is always a spiritually inviting marvel, but to my sweet cousin in the yellow dress, you see, it was home.

And so the broom with which to battle the butts had been engaged by one who wore a yellow dress beneath a bright summer's sun and a grateful prayer was prayed!

It was the least she could do—that which most would never conceive of doing.

It was an awesome prayer, indeed!

*What was originally a little sanctuary to Saint Anne was dedicated at Le Petit Cap, what was only later to become Beaupre in 1660. The basilica that stands today is actually the fifth church constructed on the site. It replaced the one that was tragically destroyed by a fire on March 29, 1922. Its basic structure was completed in 1956, but the two towering steeples were added later.*

*The first cure attributed to Sainte-Anne-de-Beaupre was that of a crippled workman in 1658, which was soon followed by the deliverance of a group of sailors from a storm. Over the years, there have been hundreds of other healings attributed to Saint Anne, and the rear of the basilica is adorned with the wheel chairs and crutches that were left behind. A comprehensive record of all of these miracles is recorded in the* Annals of Saint Anne.

*The first pilgrimage to the shrine began as far back as 1707, when Native American Indians (the First Nations) came to venerate the saint whom they called their "Grandmother in Faith." For more than three hundred years now, they return each September to commemorate that first pilgrimage. In 1876, Saint Anne was proclaimed the patron saint of Quebec itself, and one hundred years later, Cardinal Maurice Roy consecrated the finally completed, new basilica, which Pope John Paul II then blessed with a visit on September 10, 1984.*

*The present basilica contains many spectacular eighteenth-century sculptures and artworks, and the interior is a feast for the eyes, filled throughout with delightful details. The 240 stained glass windows were created with a new technique that suffuses the light beautifully, and the ceilings and sides of the church are adorned with mosaics of the life of Saint Anne, the saints of Canada, and eighty-eight different scenes capturing the life of Jesus. The ends of the wooden pews also tell the story of creation with beautifully carved figures of animals and plants and the stunning beauty of the paintings in the Immaculate Conception Chapel below literally leaves one breathless upon first sight.*

*The Frederic Doyon mural of Saint Anne, her husband Saint Joachim, and a young Mary is quite beyond imagining. It also houses a perfect replica of Michelangelo's Pieta and the tomb of the Venerable Father Alfred Pampalon, a favored patron of those struggling with alcohol and drug addictions.*

*But the focus for pilgrims is not the above, but rather the miraculous statue of Saint Anne, before the main altar, that is carved from a massive single piece of oak. Painted in bright colors, Anne wears a crown of diamonds and rubies and pearls and she is appropriately depicted carrying her daughter, the Blessed Virgin Mary.*

*Parallel to the Saint Lawrence, this basilica, which in both its architecture and its paintings so humanize the great figures of faith, is visible for miles from both sides of the river.*

*The very stones and the wood of this remarkable church somehow whisper gently to all who come there of the joys, happiness, hopes, tears, pain, and suffering of all those who place their prayers there before the Lord, His Blessed Mother, and her Mother. Within it, a universal need to explore the deeper values and meanings of life is manifested, and each and every pilgrim is powerfully struck by the understanding that they are not alone, in their respective and individual searches for happiness and peace.*

*They are struck by the realization that they journey together with all of the faithful and that the Lord longs only for them to be fulfilled and redeemed. In prayerful reflection and meditation at Sainte-Anne-de-Beaupre, such as this is found and people are invited to carry the grace that is showered upon them there home in their hearts, so as to make it an active force in their daily lives and reckonings.*

And while tours of the basilica are regularly offered, the best guide I've ever had just happens to be my cousin in the yellow dress with the broom, Mary Varick Pisaniello, who, by the way, belongs to Bruno Pisaniello, a truly wonderful man and a son of Mary Varick's ministries. She knows this basilica intimately, and her reverence for it, given the broom and the steps, has already been made well known to you. This same reverence for all of the shrines and the experience of the pilgrimages is so powerfully reflected in this extraordinary childhood reflection that she shared with me,

> My summers were the envy of all the kids. I went to school at All Saints Elementary School on Whiton Street in Jersey City. When June exams were over and I was promoted to the next grade, and summer vacation officially began, I walked down Pacific Avenue with a light and happy heart. I had a suitcase to pack for the first of the three-summer pilgrimages. Dad would leave the house before dawn to go out to Newark to the Public Service 51 Park Avenue Garage to pick up our "over the road" charter bus. It was much classier than the city line buses, with reclining seats and air-conditioning. We pilgrims were going to be traveling "first class!"

I remember waking up on the third floor of our row house at 241 Pacific Avenue to the sound of the motor running, rushing to look out of the bedroom window to see our "chariot"—interior lights all aglow, awaiting us.

Oh, the excitement and anticipation of returning "home" to those blessed, familiar Canadian shrines and the happy, holy people who would welcome us back. Father Eugene Lefebvre at the Basilica of Sainte-Anne-de-Beaupre; Father Jacques Rinfret, OMI; and Estelle Clavette, OMI, who were the heartbeat of the Pilgrim's House at Our Lady of the Cape! The Oratory of Saint Joseph also was magnificent, and I remember those marvelous circular stairwells on the exterior of the basilica that were better than any roller coaster ride or Ferris wheel for me, as I descended them as fast as my little legs would carry me. I was home, and these holy places were my playground. I knew beyond understanding that I was loved and favored by God in ways I never questioned, but somehow recognized.

Home, where her mom took them!

Home, indeed, at Sainte-Anne's and the Cape and Saint Joseph's where the pilgrims of the First Saturday Club family find themselves continuing to gather and pray and celebrate summer after summer—for sixty-three years and counting.

Now, my children can vouch for me on this, for I have long maintained and often said that my cousin Jim Varick is the funniest man I have ever known. His wit is just too fast for all of us normal human beings, and to be in his company was always a delight, because he made people laugh.

He had that great and singular gift.

He never failed to leave us laughing.

There are so many memories of being with him in Canada in my youth that come to mind, and the overwhelming majority of the same have to do with his creating havoc and trouble. He was a great tease who tortured so many nuns (but only because he loved them so). And he was a certified master at making the disabled laugh heartily at their very disabilities. He was everyone's comic foil, and he brought such joy to everyone because he had the gift of helping people get out of themselves by laughing at themselves.

No one was given a pass, neither his saintly mother nor the latest bishop to pass by.

Everyone on a pilgrimage took their hits from Jimmy.

And a Don Rickles could have gone to school simply by watching him perform, because my cousin Jim did it with the kind of heart and a class that even the great comics often lacked.

So there I am with Jim, in memory, short-sheeting beds or planting water balloon traps over doorways or stealing someone's laundry or abandoning some of our disabled fellows in the shower (for just the right amount of time, of course). We were always booby-trapping or temporarily stealing or passing along bad information.

All in the name of mayhem and fun!

But as to the sacraments and mass, of course, Jim turned on the dime and became the very icon of devotional reverence.

In fact, he had always done so. A favorite family tale of him as a child had his uncle punishing him by placing him in a closet, because he refused to stop "raising holy hell." Of course, it was just a temporary act to dissuade Jim from behaving badly, so his uncle just as quickly opened the door of the closet, because he didn't want the darkness or fear to overcome his nephew. But he did so only to hear Jim say, "Would you please shut the door? I'm saying my rosary now."

If that wasn't an "I am the master of my own destiny" retort, I don't know what is.

My most special memory of being with Jim in Canada is, however, the antithesis of all of this mayhem. It is of a couple of moments of calm and conversation with Eric Gosling, who was long the director of the volunteers at Sainte-Anne-de-Beaupre and one of the gentlest creatures on the face of the earth.

This particular summer, the Quebecois party in Canada was loudly fighting on behalf of a referendum to sever Quebec's relationship with Canada. They were loud, "We will remember our French heritage" separatists. A political junkie as I was and am, I took interest, and Eric, a Canadian through and through, and a proud flyer of the Maple Leaf, certainly and astutely saw the world differently, so we discussed Canadian politics—and also all things having to do with the basilica and the hidden meaning in *The Little Prince* and Father James Carroll's book *A Terrible Beauty*.

Yes, late at night, after all was settled at the inn—after our disabled charges had been bathed and safely secured in bed, after all was quiet, outside of the nocturnal gatherings in Aunt Mary's room, where 11:00 p.m. and 3:00 a.m. were interchangeable, we'd slip out of the inn into the still and quiet of a Beaupre night and walk the two blocks beyond the basilica to Eric's house where he had the LaBatts waiting for us, the pilgrims 3, Jim, my friend Ed Zubrow, and me.

I loved Eric, who alone in the world had a wit to match Jim's and who had a knowledge of Beaupre and the life of the basilica, to which he was so completely devoted, that was unbridled and personal.

While Eric was bilingual, his wife and children spoke French only, so I loved and took in the sounds in his house. I loved his simple, quaint living room and the kitchen that reminded me so much of the one at my own childhood at 138 Poplar Avenue. I loved the scent of his home that was not unlike that in my grandmother's house. But above all, I loved Eric and his goodness and his devotion to Mary Varick's pilgrims—to us—and to his basilica and to his faith and to his country.

And I loved that he could go toe-to-toe with Jimmy and that he told me, "Even you, yes, you, limited as you are, will pick up a thought or two from *Le Petit Prince*." And indeed, I did.

Like so many who were once associated with the First Saturday pilgrimages, Eric Gosling long ago went home to God.

But I still look for him whenever I arrive in Beaupre, for nothing ever collapses and certainly not the gifts that he so kindly gave. Yes, I look for him, confident that I'll find him lurking in the shadows, serving the needs of all he can reach, and moving the hearts and spirits of all he can touch. For if a place has a spirit, and indeed, it does, Sainte-Anne-de-Beaupre's is, of course, first and foremost, Anne's and Mary's.

But Eric's indeed is there as well, for no one ever loved Good Saint Anne more than him!

I also see my dad and mom everywhere in Canada. I see my dad, very sick and feeble with his cancer, reflecting upon the Stations and kneeling for them (on the Scala Sancta or Holy Stairs), and I hear Aunt Mary's voice sweetly resounding over the grounds, speaking of Jesus's profound love at the Cape, and I see Father Rinfret running into her arms by the pond, and there I am, in memory, breaking bread with my Uncle Bud and Aunt Anne after picking it up in the wee hours from one of the old roadside bakeries near Beaupre.

Right out of the stone ovens by the roadside, there never was a better or sweeter tasting loaf of bread.

Permit me to share one other "out of the distant recesses of my past" memories. I had to be about fifteen years old and my brother Bob, who went home to God five years ago, was sixteen. We were on a pilgrimage together, and Connie LoPresti, a double amputee, claimed the two of us. No matter what, one of us two had better be pushing her wheel chair. Or there was hell to pay. So my brother and I made a command performance for Connie and kept her laughing most of the time, which wasn't necessarily an easy task.

And lo and behold, what do I see upon my first trip back after my own fall into a wheel chair, some forty-three years removed from that 1965 pilgrimage? There was Connie still, so much older and feeble but just as volatile and demanding. Only this time, forty-three years later, she was demanding the full attention and presence of a sister act, for only Chris or Julian Franklin could push her chair and no others would be tolerated!

The more things changed, the more they had remained the same.

Connie, finally on her own after all these years, recently joined the First Saturday's heavenly masses. One imagines that God knows exactly what to expect from her and her unique and towering faithfulness.

*The original stone parish church at Our Lady of the Cape Shrine (or Cap de la Madeleine), now known as the Old Shrine, first opened for worship in 1720. It is the oldest church preserved in its integrity in all of Canada. And while a spectacular cathedral, with remarkable stained glass windows and a dome that rises 125 feet high, was raised in the latter part of the twentieth century, the Little Stone Chapel with the beautiful and miraculous statue of Mary remains the heart of the Cape to those who love her best.*

*The grounds on the banks of the Saint Lawrence are breathtaking, and the bronze statues that capture the Stations of the Cross and the Mysteries of the Rosary are moving and captivating. There is the large Rosary Bridge over a brook that commemorates the ice bridge that formed across the Saint Lawrence in March of 1879, on the heels of what had been an unusually mild winter, allowing them to get the stone for the new and larger chapel across from the south side of the river.*

*They had prayed the rosary requesting the same and so the Rosary Bridge.*

*On June 22, 1888, a statue of Mary, donated by a parishioner, was placed on the altar in the Little Old Shrine and dedicated to Mary. That very evening, while kneeling before the statue, Father Frederic, the shrine's first pilgrimage director and two others, saw the statue open its eyes to them. The "miracle of the eyes" was the first of so many miraculous events attesting to Mary's presence there. Again, some leave their wheel chairs behind, but I believe that all who walk the grounds in reverence are healed in some extraordinary way.*

It can be small or inexplicable and wholly unrecognized by the greater world out there, and yet what happens there can still be the start of a new life for an individual.

Two years ago, for instance, I whispered but a few loving words to a young girl during the candlelight procession, and she just broke down and let out all of this baggage that had been building up inside her, all of this crap that was just desperate for release. She just needed to know that she was truly loved and she was, but it wasn't just me. It was Mary, our Mother, who reached into her soul that night and turned the light on in her dark corners and gave her faith and hope.

That intervention is, by the way, now five years later, still ongoing, and it drives her spiritually to this very day.

To this very day, I might add, for that young woman and I were there brought together, purposefully brought together, and so she remains in my life and I continue to look upon her with the same fierce love that I look upon each of my own twelve children.

People are made over at the Cape, and terrible beauties are born.

By way of introduction or table setting, I will now share and then elaborate upon some of the early e-mails that my cousin Jim shared with me about his most special memories. He wrote,

> Oh Lord, so many blessed people come to mind right now as I recall Paul Russell and Frankie Fields and Sister Miriam Eymard, and Flossie and her niece Florita, and Sister Mary Bernard, a Franciscan Sister of the Handmaids of Mary Immaculate, who actually was instrumental in our meeting Mother Teresa of Calcutta. There were "Straight Ed" (who couldn't lay down) and "Flat Bill" (who couldn't rise up) and "Ed the Head," nicknames given in love and good humor to some of the outstanding pilgrims in the early days.

There were, of course, a limitless array or oh-so many others over the years—including Anne Gerhardt and Jeanette and Howie Daniels and Cecelia and Connie LoPresti and Carol Fitzgerald and the DiGangis and good old Ron Pewsey and the irrepressible Freddie Vanderhoof and the ever-devoted and devout Hank Colling and Neil Gulliksen and oh-so many other saints, who quickly moved in and out of the pilgrimage family on their way home to God.

Cecelia and Connie and Carol Fitzgerald and Freddie Vanderhoof and Hank Colling were only recently lost and are well known to today's group, and Mary Jane and Bob Gilleck and Sister Anna still provide that precious link and connection to the early days. And while all of those mentioned above have their stories, you must, at least, here be introduced to Flossie, who for years was Aunt Mary's fiercest aide de camp.

Flossie Oates was a big African-American woman from Jersey City with a heart that was ever so much bigger still.

She was a rollicking "Praise the Lord" Baptist in a sea of Catholics, who was a literal mother figure to all of Aunt Mary's children and nieces and nephews.

Hers was a life dedicated to doing good and to going above and beyond for others. To her, it wasn't just first Saturdays, it was every single day of the month. She daily visited the homes of multiple shut-ins, and she cooked their meals, and she did their shopping and ironed their clothes, and her own home was a soup kitchen for the poor, a soup kitchen for the poor that never shut its doors.

Flossie would arrange always for her legions to be picked up by the First Saturday bus—and she'd be sure to see to it that my sweet Uncle Bill Varick got the rest he needed in her room, because he'd never get it in his room with Aunt Mary.

She'd say, "Now Mary, she can put up with this nonsense, but Bill has got to drive the bus" (which he did on all of the earlier pilgrimages)—and Flossie would belt out her heavenly ascending "honey" when she saw you, and she would squeeze you in her arms and leave you with the feeling, even if only for a moment, that you of all God's creatures were most blessed—and on First Saturdays, while volunteers took care of the disabled, Flossie always took care of us children.

A favorite running joke each summer, back in the railroad trip days, had to do with the fact that my uncle and godfather and Mary Varick's oldest brother, Jim Cassidy, who worked for the railroad, used his family pass to take Flossie, north to Canada, as his wife. Now, we're talking pre–Civil Rights Days, so the conductor was usually stunned to see my slim Uncle Jim and his beautiful wife Flossie Oates, whose hugs could have splintered Uncle Jim.

Yes, my Uncle Jim, Mr. Flossie Oates, which he was proud to be.

A favorite Flossie story that must be shared had to do with the time that Bishop Stanton approached her about her receiving Holy Communion. The bishop was concerned because of our sacred rules. There was, for instance, a rule that deemed that you must be Catholic in order to receive Holy Communion. Well, Flossie, Mary's resident Baptist, insisted on receiving Communion.

The bishop approached her about this problem, but nothing he said put a dent in Flossie's armor. "Now, Bishop, honey," she said, "don't you worry none about this, because when you're in Rome, you do as the Romans do." Bishop or no bishop, Flossie, who did nothing but love and breathe community, went to communion, which, I have no doubt, was especially pleasing to the Lord.

So much for our often ridiculous rules.

*On the pilgrimage, a brief stop for Mass and a tour also is made at Saint Joseph's Oratory on Mount Royal in the city of Montreal. The basilica dome there is the highest structure in all of Montreal and one can see this beautifully imposing structure from miles away. Their carillon consists of fifty-six bells that were originally designed for the Eiffel Tower in Paris, and one can climb the 283 steps from the street to the basilica. There are ninety-nine wooden ones for those who wish to climb prayerfully on their knees, which, of course, is fortunately beyond me now. It is a spiritual and tourist destination that attracts more than two million visitors each year.*

*It all began when a small chapel was built by now Saint Brother Andre (who was only canonized two years ago) of the Congregation of the Holy Cross. When pilgrims started coming in such great numbers, work was begun on the massive church in 1914 and completed in 1966. The commanding mountain setting, sacred path, and imposing dome, complemented by a Way of the Cross of exceptional artistry, give Saint Joseph's a presence and a holy aura that is absolutely unique.*

*It is a breath of life in the heart of Montreal and a haven of peace for our all-too-often weary world.*

A second e-mail from Jim followed. This time, he wrote,

> Did you know that one of the first severely handicapped
> pilgrims was Neil Gulliksen, who lived in Jersey City with
> his Mom? Neil was in the Navy and home on leave when
> his friends called, inviting him to go for a ride. While Neil
> didn't want to go because he was tired, his Mom said that,
> "To have friends is to be a friend." A tragic accident that
> night left him a quadriplegic, and after a long and difficult
> recovery, he returned home to the need for 24-hour care.

As it turned out, Father Art Frotton of All Saints Church in
Jersey City introduced Jim to Neil and, through Jim, to the First
Saturday family. His mother fought his going to Canada, as she
felt that only she could take care of him, but Mary intervened
and Neil went and enjoyed it so. Deeply faithful and spiritual,
Neil was one of those saints, who upon his mom's untimely death,
carried that faith into the household of the good family who
took him in. That entire family converted because of Neil and his
unbridled spirit and their desire to be where Neil was—*with God.*

Then, there was a third e-mail from Jim. He wrote,

> I remember the good times that I had with Paul Russell.
> We would share a few beers and sit alongside the river in
> Princeton for an afternoon of just enjoying one another's
> company. We often solved the problems of the world in
> those conversations and shared deep theological discus-
> sions along our faith journeys. Paul, who loved God so,
> had only come to Him after he was confined to a wheel-
> chair. He developed a program to be presented in schools
> and parishes called *Welcome to my World.* It was intended
> to break down the barriers between the disabled and those
> who don't realize that they too may suffer from another
> kind of disability. We planned to take his show on the

road, but Paul, who was a spiritual director, a confidante, and friend, died much too soon.

Jim also shared the Mary Hafmeister and Yvonne stories with me. Mary Hafmeister, who had advanced cancer at the time, went on one pilgrimage only and found exactly what she was looking for at Sainte-Anne's, the strength to die in joy and peace with no regrets and no fears.

She told Aunt Mary on the return trip that, for the first time in a long time, she was truly happy as she had been assured that God was, indeed, calling her home and that her husband and children were going to be fine when she was gone. While she died shortly thereafter, in complete joy and peace as reported by her husband, as if there truly is such a thing as a beautiful death, she gave Aunt Mary a gift to return to Sainte-Anne's on her next pilgrimage. As it turns out, while I never knew Mary Hafmeister personally, her little baby Donna stayed with my family the week that she went on the pilgrimage to Canada.

So all the little Fritzkys fell in love with her baby, and we are, on some ethereal plane, therefore, connected forever, connected to the peace that she took home from Sainte-Anne-de-Beaupre with her.

The story that Jim related about Yvonne was personal to him, as he brought her to First Saturday and got her family to agree to come to Canada, despite their having rejected God because of Yvonne's disability and the grave reservations that they expressed about the trip.

They were angry, and God, after all, was to blame.

This, however, was quite a pilgrimage as my then seminarian uncles, who spread joy always, and many of their soon-to-be fellow priests were there in force, and Yvonne was in their care, climbing the steps of the prodigious and "not for the faint of heart" Scala Sancta (the Holy Stairs) when her mom got wind of it. In apoplexy, she rushed to the scene to scold all involved, but upon seeing her, Yvonne kneeling, in the arms of two seminarians, she just broke down instead. The rest of the story writes itself as Yvonne's own made their peace with God.

Committed to her stretcher always, she never stopped praying for a better world or for you or for me—for anyone or everything but herself.

There will be many more stories to relate, as Mary's own books are full of them, and there are yet legions of people who have lived these Canadian pilgrimages for forty years or more. So we have many firsthand witnesses who can shed their own light.

But to have begun with Mary's reverence and Jim's first memories points us in the right direction. Neil, Mary, Paul, and Yvonne all had much in common. They were humble people of great faith, who gathered spiritual strength out of disability and sickness and led others, who were far more fortunate than they, home again.

They were leaders and spiritual heroes, undaunted believers who lived the very gospel that Mary Varick so loved to preach. They brightly lived her theology of suffering.

Out of disability, they were called to be rainmakers of grace, rainmakers who freely gave their suffering back to God so that the goodness it fostered might then be freely showered upon others.

Just like then, there are weavers of grace among us today, wellsprings of redemption and spiritual forces for good.

Our Canadian pilgrimages, after all, have never been about the ones in the wheel chairs alone and certainly never about physical reclamation.

If that was the objective, we would have long ago bagged it.

But the disabled among us have often discovered just what their mission in life is, and they have in Canada somehow been spiritually empowered to fulfill it. And the enabled, who maybe came with holes in their own hearts and spirits, have so often been awakened and lifted, refreshed and renewed.

God works always on these journeys of Mary Varick, through the great hearts of all who go to His Mother and His Grandmother in search of Him, to touch the hearts and spirits of everyone else.

And it is no small thing to, in any way, make a difference in the life of another.

So, why Canada?

Because miracles do happen along this journey and because that is what we, redeemers, all understand to be our mission. We, through the grace of God, become the weavers of miracles. We change lives for the better. We change ourselves. And in my long experience, these personal and often-profound miracles of the heart and of the spirit that the world takes little note of never cease to be fashioned.

But we take note of them all and we give thanks. And we return because miracles are yet waiting to be born.

Like the first time, I will again take in all that Sainte-Anne-de-Beaupre and Our Lady of the Cape and Saint Joseph's Oratory have to offer. And there, in my most special places, I will commune with Aunt Mary and her good husband and my parents and so many among those I have loved on this earth, and I will look for Jim in the dark moonlight on a silent Beaupre street. I will see Mary on the steps of the basilica, and I will listen for Eric's voice and thank him once more for having loved us so.

I will look to the heavens over the banks of the Saint Lawrence, and I will embrace the fullness of this sixty-three-year living legacy of generosity and goodness and grace.

And I will be at peace!

Because nothing ever collapses and all that was fashioned for good in some sixty-four years goes on working its magic.

## Chapter 1 Placeholders

- What we have written is for those interested in the gifts of a remarkable woman who made her devotion to the Eucharist the cornerstone of her life…and for those interested in the disabled who she deemed "God's inner circle" and in the rich theology of suffering that she both developed and espoused…and for those interested in her pilgrimage journeys or the "communion of saints" that she forged through her Our Lady of Fatima First Saturday family…and for those interested in a profound story of healing and grace and peace and love or what were the driving components or gifts or forces in her life…and even for those who want to understand why there is wonder and magic at places like Sainte-Anne-de-Beaupre and Our Lady of the Cape and Saint Joseph's Oratory, the great shrines of Quebec that became second homes to her children.

- I hear his eloquent reminder that, "Nothing ever collapses." His cry that in the extraordinary genius of God's creation, spirit ever and always and only expands and enlarges.

- Just like energy, our spirits expand and explode into the all of our tomorrows.

- Out of disability, they were called to be rainmakers of grace, rainmakers who freely gave their suffering back to God so that the goodness it fostered might then be just as freely showered upon others.

- Just like then, there are weavers of grace among us today, wellsprings of redemption, and spiritual forces for good.

- Like the first time, I will soon take in all that Sainte-Anne-de-Beaupre and Our Lady of the Cape and Saint

Joseph's Oratory have to offer. And there, in my most special places, I will commune with Aunt Mary and her good husband and my parents and so many among those I have loved on this earth, and I will look for Jim in the dark moonlight on a silent Beaupre street. I will see Mary on the steps of the basilica, and I will listen for Eric's voice and thank him once more for having loved us so.

- I will look to the heavens over the banks of the Saint Lawrence, and I will embrace the fullness of this sixty-three-year living legacy of generosity and goodness and grace.

- And I will be at peace!

# 2

# A Pilgrim's Passage

This is a very Catholic story, a Catholic-to-the-bone story, and while all Mary did was rooted in the love of Jesus Christ and while it sways to beat of the music of the altar and of the Eucharist and of the Mass and while it is rooted in the soul of a defined and living faith, it remained, at one and the same time, universal.

Universal in that it is rooted in faith and devotion and in a rich love of God and in living for one's brothers and sisters and in leading a life of purpose! As such, it resonates for all people of faith—no matter their faith, no matter their particular belief.

For all Mary Varick was ultimately about was goodness and love. And God, after all, is just that—love!

The God of all is love.

Yes, her ministries, both the First Saturdays and the pilgrimages, were Catholic, and they revolved around Catholic services and forms of worship, but there were many non-Catholics who participated over the years and it was open to all. Her invitation was ecumenical.

The salient and overarching message to be extracted from Mary Varick's life is that we are, indeed, our brothers and our sisters' keepers. It is that we belong to one another and that we must confront and do all that we can to alleviate the suffering and pain of our fellows. We are not meant to lead lives of "lonely and quiet desperation." We are meant to live our lives abundantly and resoundingly and lovingly—for one another—for each other.

We are meant to live of, by, and for God with and through the help of our fellow human beings, where God lives.

In that, there is most certainly a universal application.

Like all prospective saints, some will doubt or question what is here written of Mary Varick, for it will truly be "over the top."

# In Suffering, There Is Joy

## The Root of the Theology of Suffering

But we write without apology for that, because Mary Varick was over the top. She did not live the everyday or the ordinary. She unabashedly and loudly lived a life of suffering in joy for her suffering fellows—physically, spiritually, and emotionally—in the love of Jesus, and she rejoiced always in doing so.

Note that I just wrote "suffering in joy," that she lived a life of "suffering in joy"—two words that harshly contrast, but words that found harmony in Mary. Therein lies the over the top for us, for you and I, we do not believe this to be possible. No one suffers in joy.

But Mary Varick did, and to understand her, we must understand this.

She rubbed up against the cultural norms, which would rather suggest that there is no joy to be found in suffering.

So any sarcasm or jaded questions or doubts can be checked at the door, because not a single word or syllable of what is penned here will be exaggerated.

For Mary was and ever remains our exaggeration.

Because she quite literally found joy in suffering.

In our "Preface," an attempt was made to answer the "Why we bother to write this?" question. We suggested that it makes so much sense today to write of a life that can help lead some who may be wandering or drifting or searching for a way back home to purpose and to meaning and to commitment and, maybe, even to their God. Similarly, it also is directed at helping others to renew and strengthen resolve and faith, for Mary's faith was so constant and so formidable that it poured out in a burning love.

Her story too, like her life, is a portal to grace and peace.

Who out there, by the way, anywhere out there, isn't in need of a little grace or peace or light today?

Our take was that there's a need, a real need to recapture stories like this and to reflect upon habits and behaviors that instruct and enlighten. Our weary and broken world is actually desperate for them. As to just how desperate, we may not even be aware.

In our "Preface," in all honesty, there was no concerted attempt to convince. The persuasive element or component wasn't even in play. Certainly not consciously or overtly!

# Why Not Mary Varick?

The approach taken was, is, and will be to let the life and the work and her way of being speak for itself and the ideas and themes are to flow, as it were, from a position of strength. Out of her strength! If there was an audience for Mother Teresa or Francis of Assisi or Theresa of Lisieux or John Vianney or for so many other extraordinary people of faith and of the miracles that were associated with them, then there should certainly be one for our Mary Varick, a laywoman who became a spiritual leader in the latter part of the twentieth century.

This is so, because as people are beaten back by the world and national and community and personal problems today, they need to be reassured that goodness does ultimately prevail and that

God's faith in us is somehow stronger and ever so much bigger than our own faith in Him.

So why not—we are urging people in this writing—why not? See if you can find or look to find what your heart longs for in the life of Mary Varick.

A life that was selfless, a life that inspired and moved!

Why not Mary who was relentless in her faith and equally passionate in her love of God than the greatest of any of the pronounced saints, and maybe, just maybe, even more intimate in her relationship with Mary, the Mother of God?

Why not Mary Varick who was no stranger to the miraculous?

Why not Mary who was up close and personal and very accessible to you and to me?

There was simply nothing aloof or distant or removed about Mary. She was not lost in prayer or in a convent or monastery, and there was no habit or vestment that separated her from the ordinary and the faithful. Neither was she ascetic nor angelic nor worthier than thou.

She was us!

She was just more touchable, more immediate, more impactful, more yours and mine than so many of our recognized saints were.

But just as in love with and *in life* for her God!

There was nothing ethereal about Mary Varick! Nothing at all!

She was not lost in the clouds with a halo enveloping her! She was right down there in the muck and mire with you and me.

And her church would do well to celebrate her and we do well to emulate her.

Beyond that opening argument, there was a formative chapter in which we looked at Mary through the unique prism and heart of her son Jim and of her daughter Mary and in which, the reader was introduced to the pilgrimage places to which she ventured for thirty-seven years and to a representative sampling of her early pilgrim family.

Places and people—a collage or montage of those who became home to her!

# A Way of Being

Here, we now continue our discovery of her by shining a small light on her way of being, on her immediate family, on the places where she lived—on her homes, on the books that she herself wrote, and on the rich wisdom of just one grandchild. After that, we'll proceed to reflect upon some of the larger-than-life pilgrimages and upon the stories and memories of a small army who attached themselves to and long journeyed in her "inner circle."

She was, of course, deeply spiritual, but she also was oh-so human and flawed at one and the same time, just like the rest of us. There was a low-burning Irish temper that was a most infrequent visitor, and she was certainly not above boxing people in and prodding them to dance to her music. While never one to overtly lie, she was not beyond, as it is said, "stretching it some" or either exaggerating or understating her case in order to advance her cause.

She was a player.

She was a lovable rogue or character of sorts who would machinate, manipulate, and conspire in order to advance her First Saturday Club and her pilgrimages. Her skills were such that, given the opportunity, she could get a Simon Legree to donate and she was a master at singing one's praises, at the perfect moment, in order to prompt that someone to either give more or to do more than they originally expected or anticipated.

Smiling all the time, she could play extraordinarily effective mind games. All forgivable in that the means to her ends were ultimately laudable! She was, after all, wholly interested in service and goodness and kindness, and all that was done was done for the love of and in the name of her pilgrims—her "inner circle"—her disabled.

And what was done in the name of her pilgrims, after all, was God's work, for they were most certainly His to embrace and to cherish and to take to higher ground—all of which comprised Mary's pointed mission.

I can still see the confused look on my Uncle Joe Cassidy's face at a First Saturday gathering eons ago at Saint Peter the Apostle's Church in River Edge, New Jersey, as he tried to explain to Aunt Dot why he had topped off their original one-hundred-dollar donation with another one-hundred-dollar donation with the money that had been earmarked for some new piece of furniture or trip or family need. Or my dad eerily pleading with my mom, "No, Rosie, not this time. No." But no one could effectively say no to Aunt Mary when she had them cornered. When asked directly by her, "*No*," as my friend and uncle, Mary's youngest brother, Father John Cassidy said, "somehow disappeared from the vocabulary."

Mary either did not understand or simply did not accept the word *no*.

The answer, Father John always joked, was to try to keep your distance from her.

The answer was to avoid the question altogether.

Distance was your only hope.

It is important to note that no one in her family or among her friends was rich. Among the legions or minions that she appealed to, there was no one rich. Among those she played, there was no one rich. *Those who gave to her, for the most part, gave from their own poverty.* Those who gave to her and who helped make her ministries run were largely longing for something better or hurting themselves.

That this was so—that she was largely supported by what flowed from the poverty of others is just another reason, I believe, why God loved her with a special love and why her suffering "inner circle" and all who served them never stopped smiling.

They were ever in the embrace of their God who, we dare to assume, cherished smiling with them and cherished their well-worn generosity.

But then too, keeping your distance from Mary was nigh on impossible, because she had this magnetic radar that just sucked people in, and once in her company, yes was the only possible response. I can still picture Aunt Mary arriving at our home at 138 Poplar Avenue in Hackensack with both Uncle Bill Varick and later with Jerry Sheehan, what were usually impromptu and unannounced visits.

She also was adept at using the art of surprise.

In our youth, virile young men that my brothers and I were, we took pride in helping to pull her wheelchair and her safely up the two flights of outdoor steps. Remarkably, when thinking about that, I can still picture the flowing pachysandra patch that ran up the bank from the sidewalk to our front lawn, where there was a transported, prodigious, and beautiful pine tree from Crater Lake, an array of sticker bushes, and one proud maple tree.

Flexing our muscles and pulling her up the steps, it all remains very clear and vibrant. She entered our house through the green as it were, through plants and trees, like her, that stretched out and ascended toward the heavens.

Then always positioned in the dining room, it was as if Aunt Mary held court. She always held court and not because she sought to be the center of attention, but rather because attention was naturally directed to her.

Once she settled in, the laughter would flow and a party atmosphere would fill the house. Aunt Mary and my parents would share drinks and first catch up on all things Fritzky, Varick, and Cassidy. Then invariably, at some point, Aunt Mary would sweetly set the table with a touching, moving, heartfelt story of human drama, during which you could hear a pin drop anywhere else in the house.

Outside of the mellifluous tones of Aunt Mary's voice, there were three floors of abject silence.

This was the prelude that she would use to set the table, before opening up about the next fund-raiser or the next pilgrimage or the next First Saturday gathering and the question or questions to be asked. Maybe it was about some of us going on a pilgrimage or about the need for us to sell so many books of raffle tickets or about taking in someone's baby so that they could go on the pilgrimage or simply about getting some of the disabled from some facility to the next First Saturday. The variables were limitless, and the point is simply that a question or series of questions would inevitably and tenderly be placed on the table.

Her requests were never made with a thud. They never grated on one's senses.

And my tough, gruff, World War II veteran, hard-charging disciplinarian, "No, Rosie, not this time, no" of a dad would invariably melt like butter, while my always sweet mom knowingly smiled at him. Putty in her hands, he'd say, "Why, sure, Mary," a "Why, sure, Mary" that still echoes loudly in the more pleasant membranes of my cerebral cortex. Beyond my dad's hard exterior, there was this old softie. It was a place that Mary could reach and that few did, a place that didn't fully open itself up to his own children until the later years of his life when the leukemia was bearing down on him.

It took my dad a long, long time to fully return home from the horrors of World War II. He served as a frontline medic throughout the North African and Continental campaigns, and he was in eleven distinct invasions. Yes, it took a long time for him to come home and to become who he was again, but Aunt Mary had this unique way of pulling upon the strings of who he really was always.

Had Aunt Mary's interests been different, she could have sold that proverbial ice to the Eskimos.

She could have been the greatest saleswoman in human history. But she rather traded in fashioning grace and rainmakers of peace and servants of those less fortunate. She was an "eight beatitudes" saleswoman. But along the way and for the record and this is most important to understand about her, she just lived larger. When we smiled, she smiled more broadly. And when we laughed, she laughed louder.

Oh, she had a wonderful reverberating laugh that could lighten any mood and bring light to the darkness, and she had this penetrating smile that cleansed those in her presence.

Our church, of course, may never recognize abilities such as these as extraordinary, but they were. There was something just downright miraculous in her capacity to light up a room. Just miraculous! I can close my eyes, concentrate, and see and hear it all still.

Twenty-five or twenty-six years removed, it still warms.

She was, in and of herself, a source of light and life.

To accent the above, I want to digress and share a quick story.

I married Maggie in 1981, whereupon I came to know her Aunt Eileen Kiely, one of her Mom Peg's older sisters. Eileen had long been crippled and lived a life in a wheelchair. With few social outlets available to her, we arranged in that summer of 1981 for her to go on the "handicapped (and now disabled) pilgrimage" to Canada in late July, which was her first introduction to Mary and the First Saturday family.

When we went to Immaculate Conception Church in Secaucus, then the point of departure for Canada to see her off, Eileen was like an expectant, nervous, and anxious child who was going off to summer camp. But she returned home as happy as could be and with what can only be described as a burning love for Aunt Mary. She became a First Saturday regular, and it fell to me to get her there—to the respective parish hosts—and back for years. It was one non-working escape from our extraordinary life with so many, many children that Maggie invited and welcomed.

This was the routine. All conversations—on the drive, both before and after Mass, and before and after the rosary—were dominated by one overarching and all-pervading Aunt Eileen concern. The question that was constantly asked was a variation on this theme: "Richie, can you get me close to Mary?" "Do you think you can get me close to Mary?" "Please, I want to sit by Mary at the luncheon," etc.

Preoccupied and persistent and urgent, I'd invariably get her seated right at Mary's table, which was no easy task and it required both speed and skill, as there were quite a number of Aunt Eileens in that group who longed for the same thing—to be close to Mary. Victoriously placed, she'd beam like a little child who had just won a game in the playground. Close to Aunt Mary, all was right with her world. Then too, naturally, Aunt Mary was so good at making those around her feel just that way.

There was no one to her who wasn't the *most special*.

For the record, I want the world to know that Maggie resolved my escaping from the children for First Saturdays, upon realizing that there was no reason that they couldn't go with me and take turns riding on Hank Colling's wheel chair in some church basement somewhere, in the pursuit of which, they too inevitably became relentless.

Maggie, therefore, made it her escape instead. Well played, diabolical, and successful!

So Mary Varick may not be familiar to the world, at least not yet. And while a process was instigated by priests who knew and loved her to have her goodness proclaimed by her church, it has yet to move forward. That is, of course, the same church that once freely assigned the title of saint to legions of the faithful upon the will or whim of power brokers in its hierarchy. Of late, of course, it has become much more demanding, discriminating, and exclusive.

Just two years ago, Holy Brother Andre, who performed many miracles in the name of his beloved Saint Joseph and who gave us Saint Joseph's Oratory atop Mount Royal in Montreal, finally made the grade, as did another one of my loves just this past year, Kateri Tekawitha, the Lily of the Mohawks, who I also personally revere and who is the first native North American saint. Mother Teresa, as saintly a woman who ever walked the earth, has been declared "blessed," but even she, however universally anointed, must wait and be processed.

However deserving, even she is not freely awarded the title, a title that the faithful have long attributed to her anyway.

But she was our Mary's friend and she was the loving servant of the "poorest of the poor." She is, without question, a saint, whether or not the title is officially endowed yet or not.

We all know this. How can she not be?

The point here, however, is that so too is my Aunt Mary, as all who knew her will attest. And Mother Teresa would have been the first to tell you so. After all, she asked Mary to put in a good word for her with God!

# In Her Own Words

## The Books

Her own books so clearly reflect who she was.

*My Yoke Is Easy—My Burden Light, Not Without Tears*, and *Till Death* were written over the course of two decades, and the first, the one that focused so much on family, was written and rushed to print at a time, when she fully expected that blindness was imminent. The truth is that while her sight seriously deteriorated, she never did go blind.

What is important for us to know in retrospect, however, is that Mary did not fear this. She never feared anything that God might want to toss her way. Suffering as she did from so many maladies and conditions before going home to God, the pain she alone and personally experienced over her seventy-four years was enough to fill dozens of lifetimes with angel-like sacrificial cleansings. So even blindness would never—could never—have broken her spirit, but it was one cross from which she was spared.

The first book was actually written in 1960, the same year that her youngest brother John was ordained a priest at Sacred Heart Cathedral in Newark, New Jersey; the second book in 1963, one year after her brother Francis also was ordained there; and the third, in her trilogy, eighteen years later in 1981, the year that I had the good fortune of marrying Maggie Sireno.

The copies of each that I once possessed in my youth had long ago been loaned out, summarily passed on to others, and lost.

Good books or meaningful books have this habit of getting lost on you.

In my desire to reread them in preparing for this undertaking, therefore, I reached out to my cousin Mary Pisaniello and asked to borrow hers. At first, she shipped me all three of them with the clear understanding that three of my twelve children would be sent to her and Bruno as indentured servants or collateral until such time as the books were returned.

Later, she kindly and sweetly relented and insisted that I keep them. I did so only in the full faith and trust that she had spares to fall back upon. But I have conveniently never bothered to ask.

Treasured gifts, they will not physically leave my house again, as they have now been secured in an archived collector's section of my personal library, where they may only be perused on site. There, they will remain for so long as I remain on this earth. You are kindly invited to visit should you wish to read them. For I will well share, but I will no longer *giveth* away.

Each, of course, is written in the first person, and her tone throughout is light and personal and conversational. While that is true throughout, it also should be noted that the third book—written well after her beloved Bill's death and her daughter Billie's death and when the weight and scope of service had exponentially grown—is a bit more somber. She does not write to impress or to dazzle and only occasionally relies upon poetic imagery or metaphor. To read her books is not unlike being with her in her kitchen or living room or, better still, in her room at the Auberge at Sainte-Anne's or at the Madonna House at Our Lady of the Cape, two of her most favorite places on earth, in the wee hours of the morning.

In those "wee hours of the morning" conversations, I learned much about my faith and her "inner circle" and even my own family.

On one trip in the late seventies, I learned that my father was ever so much more than the man I knew at the time and certainly worthy of more than I was giving. As a result and in time, my very way of being with my dad changed. Long before the best of him finally started to return home from those tattered fields in Europe and the horror of World War II, we had managed to grow close. Now maybe, it would have happened anyway, but Aunt Mary's place at the switching station here was never lost on me.

She let me know that I had to look deeper and to go deeper.

And please don't think that I'm throwing the word around loosely, but this surely was another miracle in my life.

In the first book, Father Rinfret, a member of the Oblates of Mary Immaculate (OMI), who grew to be Mary's dear and close personal friend, wrote the "Foreword." He did so in the later books as well, but he was joined by Bishop Peter Sutton in the third. Father Rinfret was long the director of Our Lady of the

Cape (Cap de la Madeleine) on the banks of the Saint Lawrence River in Three Rivers (Trois-Rivieres), Quebec.

The very first line of the "Foreword" was, "Congratulations," a word that was carefully and pointedly chosen by him. He did so, "In the hope that the love of God that burns in Mary will consequently burn in her readers." He believed that and he still believed it when I last saw him in front of the old chapel at the Cape after an August First Saturday Mass in 2009, twenty years after Mary Varick had gone home to God.

Happy to be with vestiges of Mary's family, he spoke of her as if he had just seen her yesterday. Her place at the heart of the table of his life had not changed. Twenty years after her death, his relationship with her remained as fresh and as intimate as one could possibly imagine.

In the year to follow, Mary's beloved Father Rinfret also celebrated his "homegoing to Jesus."

Mary once wrote a poem for Father Rinfret's twenty-fifth anniversary as a priest that was later and now long ago committed to song. And if today's First Saturday Club has an anthem, it would certainly be it. For "In host held high, what do I see—My sweet Jesus who was born for me—My Jesus who has lived for me—My Jesus who died for me."

So it was and so it remains and so it shall, tomorrow, be.

Her first book both began and ended with references to the anticipated blindness. As the first and last lines are usually instructive, the first was, "It is, indeed, a strange feeling to know that by the time anyone gets to read this manuscript, I'll be blind." While the last read, "I am not worthy, but as the darkness closes in, I'll try to be."

This book was a warm expression of thanks to God for her parents and family. She writes of a mom who daily trekked to All Saints Church for Mass and communion and of a dad who never passed by a church without stopping in. After all, as he always said, "You would not pass a friend by without giving him the time of day." She sings the praises of her brothers and sister and most keenly focuses in on the two youngest of the seven, on Francis "Skip" and John, who were to be the family priests.

She shared the overt and unabashed delight and pride that a sister had for the fact that something so wonderful about her family was so.

Not one priest, but two!

But, above all else, in the first book, she tells the tale of her unlikely and wholly unexpected love story, one that she describes as "more fantastic than any fairy tale" and of their wedding that was dedicated to the Sacred Heart of Jesus on the June 4, feast day of the Sacred Heart in 1937. If there was a star in the first book, it was, without question, Bill Varick, the great love of her life, who joined her and served as her first mate in all she sought to do to serve the disabled, those who would join her in that great effort, and, of course, her God.

It was Bill who was her portal to service.

In this first book, Mary carefully explains the theology behind the "inner circle," her *theology of suffering*, a theology that would bring so much light and hope and so much meaning and purpose to those she served. In reflecting as she wrote this story, she keenly refined her thinking and became one with this theology, one which joyfully proclaimed that the disabled, who could not do what others could, were most certainly capable of doing something far more important and special.

They were called by God to pray and to pray more than those who necessarily had to be caught up in the things of the world.

They had, in fact, been given a gift, one that richly permitted them to grow closer to God than most by simply giving God more of their time. This was a privilege that was accompanied by an even greater privilege, the ability to offer their suffering and pain up to God, so as to help sanctify and redeem others. Through this prayer and this sacrifice, grace was to be fashioned and, at least, one component or element or part of a broken world was to be cleansed and made right.

Mary didn't just preach this. She lived it, manifested it, and bore witness to it in all she said and did.

Her "inner circle," her disabled would gather on First Saturday and go to Mass and share in the Eucharist and pray the rosary as Blessed Mary had asked at Fatima. They would pray for the removal of any and all regimes that would stand in the way of free peoples who were interested in and determined to do God's work on earth.

They would pray for peace on earth and for universal brotherhood.

And then they would break bread together, enjoying a meal of roasted chicken and mashed potatoes or fresh baked lasagna or pot roast with green peas and creamed onions prepared by a team of volunteers from the host parish. Housed in either the school cafeteria or auditorium or the church basement, they would gather around tables adorned in paper with centerpieces of plastic vases in which a single fresh flower or two or three had been placed.

There, the disabled and their fellows and the volunteers who transported them and carried their wheelchairs up stone steps and down basement steps and pushed them inside and out of quiet corridors would get to know one another. There, some learned what it felt like to smile and others to laugh. There, they grew together and bonded as a family does and those without friends made friends.

Mary celebrated this relatively new staple in her life, the First Saturday Club communions that had been prompted by her beloved Bill. As to all the carrying, note that handicapped accessible was not yet in vogue back then. It would take a long time before the public consciousness began to awaken.

Mary wrote of her children, of Billie, Barbara, Jim, and Mary, especially of Billie whose school essay about her mom was on prominent display. She wrote of the early auto and then pullman train car pilgrimages and of Father John O'Brien of All Saints Church and of Neil and Anne Gulliksen and of Sister Miriam Eymard and Sister Claire Cordis and of John and Anna Fritzky, my great uncle and aunt on my dad's side who were among her first volunteers, and of Art and Claire McMahon and their son Darren and of my Uncle Jim and Uncle Joe and Uncle Bud, the three brothers who were with her from the first day.

She wrote of the earliest of the disabled and of the earliest of volunteers, of Fritz and Mary Hafmeister and Yvonne, of her seminarian brothers and their friends, Mike Darcy and Lou Fimiani on the Scala Sancta at Sainte-Anne's, of the delight that she took in the fact that six of her brother Jim and sister-in-law Helen's eight children joined her on one pilgrimage, and of having grown so that as many as thirty-seven seriously disabled pilgrims had ventured out on another pilgrimage.

The book was a testimony, a loving testimony to what had been fashioned and a call to action for the future.

She wrote of her and Bill's first New Year's Eve party in 1940, which was marked by her dad, Jim's insisting that she—Mary—not accompany them out into the cold to say good night. He told her that it was too cold for her to see them out. Lovingly, he said, "Mary, what would we do if anything ever happened to you?"

Later that day, on January 1, 1940, he succumbed to a cerebral hemorrhage at the Penn Railroad Yards in Jersey City. Leaving Mary forever with a "What would we do if anything ever happened to you?"

I came to learn later in life that this had much to do with Mary's holding on to the New Year's Eve celebrations.

It was my mom, in fact, who told me once that, "Mary celebrates New Year's in order to keep from ever letting go of our dad." This is noted especially as Aunt Mary's New Year's Eve parties became legendary. I see myself, as a little boy, in bed at Nana's next door at 243 Pacific Avenue, but unable to sleep because of the noise coming from Aunt Mary and Uncle Bill's 241 Pacific. And there I was, in a later year, being tricked by my Uncle Bill Varick who assured me that pickled herring tasted just like candy.

And I was there, with my young siblings and cousins, banging pots and pans outside, and later setting off fireworks with Uncle Buddy outside of 241 and 243 Pacific Avenue as January 1 ushered in. I also, as the years passed, well remember being part of a debauched group that stumbled down that Pacific Avenue block for Midnight Mass. And there were years of ushering in the New Year at the Colonnade in Newark with Father Don Arel's Midnight Masses, after skating across the street in an always semi-threatening Branch Brook Park.

Mary, indeed, long kept dibs on New Year's, even onto Belvidere, New Jersey, and her years there with Bruno and Mary. I know because I drove my mom and dad out one year. My mom would have walked clear across America in order to be with Mary on New Year's Eve (and though never spoken, I believe that she too was holding onto her dad along with Mary), so clear across New Jersey to Belvidere wasn't really all that far.

My growth and my rights of passage were so clearly marked and framed by my role and place at Aunt Mary's New Year's celebrations. There is a rich pathos attached to being tucked away in bed before it all began in one picture to stumbling down the street with cousins and aunts and uncles in the dead of night in the next.

The second book, *Not Without Tears*, was more of the same with many, many more names and profound thanksgivings and touching human dramas added. As she was again writing at the Cape at the dawn of spring, she began by singing the praises of the season and of the new life that it heralded, which is, notably, as rich a metaphor as can be conjured up for the Lord of Life's promise to us all. "It is spring and I am at our Lady's Shrine," she began and what then could possibly be wrong with the world.

She was with her great friend Father Rinfret at our Lady's Shrine in our Lady's arms, and it was spring. Everywhere, life was renewing itself and bearing witness to the essential passages of the Gospel and the essential gifts in the life of resurrection people.

No wonder then that she concluded this second thank-you of hers, for that is just what her books were, one in which she juxtaposed the rough-hewn tears that came with the absolute joys, with a "Deo Gratias for each day of my life."

*Till Death*, the third of Mary's books and the shortest of them, was published first in 1981 which is where Mary Varick left it, but then it was picked up again and reprinted in late 1989, with the addition of an epilogue by her daughter Mary Pisaniello. Young Mary (and she will be forever young) brought the then Mary Varick story home, as Mary too had gone home to her glory in June of that same year.

Sent to the angels and to her God and to Bill, she was joyfully released by those who so loved her on earth.

And while family and her three remaining children would especially miss her, the requiem mass that was concelebrated at Saint Lucy's in Newark was offered up in a spirit of abundant joy. Father Paul Bochicchio, the latest in a long string of faithful priests who devoted themselves to Mary's work, delivered a stirring the "Hills are alive with the sound of music," "How do you solve a problem like Mary?" eulogy that, indeed, turned tears into laughter.

Why joy? Because her life had been an uplifting prayer!

Every single trial or challenge or burden experienced on any given day had been accepted gratefully and given back to Christ, and all that she lived for and all that she accomplished was but a preparation for her own resurrection, her own passing into the living presence of her God, her own triumph. As we celebrated the wonder of her presence in our own lives, the sound of "Well done, good and faithful servant" loudly reverberated in the heavens above.

In Mary's name, we sang "Deo Gratias, Deo Gratias," and our spirits ascended and the grace of God was showered down upon us. And we felt Mary smiling so—beaming as only she could, as a bright sun and clear and shimmering blue sky invited us all to smile right back.

Earlier in the '80s, Mary had shocked her immediate family and her immediate world with the announcement that she would be marrying Jerry Sheehan, an especially devoted volunteer who had, for long, served Mary's immediate needs in the '70s, before leaving for five years to serve Mother Theresa's Missionary of Charity Brothers, after Mother Teresa herself had questioned him as to how he intended to spend his life and as to whether or not he intended to give it to God.

In response to Mother's challenge to Mary's friend, he worked with the homeless addicts and alcoholics on the streets of Los Angeles. Those were the same years that Mary largely spent with Bruno and Mary, and in Mary Pisaniello's telling, her mom had only recently determined to move back to Newark where she could be closer to her "inner circle."

New, accessible, archdiocesan-controlled apartments for the disabled were being made available to her and other members of her First Saturday family, including Connie LoPresti, a double leg amputee who had long been with the First Saturday Club. The apartments were ideally located directly across the street from Saint Lucy's and right below the Colonnade where Mary had long lived.

In a call from Jerry at that time, she told him that she was about to start a new life and would soon be moving into the Villa Victoria complex where the welcome sign had been placed by Jesus and Mary.

What better place, she noted, could there possibly be to live?

Jerry responded that he too needed to embark on a new life as he was planning to leave the order. And right then and there, after five years of separation, he said that he was leaving to come back and help her with her work. If he was to give his life to God, he determined that it was, for him, best to do so through Mary and her ministry. And as all he wanted was to be with her and to serve her cause, why not marry? Years younger with what would appear to be much more life before him, he chose a life with my aunt, one in which her getting-here-or-there worries would be forever over.

People, as people often do, were still cracking jokes about it all on the day of the wedding, but I took pride in my own wife, Maggie's singing at their wedding, and I found heavenly affirmation in the fact that my Aunt Mary's smile beamed so brightly— so much so that she, indeed, looked like a young and beautiful bride who was but in the greening and youthful spring of her life.

So young Mary wrote of this and of her mom's continued adventures and journeys in her final years! There wasn't a shrine on the North American continent that the two of them didn't get to, and Mary almost became a fixture at Guadalupe. They went to the Holy Land and to Midnight Mass on Christmas in Bethlehem, right where Christ was born, and the pilgrimages were sustained and her "inner circle" was sustained, and on every First Saturday, they continued to gather somewhere to pray and to sing and to grow in love.

In the "Epilogue," it was acknowledged that Mary's had, indeed, been a rich, full life, one that had been genuinely devoted to God and truly enjoyed at one and the same time. After all, what was there about a life for God that was not to be celebrated?

There were, of course, other pilgrimages where people rode on the bus to Canada solemnly praying for ten solid hours. Holy and somber and entirely not in keeping, I believe, with how God wants us to live. With Aunt Mary, you prayed as well and the days were filled with masses and devotions and private moments with God, but there also were celebrations and parties and silly shows and pranks and endless opportunities to hold up and to honor and to embrace each other.

There were opportunities to be both spiritual and human.

Mary Varick's *Till Death* opened with a question. "How was it, after all, that a little girl and polio victim was to have been used by God as an instrument of his love?" Then later, she asked how was it that she and Bill, after the wonder of July 17, 1951, were to become "beggars for Christ."

The answer to both questions, of course, was simply that it was God's call, God's will, His "My will be done" for her.

In the end, she suggested that God asks only for that which you yourself need in order to be fulfilled, in order to live fully. And after all, what could possibly be wrong with begging, if you were begging for God in the first place? If there were hits to be taken in doing so, then take them and smile broadly in the taking.

That is exactly what she did!

Out of poverty, she built a vessel both in and for the Kingdom of God. A vessel that touched tens of thousands of people over the years.

In the final book, she devoted much attention, first and foremost, to the suffering and loss of her beloved Bill, whose neurological problems put the family through a number of frightening episodes. There was one especially difficult time in Washington, DC, when he was actually lost for a couple of days. While sad and tragic, his gentle and happy disposition never betrayed him or Mary before his passing in 1966.

Over the years that followed, many of her pilgrims and even her beloved brothers, Father Frank "Skip" Cassidy in 1967 at just thirty-six years of age and her oldest brother and faithful pilgrim Jim in 1974, also went home to God. And then in 1977, immediately following her return to the United States, from a pilgrimage to Russia, Rome, and Lourdes, she lost her beloved daughter Billie who had battled the horror and deterioration of multiple sclerosis in the devoted care of her husband Don and her four children Don, Mike, Maryanne, and Peggy.

What they lived and dealt with was its own story, but I personally carry an indelible image of Mike and Peggy communicating with their mom by reciting the alphabet and waiting for the blink of her beautiful eyes, via which they'd translate the first word and then the words that followed. There could be no greater love than that kind of patient and blood-red love.

Each and every one of them joined in Billie's suffering. Each and every one of them paid an incalculable price.

It was, for Mary, a profound loss in what had been a decade of great losses. What it also did is beg the "Why, God?" questions, at least for us mere mortals, but not for Mary. The why it had to be that a long disabled mother who so devoted herself to the disabled had to see her own daughter completely broken and humbled by one of the harshest of all maladies! One that completely breaks down and then eliminates all bodily function until that point where there is not strength enough left to open the eyes or to take a breath!

Like Job, Mary and her family were pushed beyond all limits, only to come out whole and clean on the other side. Faith proved unshakable as always. It had been God and the Eucharist before Bill's and Skip's and Billie's and Bud's deaths, just as it was God and the Eucharist after. All that was experienced was lived in the spirit of "This day thou shalt be with me in paradise."

"*Beata Maria Virgine*," she would pray so lovingly and devotedly to that other Mary, again and again and again, until peace rolled over her like a river no matter the circumstances—no matter the cross.

Great faith, you see, is impregnable and unshakable!

In her final book, she also spent time with the Pisaniello brothers—Father Matt, the then pastor of Holy Family in Nutley and director of the Diocesan Mount Carmel Guild, and his younger brother, Bruno. Father Matt was one of those "old school" priests who could get things done and also pull financial rabbits out of his hat. Mary wrote of the many fires that he put out for her.

"How," after all, a future pastor of Holy Family would come to ask, "do you solve a problem like Mary?"

The answer, for long, had been with Father Matt's bag of tricks.

She knowingly wrote a bad check on a Saturday to a restaurant at the New York World's Fair in 1965 for the luncheon that they had served to some 330 First Saturday pilgrims. With no local parish to cover this tab, Mary was on her own at the New York World's Fair and she and her First Saturday club were flat broke.

But, by God, she still had a First Saturday Club checkbook and a pen as well.

It was, by the way, a great luncheon and unlike the usual local parish fare, but it also was one incredibly big bill. She gave it to God, wrote the check knowing that it wouldn't be deposited until Monday, went home, and called Father Matt who pulled his strings and brought her a check for deposit Monday morning.

Mary kept faith with those who delivered like this for her and paid back for such services rendered, but not without keeping her cohorts, the Father Matts of her world, jumping through loops all of the time on her behalf.

The other Pisaniello in the Pisaniello brother team was none other than our Bruno, he of a rather notorious quick wit and dry humor, who was to light up young Mary Varick's life and to marry her and to bring three children into the world with her, Laura, Barbara, and Billie. Bruno was, is, and ever shall be to those who know him a blessing.

One very funny and sweet man, he has certainly been a blessing to me.

The unprecedented and surprising trip to Russia, Rome, and Lourdes in 1977 and the earlier trip to Fatima, Lourdes, and Rome in 1967 deserve special attention. The 1967 trip and "all that could possibly go wrong" and the extraordinary 1977 Russian trip are fodder for a separate chapter, but a brief reflection on Russia is in order here.

They went because Mary was determined to "touch the suffering Christ in Russia" where worship and faith had long ago been put on trial and condemned. It was, as always, Mary's call, and she was abundantly clear as to why. They were going to make a mark for Jesus Christ in Russia, a theme that cut to the heart of the First Saturday Club's "Fatima" mission—for peace in the world and for God in the world.

They did the then unthinkable and traveled to Leningrad or Saint Petersburg by ship from Finland. There, a First Saturday Mass was offered in what was first described as the only Catholic church that was still used for worship in all of Leningrad, but later as Our Lady of Lourdes.

That small church loomed as the very heart of Catholicism in the all of a vast Russia and spiritually, with their visit, it no doubt was.

In her own writing, she largely dwelled on the interplay between her pilgrims, the small band of older parishioners, the women with the worn and wrinkled faces who were still brave enough to go to mass, and the communist youth who were there to help out, but more importantly, to watch and to keep in check. The older women at Our Lady of Lourdes, in what was but a vestige of a once parish, donned their babushkas as in days of old.

In the end, Mary believed that her group helped to show the Russian *Intourist* youth what love is and the old vestiges of that once parish what hope is. They shed a little light, they inspired, and they made a small difference in a place that had, for more than thirty years, known little but darkness. They helped bring the light of Christ back in, and in putting on Christ themselves, they couldn't help but share Him with others.

And it's nice to know that today, the light of the Lord, indeed, shines brightly in Saint Petersburg again.

Aunt Mary loved a good story and reveled in sharing them. A small sampling included the following: there's one *of* Father Matt, whose Mount Carmel Guild provided services for those who were then referred to as mentally retarded and whose speaking presence was subsequently being advertised as follows: "Come, hear the retarded priest." While obviously not intended as it sounded, he carried the label for quite some time and in great fun. She also delighted in the "tongue in cheek" poem delivered by her brother Father John Cassidy about what is was like to be related to Mary and to live in the wake of her constant storms at what was a twentieth anniversary testimonial honoring her pilgrimage work.

Her young brother brought the house down. (Oh, how I wish that I could get my hands on that poem.) She writes of Father Al Clarke and Father Don Arel and Betty Cleary and John and Jean Brown and Carmelo Rocco and Father Henry Naddeo and Bishop Peter Sutton and of a litany of other blessed souls who helped her so much and whom she loved even more.

She remembered Ed Somerhalter from the early days, whose spine was fused and who could not sit down. Not ever! "Straight Ed" as he was affectionately known once glanced over at Mary and said, "In your heaven, Mary, there will be a pair of dancing shoes and in mine, a soft, easy chair."

Mary closed out this final book, noting that it had been thirty years since the miracle that so altered her life. For fifteen of those years, she had her Bill to lean on. "As to the remaining fifteen years," she concluded, "I have ever counted on his continued help from his well-deserved place in eternity." And so it was.

More than anything else, her books pay tribute to her pilgrims and to those who either contributed or raised the money and to those who volunteered and cared for her pilgrims and especially to those who suffered in any way or fashion along the way. And so many of her pilgrims, indeed, suffered horrifically over the years, pilgrims whose loud and poignant and resonating cries of "why" gave way to "why not's" in the loving embrace of Mary's pilgrim family.

Her books were about what the unbridled love of a family can effect, about the power of love, and about the gift of grace. She hammered away at the redemptive power of silently accepting suffering in Christ's name and at the raw power of redemptive souls who sacrifice and give away the all of their lives for others.

She shined light upon the cross and the continuing resurrection made manifest in the lives of her pilgrim and disabled family.

It was about the ability of remarkable human beings to bear the unbearable, to recognize their place on the cross, and to accept that place in order to free others.

To free others, to save others, to redeem others!

Dozens of stories just like this are briefly explored as Mary devotes more attention to the ends, rather than the means. To the ends—the faith, the cross, the redemption, the grace, the Eucharist, and a proactive and loving relationship with God! Mary's love for Jesus Christ and for his Mother, Mary, and her Mother passionately manifest itself on every page.

She was, always and without question, on fire for Jesus.

Simple and focused and devoted and incredibly reverent, she moved inexorably forward, through these pages, in service to her "inner circle" and to her God. And oh, how she honors Mary and Anne and Joachim and Joseph and Bernadette and Jacinta and Lucia and all those in their lives in the process.

In her later years, most notably in the third book and beyond, her story began to read like a travelogue as she literally combed the continent and a good part of the globe, but what struck me was that no matter where she went and no matter what she did, however contrived or difficult, she wound up always in the same house, in the same place, *in the same Eucharist*.

All roads, all stories, and all challenges met took her and her companions or minions to the Eucharist, to the Lord's table, to that greatest of gifts.

As already noted, in the very moment when she was cured of the cancer, she prayed to retain her "coveted place at the foot of the cross" as a cripple.

To understand Mary at all, you must not only know this but you must also be able to embrace it. And to know her fully, you must somehow be able to rejoice in it with her as well.

For in one's suffering and in their pain and in that which most troubles, a place at that most holy foot of the cross is secured and manifested, a place where one can miraculously join with Christ and directly share in His sacred effort to redeem the world.

It is in that place where Mary Varick chose to live.

Over and over and over again in her books, she writes about her belief that her suffering disabled, her "God's inner circle" were a bountiful tool for the reconciliation of peace in the world. This again was at the heart of her First Saturday's "Fatima" mission. And she'd write that, "There is in affliction, a closeness to God that those who were healthy never experience." Or she would write that God gave her suffering pilgrims. "this special chance to know Him and to love Him and that the only choice was whether or not they were willing to sanctify their own sufferings for the love of Him."

She does not even attach the word *sacrifice* to handicapped or disabled, but rather remarkably refers to the same as a gift only, as a portal to a special grace and a special power.

It was never about sacrifice, but rather the giving of gifts.

And oh, how humbled even one as disabled as I am by what they lived and how movingly our Mary shares both their stories and the love she had for them. Then ever apologizing for her lack of eloquence, she takes us far beyond eloquence's domain into the sinew of their hearts.

But in the end, she takes us always to the Eucharist, to that place where we must live and to that place where she believed we are ultimately healed and redeemed.

# Measuring Her Life

Mary Varick's life, like all of our lives, was lived in minutes and hours and years and in homes and in places and especially in people, in legions of people. Tracking seventy-four years is easy, but the months and hours and minutes are nearly impossible to track. So we rely on the years, and they mark the time and the sweet movement of it all. So too are the homes and the places where she lived easy to track, although the places where she visited and stayed in passing are many and beyond our full grasp, as is our focus upon the all of the people who passed through her life.

We recognize that we will but scratch the surface and that is enough.

In fact, it is more than enough.

As to time, it should be noted that she squeezed ever so much more into her years and months and hours and minutes than you or me and I dare say almost anyone else ever does. She lived. She lived large, and there was a quality given to her quantity that so enriched the time she had. She used her time wisely, in praying hard and laughing loud and smiling broadly and loving richly.

And relentlessly!

She did not waste her days or even her hours or minutes.

As already noted, she was born and raised at 243 Pacific Avenue in the Lafayette section of Jersey City, New Jersey, and while residing briefly in an apartment after her marriage in 1937, she returned not long after to take up residence in the home immediately next door to the home that she grew up in at 241 Pacific Avenue, a narrow three-floor, brick-front walk-up.

Like the home she grew up in, it had great character.

Then in the mid-sixties, she took up residence in the new Colonnade Apartments in Newark, the third of the three Colonnade buildings from which she and her family overlooked Branch Brook Park which was directly below—and Sacred Heart Cathedral which was only three blocks down but clearly visible. Saint Lucy's Church was directly below the eastern front of the building (Mary's apartment faced west), so what would become her new parish was less than half a block away.

In Jersey City, it had almost been a full block.

She was getting even closer to what was always her real home. Churches and parishes and catholic communities, both small and immediate and great and worldly, formed the fabric of her life. She lived through the portal of the church.

For a time, she later lived with her daughter Mary and son-in-law, Bruno Pisaniello, in Belvidere, New Jersey. At Saint Patrick's, the church there, a hooded ramp was installed just for her, but it was all of a couple of blocks away. She returned to Newark, upon her second marriage to Jerry Sheehan in 1982 to take up residence in the then new Villa Victoria Apartments, immediately to the north of Saint Lucy's Church. In the northern shadow of the Colonnade, Villa Victoria stood those same three blocks away from the Newark Archdiocese's Sacred Heart Cathedral, where her two younger brothers, Jack and Skip, had been ordained.

Notably, she had always and rather remarkably, resided just a few stones' throw away from a church, a fact that metaphorically and poetically spoke loudly and beautifully to her connection and her devotion to the Eucharist.

## The Homes That Warmed Her

As to the places of her life, there will be no virtual tour and we are not concerned with any details, and it can be argued that she was most at home when she wasn't at home—at the shrines she loved and in houses of worship and before the altar and in the Eucharist.

In the end, nothing else mattered.

But where one lives and lays their head to rest at night and prays in the dead of night and boils the coffee in the morning says something about us all. Homes do help define people and come to take on their personalities. So, it is worth sharing a few thoughts and comments about the primary homes of Mary Varick, without relying upon anything more than my own very limited memory. But there are images that are so stark and real and vivid, images that the passage of time cannot distort.

When I, in my childhood, met Mary's childhood home at 243 Pacific Avenue in the Lafayette section of Jersey City, she and Bill and her four children were living right next door—row house-to-row house. With deep-burnt red brick fronts, the entrance to both was through a street-level door that actually opened up beneath the grand stairway that rose up to the second floors of both houses. The two homes, therefore, were not only bound spiritually but also physically.

They shared the same stairwell.

Each had an extremely small patch of grass that was guarded by a wrought iron fence in front and a small walkway that abutted the base of the grand stairway. Standing on street level, the doorway to Nana's house was to the right and the one to Aunt Mary's was to the left, again physically binding the one to the other. The grass in front of Nana's house was well manicured, while the patch in front of Aunt Mary and Uncle Bill's was well worn by the pitter-patter of little feet and their dog Smoky. There was far more dirt than grass and what grass there was certainly didn't know what it was to be manicured.

When exiting either home, All Saint's, the Roman Catholic church, where Mary was married and where her four children were baptized and where her two brothers said their first masses, was to the left, while the Greek Orthodox Catholic church, Saint Mary's, was to the right. It was but a stone's throw away while All Saint's was a good stretch of the legs.

But corner-to-corner, left or right, these homes were spiritually framed by houses of worship, just as Mary's life was. No matter what way one went, God was waiting, right there, on the corner. Symbolically, He just couldn't be escaped

What was, for me, Nana's home and Uncle Bud's home and later Aunt Anne's home was a place of wonder. Three floors and narrow but long, it was a warm, cozy, and inviting place. You entered into a living room with a comfortable sofa and easy chairs and soft lights and proceeded through a short hallway that was adorned with built-in drawers and cabinets to the right, and then proceeded into a dining room, the same room where we ate the hard rolls and butter and sticky buns that Uncle Buddy got for us long before the parents awoke, the same room where Father John said mass while we were waiting for my cousin and Mary's nephew (Joe and Dot's child) David's body to arrive home from Vietnam. It was followed by a kitchenette that was no bigger than a pantry closet and yet could produce feasts for the multitudes. The kitchenette emptied into a small enclosed backyard where rose and lilac flowers and azalea bushes bloomed.

There were no sightlines from the yard which was framed or rather enclosed by brick buildings—north, east, south, and west.

It gave one the sense that everyone on Pacific Avenue belonged to one another. And in that day and age, they actually did. As real neighbors, they were, in fact, bound both spiritually and physically.

On the second floor, there were three bedrooms, with Nana's in the rear, Bud's in the front, and a walk through guest room with two small twin beds in the middle. It was a room that I knew well, for it was where I slept when the grand events at Aunt Mary and Uncle Bill's were going on next door. The noise from the wall beyond generated this sense of peace, and I just knew that one of the single uncles, Bud at that time or John or Frank, the last two were but seminarians then, would invariably stop back over to check on me and my siblings.

They always did, each in their own time, making little people feel as special and important as whatever it was that was generating all of that noise next door.

Upstairs lied two guest bedrooms and the only bathroom in the house that separated the two guest rooms. Looking out the window to the right on the third floor, out of the front bedroom overlooking Pacific Avenue gave one the best view of the Statue of Liberty in the harbor, and the old pull-chain toilet in the small bathroom always fascinated. And why it is that I can close my eyes and still smell (pleasantly so) that bathroom is beyond me.

Now I know this is but memory playing tricks, but I swear it was as if that picture of the Sacred Heart of Jesus was looking down upon me from every wall on every floor of that house. It was Nana's gift to all of her children and to the grandchildren on their wedding days as well. In any event, you didn't think about committing even the smallest of sins in that house, because the eyes of Jesus were most certainly upon you.

There appeared to be no place whatsoever to hide from Him.

That was the home that Mary Varick lived in, the home that molded and shaped her until the day she got married. And just a couple of years later, she and Bill wound up right next door at 241 Pacific.

Needless to say, the Varick home had that messy and lived-in feel instead. And you didn't enter from street level into an inviting living room but into what was a kind of half dining room and half drawing room that couldn't quite make up its mind just what it wanted to be, because what was the dining room at 243 Pacific had been converted into a huge kitchen at 241 in order to accommodate a household with children. Those inlaid cabinets and drawers in the hall also were so stuffed that they were literally bursting at the seams, which truly paralleled and caught the essence of Aunt Mary's life and its virtual disorder. And the small backyard at the Varick home was ever so much more exciting than Nana's neatly appointed one. There was a patio of cement blocks with blades of grass filtering through the cracks and what couldn't have been much more than an in-ground cement tub, loomed to us, as the most inviting and greatest of all swimming pools.

The living room in the Varick home, which to me always bubbled with excitement, was on the front end of the second floor, and oh, do I remember the marvelous Christmas trees there, heavy laden with rich tinsel and garland. In a great family photo, in front of one of those trees, there I am along with my brothers and sisters and all of my Varick and Cassidy cousins, no more than five, nestled in the arms of Father John. Aunt Mary and Uncle Bill's bedroom was originally on the back end of the second floor, while Jimmy and the three girls had the good fortune of being on the third floor where the bathroom was.

Jimmy's was perfectly positioned to relentlessly torture his sisters, as good, bad, or indifferent, they were all up there together, beyond the sight of their parents. Jimmy's creative imagination never disappointed, and his sisters devoted much of their lives in trying to return his diabolical favors.

The advantage was Jim's.

In later years, when it must have been more difficult for Mary to get up and down the stairs, what appeared to be a double or queen bed was placed in what had been the drawing/dining room down below for her.

And that is where I often picture her, perched up in what seemed to be the symbolic center of that bed, smiling and laughing broadly and holding court again and pleasantly barking out instructions. That old Western electric phone wire also was typically draped across the front of her body. And that Sacred Heart of Jesus who loomed next door was right there in that room as well, looking upon all who entered.

In that 243 Pacific was so well ordered, it looms large on the warm and fuzzy side of memory, but it was Aunt Mary's well-worn and busy place that loomed as far more interesting and mysterious to a child. There was much more to get into! But both were homes that the Lord had truly and richly blessed, because those who lived there had so committed their lives to Him.

In doing that, they also so greatly loved each other.

When I go back and rekindle what was felt there more than forty and even fifty or sixty years ago, I find myself wishing that my own children could have known such places, because homes like that, real homes, are so rare. Homes like that became instruments of grace in their own right.

And while this ship has long passed me by, whenever I travel to that "were I a rich man" dream state, the first thing I do is go and buy 243 and 241 Pacific Avenue and invite all remnants of the Varick–Cassidy–Fritzky–Evans clan to join me there together to thank our God for what was given us all. And then, of course, I buy our own 138 Poplar in Hackensack.

There's one final note about 241 Pacific, for it was there that you are asked to picture a still young Mary Varick, laboring on crutches or in a wheel chair as she raised four young children. Making the oatmeal, setting the table, washing and ironing the clothes, getting the brood out to school, and all of the ordinary tasks demanded a second or third or fourth gear from a mom on crutches. How did she lean on the stove when she stirred the soup? How did she move the laundry? How did she turn need into defiance? What tricks she had, I do not know. Yet I do know this—she placed motherhood before disability.

When Aunt Mary and Uncle Bill and Jim and young Mary picked up stakes in the early sixties to move to the third of the then new Colonnade Apartments (that were sociologically designed to bring the middle and upper classes and wealth back into a decaying Newark), it was to allow her Billie and son-in-law Don Adriance to take up residence at 241 for their family, and there, they would raise their four children, Don, Maryanne, Mike, and Peggy.

There too, they would all have their hearts torn out in Billie's suffering.

There too, Mother Teresa would visit Billie shortly before she died.

There too, the Adriances would shadow box with God and carry their respective crosses in His name for all of our sakes.

My memories of the Colonnade also are sharp and keen. In my teenage years at Seton Hall Prep and then at Seton Hall

University, the proximity of South Orange often took me to Aunt Mary's. I often got off bus 31 on South Orange Avenue and walked clear across the Central Ward in '67 and '68 to get there. And given what happened in Newark at that time, the thought of taking that walk puzzles people, but the truth is that I never knew fear on the way to Aunt Mary's or on my way through that troubled Central Ward.

I also slept many a night on the couch in what I'd call its grand spacious living room, and I stayed there alone a couple of times for periods of time at Aunt Mary's or Jimmy's request. Apartment 1214C, it was the last door in the corner on the northwestern side of the twelfth floor which was high enough to offer a panoramic view of beautiful Branch Brook Park immediately below and to the west, a park which gets no credit, but literally has more cherry blossoms than all of Washington, DC, does. It also then had an ice skating pond that was literally Currier & Ives like. Looking north, a few blocks down, the spectacular Sacred Heart Cathedral beckoned, and the sun would beam in spectacularly in the afternoons.

You'd enter into a foyer and a fair-sized kitchen was to the right, with a dining area farther right, which opened up directly into the living area. Upon entering, bedrooms and the bath were to the left, with Aunt Mary and Uncle Bill's room at the far end of the hall. On the wall to the right in that foyer hung her Catholic Woman of the Year proclamation papers and papal pronouncements.

I remember thinking that it was an intimidating entry way, one that signaled to all to leave any dark baggage that they may have been carrying back out in the hallway.

Beyond the regular pilgrimages, it was there that she planned the first trip to Fatima and Lourdes and Rome and there that she planned the later trip to Russia and Rome and there where her First Saturday Club ministry fully matured. And like 241 Pacific, that same Sacred Heart, the one her mom gave to Mary and Bill in anticipation of their joining hands in life, still looked down upon all.

Like 241 Pacific, it was a holy place.

Her years with Bruno and Mary were largely spent in a very pleasant and well-appointed Victorian-style home in Belvidere and the final seven years with Jerry at the Villa Victoria. While years of physical decline confronted her at the villa, they remained happy years for her.

For the first time in her life, she lived in a place that was explicitly built to accommodate her wheelchair. Everything in it was built for her, so it was Jerry who had to do the adjusting there. They took full advantage of their beloved Saint Lucy's which again was right across the street and the cathedral which was but the same few blocks away.

The common denominator for all of these places was, of course, the love of God that dwelled within and the immediate access (never more than a block away with the exception of the Belvidere years, but what's a couple of blocks) to a church and to the Eucharist.

Getting to the church on time just wasn't an issue for Mary.

# The People

## Oh, Good Lord, the People

As to the people in her life, there is a discernible beginning and a rich, rich, boisterous, and abundant middle and then an equally discernible and definable end.

The Bill Varick, love of her life, and Jerry Sheehan, her rod and her shield, stories are divulged, in pieces, throughout, so we'll but reaffirm their primary place in her life here.

The people part of her story obviously begins with her dad and mom, James and Agnes Cassidy, temperate and devoted Irish Catholics. Her dad, a railroad worker and a union organizer, and her mom, a homemaker, were atypical Irish Catholics in that they prayed hard and never drank. Their distaste for the brews and whisky that saturated the better part of their race allowed them to lead a well-ordered life in which devotion to the faith drove absolutely everything. It was to God and to Jesus and to Mary and to the saints of the church that attention was first and always to be directed.

This was the primary gift that was handed down to Mary and her siblings. It was her greatest inheritance.

Faith and faith alone, the greatest of all possible gifts!

Yes, the faith was primary.

And with its being passed forward, there came greater peace of mind and more of value than anyone of those fortunes or multimillion-dollar inheritances. For all of the money in the world means little or nothing if there is no peace or purpose or goodness. It's the old "money can't buy you happiness and money can't buy you love" verity.

Money cannot buy what a relationship with God can, and the gift handed down by Mary's parents was that very relationship.

Franklin Delano Roosevelt (FDR) was a good man who was intent on righting some longstanding social wrongs, and he proved worthy of their support and so left an imprint on the Cassidys. But the more immediate impact was their Irish loyalty to political bosses and mayoral rogues like Frank Hague and John Kenny. So a big D for Democrat also was emblazoned upon the 243 Pacific Avenue Cassidys in the Hall of Records in Jersey City and Hudson County. It was, after all, an era in which the Democratic rogues played Robin Hood on behalf of the poor and the working man. So that "belonging to" also was passed down from generation to generation.

But politics and governance and debates over national income taxes, social security, public works projects, and packing the Supreme Court of the United States were small matters, indeed, when juxtaposed to matters of religion and theology.

At 243 Pacific Avenue, it was God first in the morning and God first in the evening and God first every waking moment in between.

Mary also had, as earlier noted, two older brothers, Jim and Joe; three younger brothers, Edward "Bud," Frank "Skip," and John "Jack"; and one younger sister, Rose, who was quite a few years younger, but just below her on the seven-tiered pecking order. Throughout her life, she remained close to all of her siblings, and all, to varying degrees, got pulled into the orbit of her First Saturday Club and the Canadian pilgrimages that she was to fashion and build.

But what must be understood on the people front, however, is that these relationships were rich, in that Mary so respected, loved, and revered her parents. The bond was true and sure. And the depth of the bond would be the same that would define her relationship with her siblings and while different, of course, even her husband, her children, and her friends as well. In that relationship was simply never to be taken lightly.

Relationship too was spiritual!

Relationships too were the handiwork of God, and through and in them, God revealed himself.

All six siblings remained close to Mary. Jim and Joe were good, handsome, and very bright men who married and brought eight and five children into the world, respectively. Jim and his wife Helen, who originally resided in Jersey City, close to Mary and Bill, and later in Atlantic Highlands, New Jersey, had a strong presence on the earlier pilgrimages, and many of their children and children's children are still bound to the pilgrimages up until this very day. Joe and his wife Dot raised their family on Arlington Avenue in Jersey City and only later moved to Waterbury, Connecticut, and eventually back to Cranford, New Jersey. Joe and Dot, fixtures always, maintained a steady pilgrimage and First Saturday presence over the years.

My parents had a strong presence on the earlier pilgrimages and then again later in life, while maintaining a steady First Saturday belonging. As to Bud and his Anne, they were fixtures on every pilgrimage for the disabled and at every First Saturday gathering. Bud led the group in the rosary each month, and Anne was the go-to gal on the pilgrimages whenever any kind of problem arose. As to the two young priests, they were closely involved during the early years of their priesthood and, of course, throughout their lives at what might be called the main events.

Skip died suddenly when only five years a priest in 1967, and Jack died not long after Mary herself.

What must be conveyed in but a few sentences is that each of the six lit up her life as well.

They supported Mary and her mission and her spirit, and they shared her rich faith. They were, most assuredly, better steeled in that faith because of her. She knew what they were made of and rejoiced in what they all, in their unique ways, brought to her table. Anne Cassidy was a "bull moose" who was always ready to move the world for her, Bud was a rare piece of work who made her pilgrims laugh, and those younger brothers adored her and celebrated what she evoked in their own ministries.

In a Catholic church where the priests were to be revered, they rather revered Mary, who never treaded water, and she, in turn, revered them.

As to my mom and dad, there are two images that resonate so strongly with me. The first was witnessed hundreds of times, because Mary and Mom made it a practice to talk at the end of almost every day. Throughout their lives—every day!

Every day! No matter what corner of the earth or port of call that Mary may have been in.

So the image is of my mom sitting on the bottom of the staircase near the phone that was located in our foyer, either to make or to receive the end-of-the-day phone call after all of Mary's business was settled (and long after my dad was asleep). Best friends forever, they talked practically every single night at the close of day.

So sacred was this practice that once when we were without phone service, my mom routinely left our house at 11:00 p.m. or later to walk the few blocks to Main Street where she could access a pay phone in front of Packard's Supermarket.

The second is an image of my dad, in the waning years of his life when he was so beaten back by a cancer that should have claimed him years earlier, an image that was shared by Mary Pisaniello. "Uncle Frank was not sure on his feet, and he had grown weary climbing the steep hillside *on the Scala Sancta at Sainte-Anne-de-Beaupre*. The ground also was wet and slippery and unsure because of a recent rainfall. But at the Tenth Station, your dad dropped to his knees as though he were there at Calvary on that first Good Friday. His devotion took my breath away. I remember too that he fell to his knees in Mom's hospital room at Saint Michael's just after she breathed her last breath."

Perfectly and rigidly, and even sacredly, he kneeled, no matter the pain or the steep price exacted by his cancer.

As for Jim and Helen and Joe and Dot, they enjoyed a constant presence in Mary's affairs and an abiding and humble mutual respect.

Biased as it may sound, it is doubtful that any seven siblings were ever as worthy of the love of the other six than these seven.

As to her four children, Mary herself would have been the first one to tell you that it was the four of them who were the saints in her life for simply having to put up with and endure a mother like her. In chapter 1, you were introduced to Jimmy and to the youngest of the four, Mary. So a few words about Billie and Barbara are in order!

Particularly close to my mom and dad, Don and Billie regularly visited our home in Hackensack as their family began to grow. It might sound childish or even out of place, but I remember being so taken and moved by my parents' involvement in what was the tip of the iceberg of my generation's growth. Close to all of my mom's siblings, they just seemed to have this extra barrel of love and, maybe, wisdom to share with all of my older cousins as well. While the bond tying them to Billie and Don is the most sacrosanct and overt, there also are memories of their being there for Jim and Helen's Agnes, Jimmy, and Maureen; Joe and Dot's Kathy and Susan; and Mary and Bill's Jimmy, as well as for Bud and Anne's Joe, our extraordinary Trinitarian priest.

And interestingly, while I have no direct memories of my parents having been there for Mary and Bill's Barbara, I have clear memories of my dad's intense conversations with her husband Joe.

In short, it's nice to know that they spread themselves around and extended themselves to the extended family. They tilled the fields and spread a little love and hope where both seem to have been needed.

While Billie's own immediate family was deeply scarred by her suffering, they managed as well as could be imagined, and just as her disability and her unbelievable suffering and her dying in her prime challenged and tested her own husband and children, so too did it challenge all who knew her and loved her.

There was a time when Billie was already losing the use of her legs, when Billie, Don, and the children escaped from Jersey City to our Nana's cabin at Crater Lake. The kitchen, a long, rectangular, "feed the multitudes" kind of room, overlooked the dirt road and the many paths that crisscrossed a lovely mountain cathedral of a forest that led to the lake. It also overlooked a poor excuse for a basketball court, i.e., a rim and net were attached to a tree. Don and I formed a team and successfully took on all comers for hours on end, while Billie watched through a screened window above. Smiling and laughing, she responded to Don's incessant pleas of "Billie, I need you now. Oh, Billie, how I need you now!" Spiritually, he kept calling upon the once cheerleader in her to sustain him, but it was, I realized, about ever so much more than our silly games. It was about their being there for each other in this world and about loving and carrying each other in the midst of great struggle and torment. And Billie just glowed like an angel.

There behind the window screen, she did!

She honestly glowed like an angel on that sun speckled, bright blue sky of a Crater Lake day. Excuse me for the gratuitous nature of this observation, but I think this was so because she truly was an angel and destined to be a harbinger for us.

Her suffering was no holds barred and up close and personal with God.

Meet God there, without condemnation, without retribution, without doubt, as Billie and her family did. And it was, indeed, time to shout hallelujah, glory hallelujah, for to have come through the pressure and intense suffering of that kind of tragic portal without anger or vitriol was to have walked among the blessed in the land of the living.

For her part, Barbara married young. She and her husband Joe also raised a big family that required them to work, work, and work to keep a home and hearth together. They lived that ever-demanding, always-more-than-one-job-at-a-time life. As such, they could not be as immediately involved in First Saturday family affairs, but they were rather there, as Mary insisted, for her command performances. And Barbara too, like most Varicks it seems, had to pass through the harsh and difficult shadows of her own Calvary experiences as well.

Her strong and caring and hardworking husband passed away some years ago—far too young—and her oldest daughter Debbie succumbed to a lung disease about five years ago, at far, far too tender an age.

Typically Varick, Barbara gave the mourning and the acute loss and the emptiness to God, and she found that rock upon which she could pick up the pieces and carry on. When she did, she actually joked that she "just wished that God didn't trust her so much."

But He has and He did and like Job and like Mary and like Billie, Barbara has taken every punch and responded with love only. No matter the sacrifice, no matter the price, she has had only love to give in return.

The better part of valor requires us to leave the whole of nieces, nephews, grandchildren, and great-grandchildren to a great appendix out there, but some, of course, will, as they already have, appropriately rear their heads elsewhere in the telling. So we leave family behind for now and turn to that even larger extended family of friends. And with apologies up front, we'll also look to do our best to compile a thorough disabled pilgrims and volunteers' appendix one day, for only a precious few will crop up or come to the surface as story gives way to story here.

Those noted, therefore, are among the closest of the close and but a representative sampling of the whole. We are, after all, but attempting to relate the essence of Mary's story and her contribution and not the story of all whom she loved.

To that, we could never do justice.

And we do not attempt to do so.

Why not begin with Mother Teresa?

Of course, we also could begin with Ed Somerhalter or Straight Ed or Ed the Head or our great friend Eric Gosling of all things Sainte-Anne-de-Beaupre or Brother Luke or Johanna D'Albenzio or Mary Hafmeister or Yvonne or Sister Theresa or Flossie or Ed Zubrow, who resigned as the head football coach of his then undefeated University of Pennsylvania, Ivy League champion team to take a 400 percent pay cut working with inner-city, at-risk Philadelphia youth, or Richie Fehn, Jim Varick's dear friend who turned up one day cruising in one of our own City of Hackensack police cruisers or the most obscurest of hundreds of other pilgrims over the years.

Because they all counted to Mary!

But still we begin with Mother Teresa because she is, after all, Mother Teresa, a close friend of our Lord's, who took time out to love Mary Varick, to give her Jim and Mary Varick hope for their own baby Teresa, and to pray over a dying Billie, over Mary's dying eight-year-old great-niece Sue Anne Murray, and finally over Mary herself.

There is Mother Teresa who counseled Jerry and upheld Mary and joined them in prayer and broke bread with them often.

There is Mother Teresa who sanctified and redeemed as Mary did, Mother Teresa whose "yoke," like Mary's, was "easy and whose burden was light," Mother Teresa who, like Mary, could not do all that she did for the poorest of the poor "without tears," Mother Teresa who was that most extraordinary of kindred spirits—and long before what were to become her unsolicited glory days.

So important was the relationship with Mother Teresa that she will be the fodder for special treatment later in this work in chapter 8.

Father John O'Brien, the pastor of All Saints Church in Jersey City in the 1930s and 1940s, also looms as a very important figure in Mary's life in that he both married Mary and Bill and baptized all four of their children. An early confidant and confessor, he is mentioned often in Mary's first book.

He was an early guiding light, and while Bishop Fulton J. Sheen, still the most famous of Roman Catholic televangelists was not a close personal friend of Mary, their paths, indeed, affectionately crossed and he took time out to make some special recordings of his own for Mary's pilgrims. The spiritual guidance, rich wisdom, and compassionate insight of Bishop Sheen meant a great deal to Mary and so to those in her care.

While he passed away more than thirty years ago, his legacy for Christ is timeless, and he lives large in the First Saturday Club's memory.

It is important to note that there is a letter to Mary from Bishop Sheen that will be pored over in chapter 8, along with a series of profound letters from Mother Teresa and testimony from both Bishop Peter Sutton and Father Jacques Rinfret, long the director of Our Lady of the Cape.

After Mary's death, Bishop Peter Sutton became archbishop of Keewatin-Le Pas in the provinces of northern Saskatchewan and Manitoba, Canada. He only recently resigned.

We will again hear much more from Bishop Peter Sutton in chapter 8 as we review and reflect upon the testimony that he submitted to the Newark Archdiocese in the wake of Mary's death. Suffice it to say here that his love for her was extraordinary and limitless.

There have been hundreds of priests who have actively engaged Mary's ministry in some way over the years, as either spiritual leaders on pilgrimages or as First Saturday hosts or as promoters of events. A special few did all of this and more.

So we first remember, after Mary's own brothers, Fathers John and Francis Cassidy and Fathers Bill and Mike Hornak, who too were brothers and curates in parishes in Guttenberg and Jersey City. They were the first to travel with Mary to Canada and, as such, forever held a special place in her heart.

In the later '50s, there also was Father Rob Garafallo, a then newly ordained Consalata priest who brought all of the excitement of his new priesthood to Canada and who later rejoiced in telling friends how privileged he was to have been able to say mass on the altars of such great shrines. He was especially moved by being able to say mass in Brother Andre's chapel at Saint Joseph's in Montreal.

In those early days, Mary also grew to both know and love Father Eugene Lefebvre, C.Ss.R., the pilgrimage director at

Sainte-Anne-de-Beaupre, and Father Jacques Rinfret, his coun-
terpart at the shrine of Our Lady of the Cape.

The friendship with Father Rinfret grew especially deep and
abiding and constant, as he was often an off-pilgrimage season
visitor at Mary's Jersey City and Newark homes, and it was in his
company at either the Pilgrim's House or the Madonna House at
the Cape where she went to reflect and to write her books.

Their relationship grew highly personal and rich and deep.

Theirs was an abiding spiritual love affair.

While our focus is upon that special group of priests, we
would be remiss in focusing upon Father Rinfret without men-
tioning John Normandin, the longstanding photographer at the
Cape, greeter at the Cape, tour guide at the Cape, and just down-
home, go-to guy at the Cape. John Normandin was what might
be called Father Rinfret's "*man friday*." More than that, he was
both his and Mary's special friend. Even today, his loving and
laughing presence is a fixture whenever the First Saturday Club
pilgrimage arrives at the Cape. While his son has joined him to
share the workload, John remains an institutional icon, and in
his presence, the grace and blessings to be realized, through Our
Lady, at the Cape, are immediately manifested.

What Eric, who we met in chapter 1, was to Sainte-Anne's,
John was and is, to this day, at Our Lady of the Cape.

John Normandin remains the human face, with the always
broad smile and the booming laugh and the camera hanging over
his shoulders at Our Lady of the Cape.

While you already know what Eric meant to Jim and I, he also
was extremely devoted to Aunt Mary. If she needed fresh bodies
to help her disabled, he readily provided them. I have memories of my own of having driven up early to Sainte-Anne's on
a number of occasions, in order to have my car available to run
errands for Aunt Mary during the week in both Beaupre and
Three Rivers. This was back in the travel-by-plane pilgrimage
days in the mid-seventies. Depending upon the crowd, a bus and/

or busses would meet the plane along with Eric and his Sainte-Anne's volunteers and I.

Always arriving the day before, this gave me a free night with Eric which wasn't bad at all.

Other early spiritual pilgrimage forces included Estelle Clavette, an oblate sister who long served to keep the operations at the Cape in order, and there was Yolande Richard whose gentle, sweet voice was heard ringing across the grounds in the glow of the serene and spiritually haunting evening candlelight processions. And early volunteers from the Sisters of Charity, Sister Claire Cordis and Sister Regina, were a special duo who never let the constrictions of their then tight habits restrict them from both praying and playing with their fellow pilgrims.

For some fifteen years and certainly throughout the entire decade of the '70s, Father Don Arel, OMI, was the priest who drove Mary's pilgrimage ship of state. While joined by others from time to time, his presence was the constant, and he also somehow managed to make his way to Mary's Colonnade apartment in Newark to celebrate Midnight Mass at her famous New Year's parties. During those years, he turned up even in the nooks and crannies of her life during moments of trial and pain to make a difference.

Handsome, with a rich, broad, and bright smile, he is remembered by all who were privileged to know him as very good, very kind, and so spiritually moving a priest.

Among many others involved at that time, there was, most notably, the aforementioned Father Matt Pisaniello, the "retarded priest" who pulled so many rabbits out of the hat for Mary.

In the late '70s and early '80s, the baton, over time, was directly passed to Father Paul Bochicchio who was then at Our Lady of Mercy in Jersey City. He accepted that baton with open arms and he has, more than forty-four years later, yet to pass it off to another. Hook, line, and sinker, he threw in with Mary and her Our Lady of Fatima First Saturday Club, and no matter where he was called to be by his bishop, he stayed the course with Mary.

He not only threw himself into the mix but he also threw in the youth of his parishes. His youth ministry produced a steady troupe of volunteers, beginning with the "seekers" of Our Lady of Mercy in the '70s and continuing today with the youth of Holy Family in Nutley. And the simple truth is that the young men and women of his parishes have, for long now, cared for every need of the disabled pilgrims and added life, vitality, and abundant laughter to their mutual journey.

Often joined by a group from Saint Mary's in Colts Neck, New Jersey, through the leadership of their then youth ministers Mike and Amy Lenehan, they together made an extraordinary difference for all pilgrims, both the firm and the infirm.

In all honesty, one is at a loss to do justice to describing today's Monsignor Paul, who has given so much of his life to Mary's work and who in the living present, after more than forty-four years of service, continues to do so. As such, there are, in the end, no words that suffice.

Maybe, it is enough to say that he was and remains Mary's most complete man or her "man for all seasons." And certainly, he long ago became, and more than twenty-five years after she passed remains, her *man for all reasons*. He is that most devoted of servants, whose presence and whose homilies and whose abiding spirituality have changed lives for so long and for so many. He had, as you know, the honor of eulogizing Mary, and today's pilgrims have the continued honor and privilege of his company.

One of his early "seekers" and volunteers entered the seminary to later become Monsignor Paul's priestly coconspirator. In fact, Father Kevin Carter, pastor of Saint Margaret's in Little Ferry, New Jersey, today has long been involved with Mary Varick, her mission, and her First Saturday Club—for almost as long as Monsignor Paul.

The two together, the mentor and the once acolyte, have provided a sustained spiritual leadership and stability that were simply unknown in the early years. Just as loving and committed and devoted as is Monsignor Paul, Father Kevin has contributed so much as well.

As complete a figure, his demeanor, approach, and leadership style honorably contrast with Monsignor's, and the two of them have this competitive and never-ending dog fight going on. They tease each other, lambaste each other, and do their level best, in great fun, to downright humiliate each other.

And given the opportunity, they will do just that.

Father Kevin, for instance, describes his happiest pilgrimage moment as the sight of Father Paul being led off, under armed guard, upon their landing in Leningrad (Saint Petersburg) in what was then communist Russia. "It was," he said, "the most exhilarating sight and certainly the high point of the First Saturday experience for me." He then sardonically added, "The low point, of course, after hours of joyful expectation, was having him returned to us."

One of the above two priests is more practical and by the book and better organized and more interested in getting a good night's sleep. The other is not, and their age-old battle will no doubt be renewed when the group next heads to Canada. In friendly fun, they'll do their level best, and all those with them will continue to root for both, because theirs is a battle in which everyone wins.

Needless to say, the games playing is left behind at the altar where a lifetime of friendship and respect and what is an ability to read each other's subtle cues gives way to moving spiritual experiences. When they say mass together, there is a harmony and a synergy that palpably reverberates in the souls of those attending.

Needless to say, they celebrate the mass together often.

Those who knew Mary Varick are likely to be well aware of the thing that she had about threes.

Born of her devotion to the Trinity, what came in threes was, in her mind, trebly blessed. But she often struggled to find even that one priest to attend to her pilgrimages in the '50s and '60s. As such, she would take great delight in the fact that today's pilgrimages are enjoined by three priests, as Father Frank Fano, who has enjoyed a twenty-five-year association with the First Saturday Club ever since he was a young altar boy, works with Monsignor Paul and Father Kevin.

Father Frank is a chip off the same old block, and his unbridled, youthful enthusiasm and excitement in his faith are the stuff that will enhance and enliven pilgrimages to come. He brings a light heart and a love and understanding of music and a poet's soul, and he throws it all into what is an already extraordinary mix.

Yes, Mary Varick must be celebrating and smiling down from above in the knowledge that her First Saturday pilgrimage is today regularly blessed with the support of three priests, and not just any three, but three great priests who literally light it up and who raise up her pilgrims.

Reverently, joyfully, and abundantly, they, her trinity, do this.

As to the rest of the great extended family, both then and now, a few of the preeminent volunteers either have or will pop up in this work going forward, but the gracious Flossie Oates, who hugged just a little bit harder than anyone else on the planet and left an impression on this writer that was meant to last a lifetime, deserves mention at every turn—and so again here. On the disabled side, there have, of course, been hundreds upon hundreds involved over the years, and we but touch that small representative sampling of the larger than life to give expression to the whole.

I see Neil Gulliksen, a gentle navy man whose spine was crushed in a traffic accident with friends while on leave, the first of the most traumatic cases, and I see beautiful, tortured Jeanette beside him. I see that stretcher of hers and that palpably moving gracious acceptance of great affliction that she never ceased to display.

Relegated to life in that stretcher and bed, I am reminded of her claim that there were never enough hours in the day for her to do all of the work and/or praying that she wanted to do. Her life, she insisted, was beyond full. And we are left to wonder just what magic Mary wove in inspiring pilgrims like Jeanette, who found extraordinary and unimaginable purpose in a completely broken life.

As a rule, Jeanette would outline all the causes for which she had to pray and dedicate an hour for each. Her problem, she always explained, was that there were far many more causes than there were hours. There was one hour for vocations and one to end abortion and one for the young boy in town just injured in a car accident and one for the soldiers, etc., etc., etc. The bells that hourly chimed from Holy Rosary Church in Jersey City provided the cue for her to move from one prayer to the next.

She could not move at all, yet her entire life was a prayer.

She was one especially beautiful soul.

There's Anne Gerhardt, whose heart was even bigger and who you will hear more from later…and Cecilia and Connie LoPresti, both of whom were with the club for more than thirty years and who sang their way into the hearts of thousands…and Fred Vanderhoof, a victim of severe cerebral palsy, who likewise joked his way into the hearts of thousands for more than forty-five years. A more beautiful human being never breathed air.

We just lost Hank Colling, a remarkably gracious and kind human being and my great personal friend, the friend who invited me to tackle this project and who long kept the spirit of Mary Varick alive in him. For long a quadriplegic, he had been with the First Saturday family for more than forty-seven years, before the priest invited him to go in peace at the conclusion of a Christmas Eve TV mass. He took the cue and did exactly that.

All of the above have gone home.

Among the Stalwarts, still with the club today, there also are others who have been present for equally long periods of time. There's Mary Jane Burns who wears her purple and the heart of a child, and Bob Gilleck, wonderful Bob, and Sister Anna DiCarli, whose bark belies the fact that she is all Silly Putty on the inside.

It is particularly important to note that Hank Colling had given his heart and soul, without question or complaint, to his disabled brothers and sisters and to me. Roughly half of his First Saturday years were spent with Mary and half of them had, since she passed, been spent without her.

I slice and dice the years only because a fair case can be made that pieces of Mary's spirit had been tossed Hank's way before she went home to God on that June day in '89. People who looked hard enough at Hank would, indeed, have found Mary inside him. You just couldn't miss her. For there in the heart and soul of Hank Colling, who is the most nonjudgmental and accepting man who has ever lived, you most assuredly found Mary Varick who Hank loved with such fervor.

My own wife, Maggie, once told me that, "The moment I met Hank, I knew he was someone who I could completely open myself up to, that kind of rare person with whom you could lay all of the baggage that you are carrying down without a moment's hesitation, that kind of person with whom you felt immediately comfortable."

Having pressed you with far too many names, hang in there for just a few more. When Mary went home to God, it was her Jerry Sheehan and her Bruno and Mary who picked up the pieces and carried on the First Saturday and pilgrimage program, and after Jerry went home to God not too long after Mary passed, Bruno and Mary, for a time, continued to do so. But family and life and love took them to Ohio, leaving the directorship in the capable hands of two of Mary's other relatives who were willing to keep on keeping on. Two who have now been codirectors for some eighteen years! They are her granddaughter and Billie's daughter Maryanne Adriance, and her niece and my sister Joan Fritzky Murray.

Both, to great degree, grew up in the embrace of Mary Varick and her mission. Both share the same worldview, the same rich spirituality, and the same telltale hearts.

But like Monsignor Paul and Father Kevin, they too are a bit like oil and vinegar, and their leadership styles too contrast. One says no and the other yes. One believes in rules and the other doesn't necessarily think that they're all that important. One sticks by decisions made and the other prefers to bob and weave with the changing tides. One has a just and honorable, but flint-edged sharpness and the other's edge couldn't cut through the thinnest piece of paper on her best day. But somehow, it all works anyway, because they love each other, and revere and honor their grandmother and aunt, and they are, above all else, equally fierce in their faiths.

They love the Lord, and that's not a bad common denominator at all.

# Michael Adriance

Having traveled far already, I'd like to close this chapter with a beautiful commentary that was sent by Michael Adriance, Mary's grandson. He wrote,

> I think Grandma might well be described as a selfless beggar. She was constantly seeking funds, help, and care for her beloved First Saturday Family. Out of her love for them, she humbled herself to seek assistance anywhere she could. I will never know for sure, but I don't believe this was something she was ever comfortable doing. She was, however, damned good at it! When Grandma asked for something, unless you were pure evil personified, it was hard not to succumb to her wishes, or at least feel a strong tug on your heartstrings. When she made the request, her voice dripped with honey and her face would shine with the sweet pleading of an innocent child. Looking back at all the times I recall this scene occurring, I can honestly say that I only remember her asking for assistance for others' needs.
>
> I remember being at her apartment one day. I was there for a visit with her and Jerry. During the visit, Grandma and Jerry began discussing their upcoming schedule. The heart of each day's activity was daily mass. They both seemed to know a church where they could attend mass on any given day at any given time. The Eucharist was the center of Grandma's life. I recall her discussing a day that she was not able to receive the Eucharist. In even speaking about it, she was crushed. Jesus in the Eucharist was her true love. Remember how you felt when you first fell in love and you couldn't be with the person you gave your heart to? That is how Grandma felt whenever she was not able to physically embrace her Jesus.
>
> As a teenager, I helped out on the First Saturday trips to Canada. The teens would carry the disabled on and off the bus and assist with various needs. However, we had

plenty of time to get into mischief and we often did. From time to time, someone would complain to Grandma about our antics. She would invariably come to our defense. "They are just children," she would say. "They need to have some fun" and "Look at all the good things that they do," she would add. She would then bring us aside, often laughing with us, and gently remind us that we were on a pilgrimage. She would then assure us that there was a time and place for fun and that there would be.

Grandma was on a pilgrimage to Rome when her brother, Bud, died. She was heartbroken that she could not be there. I believe it was the feast of All Souls and her path happened to pass directly into the Pope himself to whom she explained the reason for her sorrow. He handed her his personal rosaries and Grandma brought them home and gave them to Bud's wife, Anne. Grandma also became good friends with Mother Teresa's sisters. Grandma and Jerry were very helpful to them when they first established their house in the Bronx (and later Newark within eye shadow of the colonnade itself). Through the good sisters, she came to become friends with Mother Teresa herself.

She brought Mother Teresa to our house in Jersey City on at least two occasions. My Mom was limited to the bed at that time. On one of those occasions, Grandma was sitting next to the bed where my Mother was lying and Mother Teresa leaned over and spoke to her. She told her that it was her suffering and the suffering of others that gave her the strength to serve the poorest of the poor.

Michael wrote further to me about "traveling on the road to Golgatha with Jesus" and then he described himself as a "sojourner on the narrow road."

He is my cousin and Mary Varick's grandson, who so pointedly observed that "Jesus in the Eucharist was her true love." One can't help but think that his grandmother would be very, very proud of him, in that he truly knows what she lived for and proposes to live as she did—as should we all.

# The Essence of Mary's Theology

Yes, it all comes from God, but unless there are people to witness to us, it is difficult to stay the course. We redeem each other. We must redeem each other, as Mike's tender words remind us and as Mary's life so remarkably demands.

Lift high the cross and suffer for the Lord's sake and then shower his grace in the dark corners and crevices that surround so that there may be life and life abundantly.

## Chapter 2 Placeholders

- The salient and overarching message to be extracted from Mary Varick's life is that we are, indeed, our brothers and our sisters' keepers. It is that we belong to one another and that we must confront and do all we can to alleviate the suffering and pain of our fellows. We are not meant to lead lives of "lonely and quiet desperation." We are meant to live our lives abundantly and resoundingly and lovingly.

- She hammered away at the redemptive power of silently accepting suffering in Christ's name and at the raw power of redemptive souls who sacrifice and give away the all of their lives for others.

- She shined light upon the cross, and the continuing resurrection made manifest in the lives of her pilgrim and disabled family.

- It was about the ability of remarkable human beings to bear the unbearable, to recognize their place on the cross, and to accept that place in order to free others.

- Her suffering was no holds barred and up close and personal with God.

- Meet God there, without condemnation, without retribution, without doubt, as Billie and her family did. And it was, indeed, time to shout hallelujah, glory hallelujah, for to have come through the pressure of that kind of tragic portal without anger or vitriol was to have walked among the blessed in the land of the living.

- There is Mother Teresa who sanctified and redeemed as Mary did, Mother Teresa whose "yoke," like Mary's, "was easy and whose burden was light," Mother Teresa who, like Mary, could not do all that she did for the poorest of the poor "without tears," Mother Teresa who was that most extraordinary of kindred spirits!

- The Eucharist was the center of Grandma's life. I recall her discussing a day that she was not able to receive the Eucharist. In even speaking about it, she was crushed. Jesus in the Eucharist was her true love.

# 3

# Out-of-the-Box Sojourns

In her book *Till Death*, Mary Varick suggests that God's greatest gift is that, "He keeps each new tomorrow his own secret" and that all He asks of us, "in both sunshine and in shadow, is to live one day at a time sure of his unending love and confident that He will be beside us always."

And yet, in living for Him and responding to what He willed for her, she purposefully shaped extraordinary days. And while the focus upon convening the monthly First Saturday gatherings and organizing the annual pilgrimages to her beloved shrines in Quebec remained the constant in her life, her "inner circle" and its benefactors and volunteers were not afraid of stepping out of the box from time to time—to do what she referred to as the "impossible," within the confines of a faith, of course, where nothing was ever impossible with God.

Impossible to Mary was an oxymoron.

In looking back upon just three of those out-of-the-box ventures or trips over the years, where they lived the atypical or the extraordinary, it was both interesting and truly instructive to delve into the bigger picture and to look upon the contributions of Mary Varick's Our Lady of Fatima First Saturday Club in a more global context.

We do, of course, believe that, "With God, it is all one." As hard as it may be to wrap our arms around that concept, we believe it, as our God asks us to believe. With Him, the complex is made simple and all things—the good, bad, and indifferent—come home to Him.

Catholicism holds up the "mystical body of Christ." We acknowledge that we are all, in God, interconnected and that the great and the mighty and the exalted and the humblest among us are ultimately of one. Each spirit, each soul becomes, in actuality and in grace, a force for every other spirit and every other soul.

Each has the capacity to be an instrument of grace and of goodness and of love for all.

Prayer and grace and love always, somehow, someway, conspire together, in mystery, to advance the hearts and minds and capacity of the whole of humanity and to make us more worthy of a God who so perfectly loves us.

The point being reached for here is that even that which seems insignificant or small or inconsequential, in the context of the great, big, wide world out there, is, indeed, a component of the larger or greater spiritual force that shapes and moves that very world.

It was President John Kennedy who said, "On this earth, God's work must truly be our own."

We mention this because our point is that Mary Varick and the Our Lady of Fatima First Saturday Club historically and pointedly and even dramatically advanced this work—God's own work—or what President Kennedy referred to as His "work on this earth." The point is then that the work of Mary Varick and of her First Saturday Club and of what was *God's work on this earth* mattered and was of consequence both in this world and in that more important heavenly world to come.

And while we, as people of faith, look heavenward always, our God necessarily looks upon what we do down here on earth and upon how we love and sacrifice and give in His name and in the advancement of His purposes.

All of it matters. Every action and movement and word matters. Nothing is lost to or on God. All is accounted.

So, yes, the focus of the First Saturday Club was always, and remains, upon God and the things of heaven, but it is possible to consider how it also contributed to a more loving world, or rather, just how it well might have been there for a world that desperately needed it. In actuality, when considering the big picture, our world may well have been in need of tens of thousands of First Saturday Clubs, but having even this one made a difference.

*The power of one is never lost on a God, for whom it is all one.*

Whether that one is comprised of one or fifty or hundreds or a vast multitude!

With all of this in mind, we'll look at just three of the non-Canadian trips led by Mary Varick, one that was part of a pattern for a couple of decades and two that fall into that "nigh on impossible" category. The first, a simple weekend run to Washington, DC, in 1963; the second, the 1967 trip to Fatima, Lourdes, and Rome; and the third, the 1977 trip to Russia, Rome, and Lourdes.

Just three trips that we'll pause to think about and that we'll suggest the world was desperately in need of.

Yes, I do mean what I just wrote. Desperately in need of!

Mary's pilgrims need not have been conscious of this.

All of us miss much that stares us in the face as we go forward. As for Mary's pilgrims, all thought was focused upon their faith and the Mother of God and her constancy and devotion and upon the great love of Jesus and His call to us to, "Be perfect, just as your Heavenly Father is perfect." They did not necessarily have to be focused upon the needs and cries of a most imperfect world, in order to be of service to—and to attend to the needs of—that most imperfect world.

Yet these trips and that most imperfect world, a world in need of prayer and love, were of one.

They came together!

And the cause of peace itself was never lost upon a First Saturday family that was, in fact, literally created and fashioned to pray for peace always.

The ultimate mission was that illusive commodity called peace on earth. To have extended it to one was to have offered it to all. For with God, it is all one.

Mary Varick, in her book *Till Death*, did dwell upon the importance of their 1963 weekend junket to Washington, DC. Its very importance was manifested by the obvious fact that it was the only annual autumn trip to the nation's capitol that Mary ever wrote about. In that, it was a trip that her Our Lady of Fatima First Saturday Club took regularly for years—the fact that it alone was singled out bears witness to its importance. To her, this trip was ultimately to become a tale of two Johns, one whom the world little noted or knew but who had made his mark with Mary and another who was to be mourned by the entire world and who was known to Mary only spiritually and emotionally.

Two Johns, who despite their palpably different statuses on earth, would meet their God at one and the same time and as equals.

John Masalski of Jersey City was one of Mary's intrepid, early volunteers. As it happened, he called Mary on the Tuesday before that planned weekend trip to Washington to check on that Friday's schedule. When Mary advised him that Mass had been scheduled at All Saints, what had until only recently been Mary's home parish, for 5:00 p.m. prior to take-off by bus to Washington, DC, he kidded her about having to reschedule what was to him an important trip to the barbershop. Given the 5:00 p.m. start, there would be no time for him to do so on Friday after work as he had planned. Apparently, John liked Friday haircuts, so he teased Mary about the sacrifices that he made for her.

Mary remembered it as an ordinary, nondescript conversation, but one that was rendered forever sacred when she got the call from John's wife informing her that John had suddenly died while in the act of getting that very haircut at his favorite barbershop.

Rendering even Friday afternoon haircuts forever sacred as well!

She was left to dwell upon "you know not the hour" and the importance of the simplest of conversations as she and Bill attended John's funeral that Friday morning, November 22, 1963. Immediately after, Bill left to go get their bus or what was then, believe it or not, called a trolley at the Public Service garage, and Mary went home to their 51 Clifton Avenue, Newark apartment to make last-minute preparations. She was soon interrupted by an alarming call from her daughter Barbara, telling her that President John F. Kennedy had just been shot in Dallas, Texas.

Over the next couple of hours, upon learning of his death, there was a debate as to whether or not to even proceed with the trip. Despite all of the concerns, they determined to go forward, and it began with the 5:00 p.m. mass that was said by Father Tom Madison, a Graymoor friar, who was a close friend of Father Frank Cassidy.

Like Skip, he was new to the priesthood himself, and like Skip, he was a gentle people's priest who longed to make a difference.

In reflecting upon that mass, Mary suggested that two thoughts preoccupied her.

The first was that this was more than likely the very first mass said for the repose of the soul of America's first Catholic president. Of course, that was along with the repose of the soul of that other John or their John, John Masalski. In those days, the fact was that weekday afternoon masses were highly uncommon and that Mary had to receive special permission from the Archdiocese of Newark for hers.

The second thought was that the mass was ironically and appropriately being said by an African-American priest. Given John Kennedy's association with the advancement of civil rights and the fact that his historic Civil Rights Bill was then sitting before the United States Congress, this was significant, symbolic, and even inspiring.

Those were the heydays of Martin Luther King's movement and of marches and sit-ins and of beatings and of nonviolent civil disobedience and of freedom riders and of George Wallace's "Segregation today, segregation tomorrow, segregation forever." Those were the days when Kennedy's justice department had to send in federal troops in order to advance the cause of racial integration. "With all deliberate speed," they confronted the lawlessness of a "Southern Manifesto" that would illegally seek to keep African-Americans in their degraded state.

In light of the sudden death of a then charismatic and beloved president, one could not help but ponder the all of what the nation had experienced and was experiencing. Mary wrote, "As an African-American priest intoned the sacred, sacrificial words of 'Take and eat for this is my body,' you simply couldn't help but dwell upon so many stories of sacrifice during a moving mass that was highly emotional and poignant."

Mary's belief that this First Saturday Club mass was the first of many masses to be offered for President John Fitzgerald Kennedy suggested that her pilgrims, tangibly and symbolically, were among the first to give voice to the cries and prayers of a broken nation in an organized way. The First Saturday Club went to God, in and through His precious Eucharist, to pray for a beloved and fallen president, maybe—just maybe, before any and all others.

As for the weekend, what was to be joyful had been inadvertently rendered tearful and solemn. As Mary's pilgrims headed down I-95 in a coming of winter's darkness, all were aware that their president's body was somewhere in the air above them on its way home to where they were heading and to where kings and princes and prime ministers and leaders from around the world would soon be descending.

John Masalski's brother and sister paupers were, indeed, joining the princes.

The next morning, mass for the group would be celebrated at the spectacular National Shrine of the Immaculate Conception, and later, they would be among the stunned and silent throngs of mourners who watched on Pennsylvania Avenue, as the caisson rolled by and that riderless black horse accompanied the fallen president, John Fitzgerald Kennedy, from the White House to the United States Capitol. Those infamous and dark days of November 22–25 would live large and forever in the nation's memory and history, but even more so in the minds and hearts of the First Saturday Club members who were there to be a part of it that weekend.

Memories of that weekend remain stark and clear, as all people, all across America, stayed glued to their TV sets in order to join in the ceremonies and to emotionally and spiritually participate—and the First Saturday Club was there, doing its part to mend and to heal by prayerfully going to God.

Mary would later write, "For reasons unknown, God brought me close to the broken heart of our nation that weekend."

Spiritually, one can't help but think that it just might have been that the nation needed her and the prayers and redemptive spirits and glad hearts of those who accompanied her. As to their belonging to the heart of a living history, the connectivity and synergy remain forever palpable and powerful!

I can personally relate to this in that I, at the age of fourteen, went on the Washington trip in 1964 and that it was still, a year removed, tearful and mournful, and solemn. The impact of John Fitzgerald Kennedy's death was that deep and that formidable and sages and historians, and philosophers, in what is now more than fifty years removed, still argue about what was lost in losing him.

Suffice it to say that the answer is much!

The particular impacts on an evolving history are of no consequence to us here, but that the First Saturday family and its intimate relationship with God enjoined that moment in history, that moment of loss and need and peril, in prayer, was of great consequence.

The moment demanded prayer. More than anything else, it demanded prayer. And who better to help fill that demand, who better to help sustain the heart and soul of a wounded nation and people than Jersey City's and Newark's Our Lady of Fatima First Saturday Club.

In suggesting this, we are not overplaying our hand, but honestly reflecting upon the spiritual cry that so accompanied that moment in history, a powerful and a sacred moment for a nation that was appropriately colored by the sacredness of Father Tom Madison's mass and the Washington sojourn of Mary Varick's pilgrims.

As to the next trip, an article surfaced in the December 7, 1965 issue of the *Jersey Journal*, heralding the fact that the "Flying Wheelchair of Jersey City" and its environs are really moving now. The owner-occupant, Mrs. William Varick, has started planning for the biggest adventure of her life. The adventure was to be a junket to Europe in the summer of 1967 for her invalid family. There were great plans to make and much money to raise.

To that end, there was another article in the same paper, more than a year later, on February 14 of 1967, featuring the generous, ecumenical efforts of the Mount Pigsah "African Methodist Episcopal" or AME Celestial Choir to raise money for the First Saturday Club's European tour fund.

Note this clearly, Episcopal and Methodist African-Americans were to raise money for a Catholic-based contingent of disabled pilgrims who longed to visit the great shrines of their church. Yes, Catholic to the bone, I have written. But there also was something ecumenical to the bone about them, because Mary Varick casted the widest of nets.

A very detailed piece about Mary and the coming trip appeared in a feature story in the *Sunday Star-Ledger* of April 30 of 1967. The reporter, Jean Joyce, did her homework and came to truly know Mary and her "Love God joyously," "I say, God, use me whatever way you want and I won't worry and I don't," and "Oh ye of little faith." She wrote of her bright blue eyes that "sparkled mischievously" and of "her incredible ability to move her listener to tears of grief or laughter" and of a life that had been described as "rollicking and wonderful." She wrote of "an oversized heart that spills over with love" and of their need for money in order to take her "beloved family" of invalids to Europe.

Mrs. John Peduto, a prominent volunteer at the time, also was quoted. She said, "The First Saturday Club is something that you have to see and experience before you understand. They made me realize that I wasn't doing enough. This is real religion." She and Mary both focused upon their desperate pursuit of the "impossible that summer"—a pilgrimage to Fatima, Lourdes, and Rome. The article closed with a pitch for a May 8 fund-raising card party at Sacred Heart's parish hall.

On the back of choirs and card parties and remortgages and great debt, the impossible was realized.

On June 30, 1967, 207 First Saturday pilgrims flew across the Atlantic to Fatima, Lourdes, and Rome. Rather remarkably, 67 of the 207, nearly a third, were disabled and most of them were in wheel chairs, with two, Sister Miriam Eymard and Neil Gulliksen, on stretchers. Nine of the 207, led by Bishop Martin Stanton, were priests.

It bears repeating—67 of the 207 or nearly a third were severely disabled

Forty-seven years removed now, none of the disabled who made that trip are still with us today, as Hank Colling just passed away a couple of Christmas Eves ago and Freddy Vanderhoof did so in 2011. Joan Murray, who helps to direct the club today, was among the other faithful and hardworking sojourners on that trip and others still around include Mary and Jim Varick and Dot Cassidy, but the overwhelming majority of these 1967 pilgrims long ago went home to God.

It's interesting to juxtapose Mary Varick's commentary about the trip in her book with the commentary of others who were there. Mary acknowledges the travails and hardships, while preferring to keep her eyes clearly focused upon the rich spiritual bounty and blessings. The others gratefully bear witness to the bounty and the blessings, while first venting about the incredible difficulties and challenges. Mary and everyone else, as it were, went home by different roads. Mary cried later, while they understandably cried first.

In the end, they do get to the same place, but they get there in different ways. For the group, the cup was always half empty, and for Mary, it was always half full.

When talking to Hank Colling about this seeming phenomenon, he suggested that Mary Varick's view of everything was rose colored. She couldn't help but focus upon anything but the good, he insists, for it was her nature to do just that. Whatever the secret to be unveiled in the new day, be it sunshine or shadow, it was, to Mary, still a gift from God and it was, therefore, to be gratefully embraced.

Simply put, if there was anyone who knew how to accent the positive, it was Mary Varick.

What made Hank the perfect mirror through which to capture the true sum and substance of that 1967 trip was that it was his very first Our Lady of Fatima First Saturday Club experience. His parents had read an article about it in the *Advocate*, Newark Archdiocesan's newspaper, and they determined to take Hank themselves.

Lourdes and Fatima, after all, held out the faint but still-possible promise of a miracle or cure for their beloved son, who was still new to the quadriplegic world.

He's perfect for us, because no matter how crazed the circumstances seemed to him, he stayed when his parents had to return to the States due to a death in the family. He's perfect, because no matter how disorganized and nightmarish, he enjoyed and celebrated and managed to fall in love with a disorganized contingent that was, forever thereafter, to remain at the heart and center of his life. He was perfect, because he bore witness to the fact that no matter how bad the trip was practically speaking, it was over the top and monumental spiritually speaking.

In the end, the disorganized, outrageous, trouble-plagued pilgrimage abundantly delivered for them all.

Having had the privilege and pleasure of speaking with Hank about that trip a number of times before we lost him and his always wonderful company, his usual and patented response was that, "It was a disorganized disaster." He also freely described it as "nightmarish." And he almost gleefully talked about spending all night waiting in an airport in Portugal only to board a "Spantax Airlines" World War II reject of a plane at dawn, a plane that later greeted disembarking pilgrims with huge blobs of oil that were being summarily ejected from its sputtering engines. That so many were greeted that same way did not detract from the indignity of it, but ever the positive spinner, Mary Varick wrote that everyone simply decided to wear polka dot apparel that day.

Hank also rode on busses that broke down, and in both Fatima and Lourdes, he arrived at hotels only to discover that they could not accommodate him, leaving him to endure long waits, once in the rain and sun and once in blazing sunshine alone. In one case, the hotel elevator couldn't accommodate his wheelchair at all, and in another case, he simply refused to limit his movement to the barrier presented by fourteen steps outside and only staircases and no elevator within.

"The volunteers were already being pushed to the brink, so it just wasn't right and I didn't come all the way to Portugal to be stuck in a five-by-seven-foot room," he said.

Hank also shared the following note with me, one that paints a telling picture,

> When we arrived in Portugal, all the busses that were supposed to take us on the 4-hour ride to Fatima had gone home, so it took many hours of waiting. While Mary and company lined up transportation for us, I can remember sitting on the plane waiting to be carried off in what was stifling heat. And when my turn finally came to be put on the airport bus, I had to wait for several hours more in that awful heat, before the over-the-road coach transported us the four hours to the little Village of Fatima.
>
> The trip to Fatima was quite a journey. The roads were so narrow and the bus would scrape the houses in the small villages that we traveled through. Actually, it was quite exciting, despite the lack of air-conditioning and the terrible heat. I sat next to Dottie Healy and every time the bus went around a curve, I would slide either into Dottie's lap or start falling into the aisle. Finally somebody got their hands on a big strap and they tied my upper torso to the seat. What a trip. Dottie and I laughed all the way.
>
> The laughter and the goodness and the grace of the company helped us survive the constant waiting for rooms, for food, for transportation, for help, and for anything and everything you can imagine.

In fairness, Mary also freely acknowledged all of these problems and issues.

She just chose to spin the tales more mildly and to keep the eye on the truly beautiful and spiritually uplifting prize. Hank gets there too and so do Joan and Dot, who just wonderfully celebrated her ninety-sixth birthday, and everyone else, after first, in laughter, recalling their particular or favorite or most closely held disaster. Dot Cassidy's first recollection was of a Fatima tour official repeating the words, "Most disorganized, most disorganized, most disorganized" again and again and again, while it was the flight boarding, unboarding, and horrific delays that sat on the top of the despair charts for Joan Murray.

Dot recalls that tour official shaking his head in disbelief and personally admonishing all he encountered for their failings. So much so that a few actually cheered when Bud Cassidy, Mary's brother, approached him, stood up to him, and said, "You may be disappointed in us, but we are far more disappointed in you." As to Joan's dismay over the long waits, she said, "It was just so hard on so many of the disabled who weren't used to being in their chairs for so long, but their spirits overcame and what was a terrible hardship was treated, as time passed, as an exciting adventure."

To Mary, of course, the all of these trials only presented them, each and every one, with the opportunity to give even more to God.

And what could possibly be wrong with that?

Believing that we've already done some measure of justice to the whole, we will not laundry list all of the problems and both the minor and the major disasters. Such an effort could very well result in a book of its own. So, a close peak at day 1 alone will satisfy our need to play *Saturday Night Live* with this journey.

It began well with mass at the chapel of Our Lady of the Skies at Kennedy Airport. But the 207 had been assigned to three relatively close flights, with the last scheduled to depart at 8:30 p.m. But after a six-hour delay, due to some radar malfunction, it was 2:30 a.m. before the third leg of the crew lofted into the friendly skies, which led to a problem on the receiving end in Portugal as the busses that were scheduled to take them to Fatima disappeared. Upon arriving, there was, therefore, another multihour delay in Portugal rearranging local transport to Fatima.

Then upon finally arriving in Fatima after hours on bumpy, mountainous, and cobblestone roads, the crème de la crème of traveling conundrums surfaced, as all of the alleged accessible and first-class accommodations simply could not accommodate the disabled at all. With each facility, there seemed be a different problem and rearranging accommodations for the disabled elsewhere was, indeed, a nightmare.

Many of them wound up having to be placed in the hospital on the shrine grounds. So the First Saturday group was spread out and about, and while they could be brought together for mass, that was about it. To make matters worse, the director of tourism at the shrine passed away right before the First Saturday group's arrival, resulting in the entire staff disappearing for his funeral.

Getting help with the simplest of problems or accessing even basic information, therefore, became largely impossible. And as Mary noted in her book, Estelle Clavette, an oblate from Our Lady of the Cape, literally commandeered control of the Fatima Hospital in order to care for the members of Mary's "inner circle" who were displaced there.

Maybe because of these circumstances, many in the group were disappointed in Fatima itself. For indeed, First Saturday members had always come together in faith and in devotion always to fulfill their commitment, in prayer, to fostering peace in a world that desperately longed for it, but they also came together, in solidarity and camaraderie, to be for each other in friendship and love.

That second component, the human and personal one, was unexpectedly lost to them in Portugal.

This was to improve some at Lourdes, and it got better still in the Eternal City of Rome where the group was, in large part, finally able to come together at Domus Pacis, a retreat house. There, even the handfuls who were domiciled elsewhere, at least, had access to Domus Pacis.

So in Rome, the club and its 207 finally became one again.

That Fatima disappointed some was sad, for in a very real way, Mary looked upon it as the true home or birthplace of her "inner circle."

The thoughts that the blessed Mother shared with Jacinta and Francisco Marto and Lucia dos Santos had given voice and expression to the literal mission of her First Saturday Club. Theirs was a Fatima theology and a Fatima call to action, as they were, after all, the Our Lady of Fatima First Saturday Club. "I am the Lady of the Rosary," she had said, the same rosary that Mary's group pledged to pray with—for as long as there were days, for peace in the world.

For a focused Mary Varick, therefore, the First Saturday mass that was celebrated there at the Shrine of Our Lady of the Rosary in July of 1967, the one hundredth consecutive such First Saturday mass in the fiftieth anniversary year of the 1917 apparitions at Fatima, was the culmination of what Mary consistently referred to as her *impossible dream.*

Both practically and spiritually bound to that site, it was at that particular mass that what was held most dear to her 207 was reaffirmed, pronounced, upheld, and unabashedly shared with the world.

"Our lives of suffering," wrote Mary, "were to be given to Jesus, through Mary, our Mother in prayer for peace in the world." No matter the secret to be unveiled in any new day for Mary's contingent—that was the constant that had to be at the epicenter of each and every day. Oh, how powerfully and profoundly it was manifested, Mary felt, on that July First Saturday at Fatima, where her "inner circle" enjoyed the privilege of coming home to Our Lady of the Rosary.

So much so that Mary wrote that it was as if the song "The Impossible Dream" was literally playing and resounding inside her as if it were her own. "To reach the unreachable star," indeed! The Our Lady of Fatima First Saturday Club of Newark, New Jersey, was praying the rosary in Fatima itself. What could have been more unreachable to a Newark-based group whose lives had already been physically broken and forever challenged.

So moved was a Sister Anna Lawrence that she wrote Mary to say, "Today, we are in Fatima where our Blessed Mother honored the earth with her presence fifty years ago." She knew then that Mary Varick's pilgrims and her "inner circle" would make it as well and cross the ocean to observe the First Saturday of July 1967 upon the very spot where she pleaded for prayers and for penance."

For Mary Varick, it was the spot, not the only but certainly the most important and the most significant of all.

While life improved only slightly for her pilgrims in Lourdes, Mary noted that Father Don Arel and Estelle Clavette again had to pull rabbits out of the air in order to get the accommodations to finally accommodate. To Mary, who was, of course, Fatima driven, even the compelling beauty of Lourdes and its basilica and the glorious Grotto at Massabielle where Bernadette Soubirous knelt before the *Immaculate Conception*, while wonderful and full of grace, could not compare with her Fatima.

Fatima, after all, was home!

Rome, however, and the seven days spent there, seemed to finally bring order to a trip that had previously moved forward in a state of disordered flux and angst.

In the current travel guides, they criticize the extremely small rooms and the showers that are difficult to move around in at Domus Pacis, but that didn't seem to matter to Mary's minions who were overwhelmingly ecstatic to simply have found a clean place where they could finally be together. And the distance from the heart of the ancient city and the heart of Saint Peter's itself didn't seem to matter either, for they were finally home again with each other.

They enjoyed tours of the city by day and by night, and they came together for a reception at Via Venito, and masses were said by their nine priests at locations all across the city, but largely at Santa Susanna, where they befriended a contingent of Irish seminarians who wound up pushing many a wheelchair that week.

The sights, of course, in their sheer beauty and in their holiness, moved many to tears.

But there are always detractors, and there was one sardonic pilgrim who was on her way out of the Sistine Chapel while another was on her way in who reportedly and caustically said, "It looks better in the postcards." That said, the overwhelming majority, however, were rather "stunned and numbed" by its incomparable beauty.

Some remember the Irish nurses who volunteered at Fatima... and a few remember being moved by the wearing of the black by the Portuguese women in Fatima, who they discovered wore black both when their husbands and sons were out to sea and again when they died...and a few remember the soups that Estelle Clavette prepared at the hospitals in both Fatima and Lourdes...and one remembered the anxiety on the faces of the men who took their gregarious Anne Gerhardt down five floors on a stretcher on the fire escape after an elevator broke down in Lourdes...and Mary Varick sang the praises of Jerry Sheehan, with whom she was going to have history...And everyone was amazed by the extraordinary devotion of the beautiful and tireless Sis Dakes who never left Neil Gulliksen's side after he grew desperately ill in Lourdes.

Forty-seven years removed, Dot Cassidy, now ninety-six years old, got emotional and almost tearful, recalling the site of the procession in Lourdes which she wished, "All the youth of the world could witness today, because there was a holiness about it that could turn them away from hateful ways."

Forty-seven years removed, there is no doubt that all took home images and memories and impactful moments which forever colored and shaped their lives.

There was oh-so much to remember but no one who was, as Mary suggested, blessed to be on that trip could possibly forget the remarkable audience that they had with Pope Paul VI.

The pope was directed to Mary, who got to personally introduce her suffering "inner circle" and to present him with an inscribed parchment that contained a message from the Our Lady of Fatima First Saturday Club. The club's own Judy Dadek had meticulously and beautifully brush painted it with her teeth. But it's what followed that stunned, as the pope took the time out to personally bless each of the disabled. They watched in awe as he knelt down to kiss Neil Gulliksen and Sister Myriam, who he also privately prayed with, and they watched joyfully as he knelt down again and clasped the hands and kissed the head of a young boy on the trip who could neither speak nor hear. Everyone watched as a profoundly moved and emotionally engaged heir to the throne of Saint Peter embraced their "inner circle" with deep affection and heartfelt emotion.

"In my life," said Joan Murray, "it remains one of the most special and unforgettable moments. Everyone there was completely blown away by our pope's love and gentleness."

They saw Jesus in him; they all saw Jesus in a pope who was so fully and humbly human!

And so, all of the drama of delays and no accommodations and planes that needed new engines and bumps on the road—and oh, how bumps on the road savage the rear ends and backs of those who are wheelchair bound—and busses that broke down and the inability to find each other melted away in the presence of a surprisingly up close and personal and very human and loving pontiff.

Interestingly, there was a subliminal connection that bound Pope Paul VI to this humble contingent of 207, for he too was especially devoted to Mary. He introduced three Marian encyclicals, and it was he who proclaimed Mary *the Mother of the Church* in the Vatican Council. Then too, he sought dialogue with the world, with other Christians, other religions, and even atheists, excluding nobody. He saw himself as a humble servant for a suffering humanity, and he demanded significant changes of the rich in America and Europe in favor of the poor in the Third World. He insisted that his church become a force for social justice.

Out of the inner city themselves, the First Saturday Club and its pontiff were, therefore, kindred spirits.

After the audience with him, there was a scheduled tour of Saint Peter's in the afternoon that led Mary, who had no fear of requesting anything of anybody, to ask for permission for her group to have a box luncheon picnic on the grounds. Permission was remarkably granted to do what no one there recalled ever happening before, so after their blessed time with the pope, they retired to his Papal Gardens to enjoy "pickin' chicken and beer." What a contrast! Beer in the Papal Gardens, unthinkable and unimaginable, but somehow real to 207 pilgrims who were permitted to joyfully embrace the Papal Gardens, in a manner that no one before ever had!

"I kept pleading with everyone to please leave no beer cans in the Pope's flowers," wrote Mary.

Joan Murray inadvertently offered an explanatory footnote, as to what made this trip, aside from the destinations, very different. She did so, when I asked what personal memories she had of our Aunt Mary there. She explained that it wasn't like Canada, where the typical day ended in the wee hours in Aunt Mary's room.

"In Europe, I don't remember having a single personal moment with Aunt Mary, and I was never in her room. For the most part, we weren't even together, and when we were together again in Rome, we were all preoccupied with those in our care." It was, she explained without a hint of complaint, from beginning to end, a high-octane and high-pressure venture for the volunteers.

Nineteen sixty-seven was an unforgettable year for America, and while the First Saturday Club was off in Europe, things were breaking down at home, culturally, spiritually, and practically. The music was loud and scaring some, the drug culture was claiming too many of the nation's youth, the proponents of free love were threatening morality, and the politics of Civil Rights and Vietnam were dividing and tearing apart a shaky *e pluribus unum*.

One noted historian suggested that outside of the Great American Civil War, America had never been closer to coming apart than it was in the mid-sixties.

Despite Martin Luther King's nonviolent approach to garnering long-denied freedoms and liberties, one hundred years of bigotry and racism and the outright oppression of Jim Crow laws and the "see no evil and hear no evil" denial of "separate but equal," America finally exploded in 1967. Race riots left the inner cities of the nation burning, and no corner of the nation escaped unscathed.

On the streets of the First Saturday Club's Newark alone, twenty-six were left dead, and 725 wounded when the city erupted while the First Saturday Club was in Europe. Seventeen were left dead within eye shadow of Mary Varick's Colonnade, in her neighboring Central Ward.

It is ironic and maybe even telling, to those interested in going deep, that this violence erupted at the very time that this solemn pilgrimage progressed.

What was happening at home also was compounded by what was happening in Vietnam. Wiser and better-informed citizens were increasingly questioning the wisdom of America's engagement there and the flawed psychology of a *domino theory* that invited all to quake at the steady advance of communist ideology. President Johnson's friendship with President Diem of South Vietnam and our failure to understand Ho Chi Minh of North Vietnam blinded us and committed us to a policy of utter madness.

The suffering in Vietnam reached its apex during the *TET Offensive* of the North Vietnamese in the summer of 1967. The blood flowed more freely and the death tolls rose dramatically, and the dying were brought home to a tired and beleaguered nation every night on the evening news.

So while a Mary Varick had every reason to look upon 1967 as the greatest year for her First Saturday Club, it was undeniably the toughest year, outside of those Civil War years, for a breaking and challenged America.

So we must wrap our arms around the disparity of the solemnity and holiness and grace that enveloped 207 American pilgrims who watched in awe as the pope blessed their own in Rome and weigh it against the violence, blood, and carnage of riots and war and chaos. 207 looked, through Mary, to God and prayed for peace in a nation that just happened to be desperately longing for some peace.

The juxtaposition of these two extremes overwhelms and can only call upon us, as a people faith, to surmise that it must have been the prayers and the goodness and faith of the former and those like them that inevitably, through the grace of God, healed the brokenness of the latter. Evil and mean-spiritedness and hate and bloodshed can only be setback and eliminated over time, when the light of goodness and the love of God take precedence.

There is, therefore, this author sincerely maintains, a stark connection between the humble suffering of an inner circle and their love of God and the Eucharist and their prayers and a TET Offensive and the twenty-six dead in a racial uprising on the streets of their own Newark. The light of the Our Lady of Fatima First Saturday Club and that from many other centers of energy and daring simply needed to shine in order to bring peace to the hot cities of America and to the ravaged landscape of Vietnam.

Oh yes, love is the answer. Love is always the answer.

As it happened, I was in Newark, living in a Cursillo Retreat House and working in the projects as part of Catholic Youth Service's (CYS) summer project, when the riot broke out. I heard the guns throughout the night, and I rode a bus that was almost overturned by an angry mob. And friends from my neighborhood in Hackensack began falling and dying in Vietnam. My brother Frank, with whom I had long shared a room was, as those who served in Vietnam so casually said, "In Country," when Mary's pilgrims were in Europe. I was well aware of and deeply moved by all that was crumbling around me.

As to the 207, I was there at the airport to help when they returned, there among the many who welcomed them home, but largely unaware of the great service they had done for all of us in a then very sad America that so longed for healing and peace.

In a thank-you to Mary forwarded later that July, perhaps William and Franck of WADO Hispanic Radio put it best when they wrote, "It is difficult to express our gratitude for the wonderful pilgrimage. No doubt God must be very pleased with you for making it possible. Everyone could see the spiritual graces that were so abundantly showered upon us all."

It was ten years later, in another summer that Mary Varick was to lead another contingent across the Atlantic in response to their Fatima mission. Mary wrote that it was their objective "to bring a suffering Christ in our world to touch the suffering Christ in Russia."

She wanted to tangibly answer Our Lady of Fatima's call to recite the rosary in that cold and distant and removed land. A free people who were free to practice their faith longed to purposefully reignite that faith in a land where that very freedom was denied.

Remarkably, Mary Varick and her humble band of brethren, "inner circle," and volunteers alike, had, through diplomatic channels, won the right to do so. Initially, they looked to Moscow, but they were redirected to Leningrad, the once and future city of Saint Petersburg and the once capital of Russia, where the Virgin Mary once reigned as the Queen of Russia.

So the change from Moscow to Leningrad seemed fitting for a group that was named for that very same Queen.

As early as January of 1977, this journey had been but a nagging dream of Mary Varick, but it suddenly became real at the January First Saturday in 1977 at Our Lady of Mercy, in Jersey

City, when Father Paul Bochicchio presented Mary with a check for one thousand dollars that she immediately determined to use as seed to inaugurate the Russian fund. All kind of steps were taken to raise an immediate goal of seventy-seven thousand dollars, but they were far from achieving that goal, until the deal was finally sealed when Bruno and Mary Pisaniello took out a second mortgage on their beautiful home in Belvidere, New Jersey, where the mountains most certainly, but quietly proclaimed, "Oh ye of great faith."

But when the time came, leaving was difficult for Mary in that her beautiful daughter Billie Adriance's multiple sclerosis was in its latter stages and she was very, very sick.

It so happened that Mother Teresa visited Billie with Mary in her familiar Jersey City, 241 Pacific Avenue home, only a week before their planned departure.

When Mary expressed her "misgivings" about leaving Billie as she was, Mother Teresa said, "There is nothing you can do for Billie. Leave her in Jesus's care and do the work that you planned to do for God."

In a handwritten note left by Mary Varick about her relationship with Mother Teresa, she relates no less than four visits by Mother to Billie's side at varying stages of her disease. Upon one of them, she profoundly said, "It is you, Billie, you and your suffering that give me the strength to do what I do for the poorest of the poor." After this final visit, Mary wrote, "I journeyed thousands of miles in the days that followed, but my heart and soul spent much of that time with my Billie."

The distance only served to bring her closer.

As it happened, Billie would go home to God five days after Mary's return. Not long after, Mother Teresa wrote her friend Mary to say, "You know that I would have been there if I could. But now we are both so much richer with Billie there to intercede for us."

This time, it was but sixty people and five priests and one flight—so smaller, more manageable, and more organized. And far easier to keep together!

The first night was spent in Helsinki, Finland, and then, they traveled by boat on the Baltic Sea to Saint Petersburg. Interestingly, Mary wrote that the first time that she had ever heard the haunting and powerful hymn "Be Not Afraid" was during mass as they sailed on the *SS Ilmator* to Russia. How appropriate those words were, for truly they did not know what they would find or face at the time.

They were truly sailing into an unknown!

Reality struck when they entered the harbor to be met by a phalanx of armed guards and military officials, and there was discomfort as they waited for a long time before being allowed to disembark. It was a discomfort that grew as all had to surrender their passports in exchange for temporary visas, although they were staying but a short two days. It was a discomfort that further escalated when Father Paul was marched off, under guard, to be interrogated by Russian officials.

And while then teenager and today's Father Kevin Carter gets a lot of mileage out of his joke that the site of Father Paul being marched off under armed guard was his happiest memory, indeed, feelings were quite different at that time, as all were confused and worried. A team of young Intourist guides were assigned to the group to allegedly assist, but actually and clearly to guard.

Cool and distant and removed at first, they didn't warm up or let their guards down until the conclusion of an extraordinary mass at the only functioning Catholic church in Saint Petersburg, Our Lady of Lourdes.

There, the only locals attending were elderly women with tired, worn, and wrinkled faces. Early twentieth-century babushkas adorned their heads, and they too, like the young Intourist guides, only seemed to come to life at the end of a mass that was profoundly moving.

The pronounced absence of men and youth in their sparse congregation bore witness to the near tragic impact that the Soviet government had upon the mere celebration of faith. Here was a land where faith and hope and, in so many respects, even love had been exiled. Here was a land where only old women, in sparse numbers, had the courage to publicly keep faith with their Lord.

So the fact that this celebration of the mass, in their beautiful, old, and captive church, Our Lady of Lourdes, was so powerfully emotional made a mighty difference, explained Mary—"for us, for the Russian women who dared to join us, and for the Intourist guards whose coldness summarily melted away. The spirit of that mass moved even those who did not expect to be moved."

Mary Varick wrote in her book that it was as if her group turned a light back on in Leningrad or Saint Petersburg and that prior barriers and fears and negativity just seemed to melt away in the very church where they had come to embrace a suffering Christ in Russia.

While forever unknown, it can certainly be argued that they clearly recaptured a soul or two or more for God and in the name of peace.

Upon leaving that church with good feeling swelling all around, one elderly woman all but pleaded with Father Al Clarke in the hope of receiving the crucifix that he wore. But having been coldly and harshly warned by their military not to leave the smallest thing behind, he had to resist his incredible desire to give it to her.

Upon boarding the bus, he sat down in despair next to Mary and said that he now knew what Peter must have felt like when he denied Jesus three times.

For he too, in denying her, had denied Christ. He confessed to Mary. At least, that is what it felt like to him, and he couldn't help but cry.

At that same time, as they were leaving that mass, Mary Pisaniello said, "There was another elderly lady who approached my Barbara with the gift of a well-worn holy card. She pressed it into her hands and implored Barbara and her generation to carry on the faith and not to allow it to fade or fail. Her eyes were incredible, as you saw the desperation and the pleading and the hope in them. Her eyes spoke volumes. Such a treasure from a woman who knew all too well that she could never replace that religious article was so remarkable."

Such were the highs and lows and the sadness of Russia!

There, the tangible light of a faith that refused to die despite decades of oppression—and there, the longing for faith and for the light of Christ in the faces and hearts of those who had, for all too long, been denied Him.

There was much more to the trip as they enjoyed a long stay in Rome and another audience with their beloved Pope Paul VI, who while older and worn, remained just as gentle and warm. Then it was back to the Grotto at Massabielle, but interestingly to the Russian Rite Shrine at Lourdes where the sixty received a great ovation from a crowd that was told that they had only recently celebrated mass at the church of Our Lady of Lourdes in Saint Petersburg in Russia. It was a very special moment that was followed by another tangibly holy procession.

And while the trip was largely spent in Rome and Lourdes, it had always been about Communist Russia, a land where they dared to hold even heaven hostage.

Mary Varick would later write that, "We went from the Grotto at Lourdes in 1967, to Our Lady of Lourdes in Saint Petersburg in 1977, to the Russian Rite Chapel at Our Lady of Lourdes in France, and finally, a few months later in the fall of 1977, to a First Saturday gathering at Our Lady of Lourdes in Mountainside, New Jersey." There, they were hosted by her brother, Father John Cassidy, whose homily, Mary noted, was that day among the most stirring she had ever heard.

This passing from Lourdes to Lourdes to Lourdes in 1977 warrants comment, for while Mary wrote of her club's spiritual belonging to Fatima, it was at Sainte-Anne-de-Beaupre in Quebec where all of this began, at Sainte-Anne-de-Beaupre which had long been popularly referred to as the *Lourdes of North America* in years gone by.

So the journey that carried Mary's "inner circle" to three (her beloved Trinity) Our Lady of Lourdes churches in three (her beloved Trinity) different countries in rapid succession in 1977 actually began at another Lourdes in another country in 1951.

Even Mary never made this connection. At least not in her writing! But it still stares us in the face, this link between Beaupre and Lourdes, between beautiful Saint Anne and Bernadette, and between these two most holy places that uniquely claimed and carried the First Saturday family in 1977.

Mary was cured at the *Lourdes of North America*, what was to her, ever and always and rightfully, a beloved Sainte-Anne-de-Beaupre. But we know—*and it's so nice to know*—that there was even more to the already profound ties that bound her First Saturday family to Lourdes in 1977.

The waters of Lourdes that Saint Bernadette drew from the earth in the Grotto at Massabielle, indeed, run wide and deep in the hearts and souls and spirits of the Our Lady of Fatima First Saturday Club.

As to the gift of their prayers in Russia, it's enough to simply look at where Russia was in 1977.

Leonid Brezhnev had already ushered in the doctrines of détente and perestroika, and they were, indeed, opening up to the west. The winds of change and understanding were blowing through their politics.

But they were a long way from home, and it was only two years later that they would sadly move their armies into Afghanistan in a horrific attempt to subjugate a people. It was an attempt that resulted in the deaths of hundreds of thousands and in the dislocation of millions. And it would be more than a decade before that infamous wall finally fell in Berlin, and the USSR gave up the ghost of a long-failed attempt to control the free peoples of a region with an oppressive iron fist.

But more importantly for us, it was in 1977 that Menachem Begin became the prime minister of Israel and that he and Anwar Sadat, the president of Egypt, with the great help of President Jimmy Carter, engineered a monumental peace treaty that changed the Middle Eastern paradigm in a wholly unprecedented and extraordinary way.

Make no mistake about it, prayers for peace and peace itself came together there in 1977. There in the bountiful mix that gave rise to this very welcome advance for peace in the world—were most certainly to be found—the prayers of an Our Lady of Fatima First Saturday Club in a distant Russia!

So huge was it that thirty-seven years later, we are still waiting for the next shoe to drop advancing peace in the Middle East. As to the Unites States of America and Russia in 1977, the rhetoric was definitely toning down, tensions were finally softening, and more progress was being made on nuclear disarmament issues. Sure, we had a long way to go and Russia was still going to cause great messes (as would we as well at times), but they were, at least, abandoning their Cold War rhetoric and their hard lines.

The promise of great change was in the air.

So for an organization that was founded in the heart of a Cold War, under Blessed Mary's banner, in the interest of bringing peace to the world, 1977 was a very, very good year. No longer were we looking over our heads, like Chicken Little, waiting for the bombs to drop and the sky to fall. No longer were little children placing paper bags over their heads in church basements during air raids in preparation for an anticipated nuclear holocaust.

The cause of peace had, indeed, been advanced.

It's interesting to note that we paused here to focus on the impact of just a few out of the box or different pilgrimages, while it can be argued that each and every one of the pilgrimages, from the early fifties until today, also has impacted and been a force for good in this world.

So permit me to share a note about just one more trip, the final Canadian pilgrimage of 1976, the last of the pilgrimages before Russia. For I know that my aunt, Mary Varick, revered having family with her.

She reveled in giving her family members the greatest gift that she had to offer to them—her pilgrimages.

That year was important, because it may have been the last that her mother, Agnes Cassidy, was with her and there too was her brother Joe and his wife Dot as well as her ever-faithful brother Bud and his equally faithful Anne. Her daughter Billie, in the grip of multiple sclerosis, was there on a stretcher along with her husband Don Adriance and all four of their children, Don, Mike, Maryanne (one of today's codirectors), and Peggy. Bruno and Mary Pisaniello also were there with their children, Laura and Barbara. So too was Mary's son Jimmy and his Mary.

As Mary reflected upon the Stations of the Cross on that trip and came to the station where Jesus met His Mother, she could not help but think of the three mothers representing three generations of one family who stood before Him there—Mary's mother who was in a wheelchair, Mary herself in a wheelchair, and her Billie upon a stretcher. Three generations, in suffering, humbly taking their place beneath the cross! Powerful and poignant, there was no need to say more.

This particular trip, with so much family present, must have been extremely enjoyable for Mary, for to be in the embrace of family was, to her, to be in the arms of Jesus.

Mary believed that the gifts and grace of a loving God were constantly showered upon us and that the secret we waited to discover in each new day, in sunshine and in shadow and in joy and in tragedy, wasn't really a secret at all.

It was only the constancy of Our Lord's presence and love.

It was a promise that was being readily and steadily fulfilled.

What was a secret was only what we ourselves were to bring to each day.

It was God who was the constant and we who were the variable.

As to what Mary was able to bring to her days, she suggested that it could never get any better than Russia. She wrote, "Jesus was there. I met Him there, you see." In the Eucharist, her greatest love, she found Him there, and in her heart and soul, she rejoiced in Him there.

"Never better than Russia," she proclaimed.

There are thousands, given what was brought to their days with or through Mary, who might argue with her. And her attachments to Our Lady of the Cape and Sainte-Anne-de-Beaupre were far more sacred and richly personal. But to help bring Christ and His Light home to a land from which He had long been exiled—a suffering Christ—Russia was, somehow, her high water mark.

"God needs you in Russia!" said Mother Teresa. And so did we! And so it was.

In her epilogue, Mary Pisaniello would open the closing of Mary's final book with words that Mary Varick often voiced about her most important and personal pilgrimage to come—her journey home,

"Remember, my Jesus, I am ready whenever you are."

She was, without doubt, ready! Ready for what would be her greatest pilgrimage and her greatest journey. Ready for ever so much more than '77 or '67' or '63! Ready for her homecoming and the embrace of her Jesus to whom she had given her all.

With the profoundest of faiths, she must have taken that last journey with the strength that comes from knowing. As to the end of her earthly sojourn, we imagine it beautiful and glorious and magnificent. We imagine it and we fall short, for it must have been beyond words, beyond expression, beyond our comprehension or imagination.

Her daughter, Mary, closed the book on her life and on her final journey, both practically and figuratively, with these—simple, clear, and definitive words—these words...

"What a peaceful way to live and to die."

## Chapter 3 Placeholders

- For a focused Mary Varick, therefore, the First Saturday mass that was celebrated there at the Shrine of Our Lady of the Rosary in July of 1967, the one hundredth consecutive such First Saturday mass in the fiftieth anniversary year of the 1917 apparitions at Fatima, was the culmination of what Mary consistently referred to as her *impossible dream.*

- They watched in awe as he knelt down to kiss Neil Gulliksen and Sister Myriam, who he also privately prayed with, and they watched joyfully as he knelt down again and clasped the hands and kissed the head of a young boy on the trip who could neither speak nor hear. Everyone watched as a profoundly moved and emotionally engaged heir to the throne of Saint Peter embraced their "inner circle" with deep affection and heartfelt emotion.

- "In Europe, I don't remember having a single personal moment with Aunt Mary, and I was never in her room. For the most part, we weren't even together, and when we were together again in Rome, we were all preoccupied with those in our care." It was, she explained without a hint of complaint, from beginning to end, a high-octane and high-pressure venture.

- So we must wrap our arms around the disparity of the solemnity and holiness and grace that enveloped 207 American pilgrims who watched in awe as the pope blessed their own in Rome amidst the violence, blood, and carnage of riots and war and chaos.

- The journey that carried Mary's "inner circle" to three (her beloved Trinity) Our Lady of Lourdes churches in three (her beloved Trinity) different countries in rapid succession in 1977 actually began at another Lourdes in another country in 1951.

- Even Mary never made this connection. At least not in her writing! But it still stares us in the face, this link between Beaupre and Lourdes, between beautiful Saint Anne and Bernadette, and between these two most holy places that uniquely claimed and carried the First Saturday family in 1977.

- For an organization that was founded in the heart of a Cold War, under Blessed Mary's banner, in the interest of bringing peace to the world, 1977 was a very good year. No longer were we looking over our heads, like Chicken Little, waiting for the bombs to drop and the sky to fall. No longer were little children placing paper bags over their heads in church basements during air raids in preparation for an anticipated nuclear holocaust.

- "God needs you in Russia!" said Mother Theresa. And so did we! And so it was.

# 4

# The Voices of the Faithful

A couple of months after Mary's funeral, a small group or representative sampling of her *First Saturday* faithful gathered to grieve together and to lean on one another and to speak of all things Mary. They came together to bear witness to a special soul they so loved in a communal atmosphere.

It should be noted that this was an organized gathering, as a videographer was there to capture it all, and a pleasant gentleman, whose name remains unknown to me, was there to both moderate and facilitate the conversation. My guess is that it may have been part of an early and concerted effort to gather testimony for Father Kevin Carter who was fostering the effort to move Mary Varick's cause for sainthood.

In sorrow especially, this small group or contingent from the First Saturday Club family gathered together to speak about their recently lost friend, Mary Varick, for when a great loss had been suffered, it is not good that one should be alone.

One by one, they talked about what Mary meant to them, and one by one, they shared a few heartfelt stories about her, those stories that were right off the top of their heads, those that first came to mind. Some were humorous and some moving, and all were meaningful.

It is, for the record, the stories that first come to our minds that speak volumes and that speak the loudest.

Having been called by God and having left this earth on June 27, 1989, what follows is what this contingent who loved her first wanted or most wanted to tell the world and you about her.

Among the group was *Howie Daniels*, a paraplegic and character of the first sort who Mary had rescued from Pollock Hospital in Jersey City in the sixties—*Flossie Oates*, a Jersey City African-American Baptist woman, who served the poor of Jersey City and who had, over the years, been Mary's volunteer's volunteer and a lover of all of Mary's babies—*Hank Colling*, a quadriplegic and my dear and inspiring friend, who tragically fell off a roof while working for what was then New Jersey Bell at the tender young age of twenty-three—*Frances D'Amato*, who met Mary through the Saint Francis Society and joined forces with her, for the first time, on the infamous 1967 pilgrimage to Fatima, Lourdes, and Rome—*Anne Gerhardt*, who saw herself as "a very big woman with an even bigger heart" and who took no small measure of joy in referring to herself as Mary's best friend—and *Anne Toth*, a very humble and deeply faithful, non-Catholic victim of muscular dystrophy whose very first First Saturday just happened to be when a small crowd of 330 gathered at the New York World's Fair for mass in 1965.

With the passing of Hank Colling just this past Christmas in 2012, I must start by noting that each of these six, these once linchpins or leaders of Mary Varick's First Saturday Club family, has now enjoyed their own "homegoing to Jesus" as well. That's how Mother Teresa spoke of Mary's death, and it is how I now choose to look upon the deaths of these six as well. Each shares Mary's legacy. They own a piece of it, and they have, I no doubt trust and pray, joined her in paradise.

In so many ways, these six were truly representative of the whole and certainly representative of the caliber, quality, and richness of the people who comprised the *Our Lady of Fatima*

*First Saturday Club in 1989.* They were good people with big hearts, and like Mary herself, each was deeply faithful.

In Mary Varick's presence, all of them shined, for she invited all who joined her and who both prayed and played with her to shine and to celebrate.

With Mary, one could not help but expand or ascend.

Thinking about this group compels me to share an aside that colors all that I write and that I must be open about. Of Mary Varick's sanctity, I have no doubt, but as I regularly dwell on this subject or thought of sainthood, I am consistently shaken and moved by so many who also were so tangibly saint-like. I think of Hank or Flossie or Yvonne or Jeanette or Bill Varick or their Billie or Neil or Paul Russell or Freddie Vanderhoof and countless others, and I can't help but see the saint who resided in them as well.

If you knew Hank or Flossie or Jeanette, you would agree. You couldn't help but agree, for they truly were saints. Wholly devoted, reverently devoted to the love of God.

Maybe, it's simply because I'm too inclusive or open or liberal, but I cannot help but see what I see. I just can't help it, and I can't help celebrating it—because they loved so greatly or suffered so mightily for others or literally lived Aunt Mary's theology of suffering and so faithfully carried the cross.

They were special, they were holy, and they were Mary's.

Led by my sister Joan, there also remains a saintly contingent among today's Our Lady of Fatima First Saturday Club.

Mary Varick, you see, helped to fashion and to shape saints. Now, she didn't make them, but she most certainly awoke the very best that was in them. She drew people to herself, and she invited the saint that was lingering inside them to surface. In goodness and in kindness and in mercy and in sacrifice, she did this again and again. She did this and God witnessed it.

Of Mary Varick's First Saturday Club and family, He witnessed infinitely more!

This writer's "takeaway" lines about Mary Varick that have been so lovingly shared by these six requires no literary elaboration. For the impactful nature of the following truly speaks for itself.

Each of the six had found life in the spirit and in their God, through the intercession and actions of Mary Varick.

Many speak pointedly of having been saved by Mary and the words of all relate to this very phenomenon of having been saved.

It is, we must emphasize, no simple thing to save a life.

One, therefore, assumes that it must not be easy to save a life, and yet the facts suggest otherwise, as Mary Varick was clearly a rainmaker of such miracles. She saved lives, and those "saved by" willingly and loudly attest to the same.

But only with God's help, Mary would protest. A God with whom and through whom all things are possible.

*Howie Daniels* said, "She took me out of the darkness. And where there had been only darkness, she brought this bright light. *She saved me*," and,

*Flossie Oates* said, "Mary was just like the Blessed Mother herself to me. She changed my life in every imaginable way. *She was like the savior*," and,

*Hank Colling* said, "If she hadn't come into my life, I'd be dead. *She saved me*," and,

*Frances Damato* said, "She tried to bring us to love and she inspired us to pray," and,

*Anne Gerhardt* said, "She taught me that the all of my life is a pilgrimage," and "While Midas may have turned everything to gold, it was Mary who turned everything to love," and finally,

*Anne Toth* said, "Mary taught me how to leap over barriers, and she added a spiritual quality or dimension to my life that made all the difference for me."

Such things, of course, are said of saints.

Make no mistake about it. The words of these six are spoken of saints. And I need say nothing more about it.

The thing, as the Romans used to say, speaks for itself.

In taking them to the mass and to the Eucharist and to the rosary and to each other, Mary Varick redefined their very lives and redeemed them.

In taking them to Sainte-Anne-de-Beaupre and Our Lady of the Cape and Saint Joseph's Oratory and a hundred archdiocesan parishes, Mary did this. In bringing them home into the heart of each other's peace and joy and love, Mary did this. "Without her, I'd be dead," they said. "She brought me out of darkness and into the light," they said. "She taught me to embrace life and to leap over barriers and to become pilgrim people and to love one another more fully," they said. "She saved me," they said.

She was "like the Blessed Mother herself," an instrument and limitless wellspring of grace.

Looking back upon the autumn of 1989, here, in 2014, I have already noted that of this group, exactly twenty-five years removed from this gathering, all have gone home to God and to the embrace of Jesus Christ and His Mother Mary to whom each of them dedicated their very existence and, no doubt, to the welcoming arms of their great friend, Mary Varick, to whom they were so devoted—to Mary who was the very face of Jesus to them.

All of this was fostered in profound humility, colored in humility, spoken in humility. While what was said of Mary was extraordinary and wonderful, there was no boast or brag in it. They spoke of wonder and of miracles and of sanctity and of grace, but first and foremost, they spoke the truth of Mary and her ministry which was humbly manifested always. They spoke of the brightness and power of what great love can, through the intercession of the Lord, produce. All that Mary did was first given to God, but oh, what power, instruments of great love, like Mary Varick, had been given, by God, to do great and good and even extraordinary things.

These six spoke of such things.

*Hank Colling,* who was an instrumental and spiritual force behind what I write, raised five adopted children with his remarkable wife Mary, quite an unusual and extraordinary feat for a quadriplegic. Despite his suffering a great deal in his final years, largely with respiratory complications and cancer, his bright light and beaming smile continued to embrace all comers. As faithful a man as there was on this planet, he proclaimed always that he was an apostle of Mary Varick and that he had never stopped trying to do justice to the work that they once did together, work that defined his life.

Most of the stories that he focused upon in this gathering were of the trials and tribulations he faced, as a young man and young victim of disability, on the historic and the still-not-fully-digested pilgrimage to Fatima, Lourdes, and Rome in 1967, all of which was somewhat comprehensively recaptured in a previous chapter.

So don't think that Hank Colling was either silent during this conversation or mistreated in our recording of the same.

Beyond waxing poetically about his first journey with Mary Varick in 1967, he shared a few other profound observations about what she did for him and his response to the same.

At a time in his life when Hank doubted everything, he said that, "Mary Varick gave me both the faith and strength to carry on." And having helped him to tap the faith and strength necessary to go forward, he said that, "Mary Varick, by her good example, brought me to goodness, to holiness, and to joy." And when she prayed or reflected upon the Stations of the Cross, he said, "It was like being in heaven."

I can't help but hear what Hank so lovingly said, during this conversation, about Mary's prayers and recall his own desire to reflect upon those same Stations of the Cross for her when he was last in Canada a few summers ago. He had prayed and felt that it was something that Mary needed him to do for her. His desire was palpable and stunning in its own right, but at Sainte-Anne's on the Scala Sancta on a very windy and rainy day, he was relegated to using their public address system and every time he began to speak, it cut out on him and the wind rattled the paper upon which his notes were framed.

Time after time, it cut out on him, until he had nowhere to go with it. Time after time, the wind played tricks with his notes.

Sitting right next to him, he looked as if he were ready to cry, and he felt as if he had failed Mary Varick who had that day, he believed, asked him to do this for her. I felt so bad for him, and I liked to believe and I told him that people somehow heard what was in his heart and what he was not given a chance to articulate.

For what is in the heart is often spoken without words.

But oh, how Hank longed to do Mary's work for her that day. How he longed to carry on for Mary, who never stopped stirring inside him.

Please note that there is much more about Hank's relationship with Mary and her impact upon him that is related throughout the body of this work, as Hank's own passion was, as we purposefully continue to note, the driving force behind the very pursuit of this effort to leave a spiritually inspired account of Mary Varick's life and ministry for posterity

*Howie Daniels's* stories were, for the most part, deeply family oriented, and the bulk of them had to do with Mary's oldest child Billie, her husband Don, their four children—Don, Maryanne, Michael, and Peggy, and their collective grappling with Billie's great suffering with multiple sclerosis. He said that you couldn't help but stand in awe of them and of their faith and of the love that they so clearly shared. "To have watched," he said, "Billie's young children communicating with her, when all she was capable of doing was to blink her eyes in order to indicate the letter of the alphabet that she wanted to convey, was just remarkable."

Patiently, oh how patiently, he noted, they'd hover over Billie, eyeball-to-eyeball, in order to help. "And to see little Maryanne, who was little more than a child herself, assume the mother's role and the mother's workload, just made me want to cry," he added.

But above all, he suggested that there could have been no greater blessing than in simply "having the blessing" of watching Mary with her Billie during what were the darkest and most incomprehensible of days for Billie physically. There was, he explained, a kind of aura in the room, as the grace that the two of them fashioned together became so strong and palpable, so thick that it was as if you could just reach out and touch the grace itself.

Imagine that, a grace so big that you could physically, as well as spiritually, embrace it.

Imagine that, physically embracing something so profoundly and utterly spiritual!

Yes, this grace, Mary and Billie's grace, was so strong and so rich that you could grab hold of it as it pressed up against all present. So rich that you could draw it to yourself and literally drink it in! What happened between the two of them as Billie was preparing to die, Howie Daniels suggested, was just like that.

It was holy and profound and sacred and no description does it justice.

"I'd look at the two of them," he added, "and swear that I was in the presence of not one, but two saints."

In the grip of unbelievable suffering and in the face of imminent death and great loss, no daughter and mother could ever have exhibited a more passionate or tangible and living love than they did. Their two hearts and their two souls were one.

They reached inside the depths of the other and assumed each other's pain.

The physical suffering of the daughter and the emotional suffering of the mother conspired together to create something so spiritually beautiful and immeasurable and sacred.

And Mother Teresa of Calcutta, Howie reminded us, also had been there to anoint it with her prayers and her own grace.

I just think about this, and having known the two of them, I can only imagine what it was like. But I can tell you what I know now. In simply trying to write of it and to paint a picture of their imparted holiness, the very earth moves beneath me. My insides swell and the sky brightens and the earth shakes, and I think that I am, at one and the same time, so blessed and yet so unworthy. For I am so far removed from living as magnificently as they!

Then in speaking about Mary's reflections upon the Stations of the Cross, Howie nearly began to cry, and he seemed, at first, to be reaching out for words that he could not find—words that might do justice to Mary's words. But he collected himself and eventually said, "How lucky I was to have the opportunity to hear Mary do the stations and how sorry I feel for those who never got the opportunity to do so."

"Whenever I did, I felt as if I was listening to Christ himself," he said. (In a later chapter, we will share the very words that Mary did use. And the words will speak to us still, but what we cannot share is that rich and moving ebb and flow of her voice, the inflections, those always misty eyes, the facial expressions that said ever so much more than mere words ever could, and the literal and tangible love that poured out of her).

In Mary's presence, all of that was taken in as it colored and dressed her words.

Howie smiled when he pointed out that so many people who weren't even a part of Mary's group would stop in their tracks the moment they heard her voice on the grounds of the Cape or Sainte-Anne's. "Our numbers," he said, "would always double or triple between the first and fourteenth stations." Because Mary Varick just captivated people and brought them closer to their God.

Howie also had memories of Mary's Bill to share.

Back in the old days, when Bill Varick himself drove the bus or trolley, with the old standard and grinding transmission over the rough-cut country lanes and byways that predated today's highways, there were many thorny and sticky travails while driving. We might also point out that it was pre–air-conditioning (summer months) and pre–bathroom-on-board days.

In short, the trip itself was not for the faint of heart.

Bill's worries and fears were, naturally, reserved for and shared with Mary alone, the leader of the pack. Riding, as was her custom, in the front row on the right where she could be beside Bill always, Bill could literally whisper his concerns to her.

As it happened, Howie himself had long fought for the front row left, which, first and foremost, enabled him to be with Mary but also to be where the action was. He said that he had often been in position to hear Bill express his fears to Mary, as they drove on some roads that weren't even fit for a horse to use, much less a huge bus.

But always, Mary's response was the same, for God, she assured Bill, was on their side. It was as simple as that. "Don't worry, Bill," she'd say all the time. "God will see us through."

"Don't worry, Bill. There's no need to be afraid of the road or the transmission. God is with us." And so He was.

Upon first reading the above memory of Howie, Mary Pisaniello was kind enough to add her own memory of the same. She wrote,

> I remain so familiar with what Howie described (later he preferred to be addressed as Howard). I remember some of those nightmare road situations my father encountered that literally made the man sweat. He was far too dignified a gentleman to ever sweat. One such incident was on

the way to Saint Joachim's, north of Beaupre, where a very narrow bridge was under repair. It had no side rails as of yet, and it was down to one lane (from my perspective, suitable only for a bicycle). There were no alternate routes to travel and no place to turn that bus around (no power steering or automatic shifting at the time). He stopped and turned to Mom who encouraged him, literally sitting at the edge of her front seat as though operating that bus herself, talking to and praying with him, and all of the passengers on board for that matter. And slowly, across that water, we went. Once on the other side, he pulled the bus to the side of the road and stepped off the bus to regain his composure. He was pale and shaken and probably already anticipating with dread the return trip to Beaupre.

As it turns out, those precious few who were there from the beginning all have their moments of dread to share.

Poor Bill Varick's heart took a beating, and the early journeys may well have taken years off his life, but he never failed and never disappointed that "full speed ahead and 'God is ever on our side'" wife of his.

But the most important Howie Daniels's story was not elaborated upon, likely because it was too personal and too deep. But he hedged no bets in conveying its outcome. "I had given up on God," he said. "I was lost. It was Mary who brought me back to God and back home."

No one, he insisted, could do more for another person than that. "She did the impossible," he said. "Mary Varick gave me my God. She was a great, great lady!"

Mary Varick and *Flossie Oates* had long been kindred spirits. In fact, they met and were drawn to each other fully twenty years before Mary's Beaupre miracle and twenty-one years before the first pilgrimage and twenty-nine years before the "first" First Saturday gathering.

Even before her marriage to Bill and before the full greening or youthful spring of Mary's life, these two had consecrated a friendship.

What brought them together when Mary was still in her teens, we do not know and we probably never will. We know only that they did, because Flossie herself told us so, proud and sure, as she was, of the fact that there friendship was born in 1931, in the height of the Great Depression and fully a decade before the Great War.

Maybe, they first met when Mary was at the Medical Center recuperating from an infamous surgery that did not work. Flossie well could have been an aide or volunteer there. Certainly a volunteer, as she volunteered for everything. And maybe, Jimmy, Barbara, or Mary will fill in this blank, but it is of no consequence. What is of consequence only is that these two, who moved in very different circles in a world that was much more deeply segregated at the time, here both ethnically and religiously segregated, indeed, joined hands and lives and spirits for a lifetime.

And so deep was their connection, it left Flossie saying, in the wake of Mary's passing, "What am I gonna do now? Just what am I gonna do now?"

What Babe Ruth is to baseball or Bobby Orr is to hockey or Abraham Lincoln is to the history of the United States of America, Flossie Oates forever is to the Our Lady of Fatima First Saturday Club. She was the hero, the greatest player, the MVP, the larger-than-life icon of the past who is to be forever heralded by those who never knew her, because she was just that big and truly worthy of commemoration.

For Flossie Oates was, indeed, the champion who gave 1,000 percent every time!

In Jersey City, she tended to shut-ins, and she cooked for the homeless and elderly and washed and ironed their clothes. She was a mother to all kinds of outcasts, and she embraced every comer in need in an almost infinite variety of ways. With a severely disabled niece of her own, Florita, who she loved deeply, her bond with what Mary Varick fashioned was only natural, but she didn't just bond. She came almost immediately to serve as both Mary and Bill Varick's aide-de-camp.

*She was the enforcer, the troubleshooter, the lead blocker, the distraction, the way, the bouncer—she was whatever Mary and Bill Varick needed her to be in any given moment.*

A "praise the Lord," broad-shouldered, big-hearted, buxom Baptist, she was some kind of piece of work for this planet.

Unforgettable to all who knew her!

Again, she did much of their troubleshooting, she covered tracks that needed covering when necessary, and she didn't mind cleaning up the messes that they often left behind.

Big, bright, joyful, with the booming voice of a spiritual Baptist who expected her prayers to be heard, she also served as a second mother to Mary's children and to Mary's nieces and nephews and to whomsoever in the club was in need of a bit of tender loving care at any moment in time.

The truth is that she is—in the depth of my memory—love personified. She was love, and in her company, a child—and I was, indeed, a child—was protected, secure, safe, and home.

Some of my memories are hazy, like being farmed out to be with her in her Jersey City apartment to be cared for, but others are neatly and crisply frozen in time and clear. I see her in so many kitchens that serviced so many Catholic school cafeterias and auditoriums. She ruled in those kitchens. I see her in so many churches, never sitting, but rather always standing, as she was, ever and always, the most likely to exit with the disabled person most in need of tending to. I see her "fussing" with stuff in Aunt Mary's home, and again, my apologies, for what that stuff was, I do not know. I know only that if my Aunt Mary had stuff that needed to be "fussed" with, Flossie was either likely to be there or well on her way.

I have this memory of being in the kitchen on the back end of the first floor of their Pacific Avenue home, as Flossie entered with a flourish from the front door. While only at the door, her presence seemed to envelop every square inch of that first floor almost instantaneously. I was as far away as one could be from that front door, but *poof*, Flossie was suddenly everywhere. Oh, what a commanding presence Flossie Oates had. Beyond her sheer presence, I remember the first seven words she bellowed out that day. They were so clearly delivered and so memorable that I could never forget them. She did not utter by the way—she bellowed and she commanded attention. I think because she was so worthy of it.

*"Honey, why didn't you call me sooner?"* she said.

That's it. I've got nothing more. I don't know the what or the why or the wherefore, but doesn't that say all we need to know.

To this day and I never saw Flossie again after Aunt Mary's funeral, I never lose the feeling of being enfolded, safely and warmly, in one of Flossie's full body hugs, nor do I ever lose the sound of her booming voice or of her "Richie, honey." To her, I was never a mere or plain Rich or Richie, but rather a "Richie, honey." And what was the Richie of my preteen and high school youth forever remained blessed to be a "honey."

The rest of the known universe to her was similarly honored with that same tag or title. We were all "honeys." It was "Mary, honey" and "Bill, honey" and "Father, honey" or even "Bishop, honey" for that matter or just plain "honey" if she wasn't sure of your name.

In this gathering, Flossie's memories were, I believe somewhat typically or appropriately, all over the place.

She first recalled Mary's historic battle with Cardinal Spellman and with the general manager of New York's Grand Central

Station to win the right to have mass said there for her departing pilgrims before they boarded the trains on their way to Canada. She did win that fight, having played both sides against the middle, and that was a first, recalled Flossie, as was the mass said at the New York City World's Fair, as was the mass at the John F. Kennedy International Airport, and as was the mass for a foreign tour group in Leningrad or what is today's Saint Petersburg.

All were among Mary's firsts.

But Flossie's espoused favorite memories were of traveling on that train that left Grand Central Station as Mrs. James Cassidy and of hiding Bill Varick in her room. As noted already in this work, what an unlikely couple were Mary's frail, thin, soft-spoken oldest brother Jim and this particular wife of his who may well have been the most vivacious African-American Baptist woman in all of Jersey City.

But "Husband, honey" he was, and she enjoyed every moment of it. And that they got to take advantage of Jim's Penn Central Railroad employee spousal pass was all well and good to Flossie. In fact, anything that served Mary's cause was all well and good with Flossie.

As to hiding Bill Varick, she spoke very seriously about this as if she still longed to take care of her friend who had gone home to God so long ago. But it was still up close and personal to Flossie. She said, "My poor Bill—that good man simply couldn't get a moment's break or rest. First of all, he was hounded all the time and constantly bombarded with 'Bill this' and 'Bill that,' but what was worse for him is that he roomed with Mary, of course, who lived in a constant whirlwind. Now, Mary thrived on—even loved—the energy in that whirlwind, but Bill needed a break from it every now and then, and my room became his haven."

And there you have it—Flossie and her marriage of convenience to Mary's brother Jim and her prospectively scandalous relationship with Mary's husband Bill.

Of course, one could well have said of Flossie just what she so thoughtfully said of Mary Varick that afternoon. "When it came to helping people and Mary Varick," she suggested, "there was never ever a stone unturned."

*"Mary," Flossie added, "was a woman who made us feel like people and who changed my life in every possible way."*

Joined at the hip, in goodness and in service to others, throughout all of their days together, Flossie then sadly and movingly asked just what she was going to do without her beloved Mary, to whom she had "given her heart" a long time ago. "There is nothing I wouldn't have done for that woman," she said. Of course, the "What am I gonna do?" line of Flossie was ultimately a self-fulfilling affirmation.

For there was no other possible course of action for her than to go on giving until the day that she died! After all, that "giving until it hurts" devotion is what brought her to Mary in the first place.

For the record, if ever there was a person worthy of the title "honey," it was Flossie.

Before closing this brief segment on Flossie's contributions to this incredible discussion on what Mary Varick meant to six friends and followers of hers, I cannot help but note that I am fascinated by the depths and wonder of her line that, "Mary was a woman who made us feel like people."

And oh, the way Flossie said it, suggesting intricacies and tributaries that could well carry us beyond the initial depths and wonder, and so fascinate reflective minds forever. So simple a phrase—so basic—and yet so stunningly profound at the same time! For God created us "To be His people" and yet a messenger from and of God is often needed "To bring out the people in us," which is an act of blessing and sanctification and redemption.

Suffice it to say that in a fairer and freer world, where time was of no consequence, I would philosophize and reflect upon this one line of Flossie's at great length. So, in here sparing you that, it is enough to suggest that there are powers and worlds to explore in just what it is that "makes us feel like people!"

Suffice it to say, in closing, that Flossie too made people feel like people. She made me feel like people. She enfolded me in bear hugs and she loved me and she watched over me and I loved her back. I was just a kid, and yet for what she was to me, I will love Flossie Oates forever.

To paint a picture of *Anne Gerhardt* is not easy, because no writer ever wants to appear mean. So, knowing that it matters nothing to her and is of no real consequence, we'll say it loudly and clearly right here at the outset—Anne Gerhardt was a very, very big woman.

Again, she was a very, very big woman.

But she also had an even bigger sense of humor and a heart that was even greater still. She was beautiful. And she took care to accent that beauty and so she dressed to the nines.

All of the time and every time, to the nines!

The makeup was always carefully applied, and she wore flowing and colorful dresses that suggested that she was, ever and always, a lady.

She met Mary, in the dark and lonely days when her muscular dystrophy was new to her and after her husband had left in the wake of her diagnosis, "he saw no life for the two of us any longer." Coldhearted and mean-spirited, he was as removed from being worthy of her as was the most heinous of criminals. Anne spoke of this and of what it was like to read Mary's first book and then meet her in the wake of all of these compelling life's changes. She remembered the minutest of details.

But most importantly, she remembered that Mary Varick came into her life when it appeared to be collapsing.

"She blew in when everyone and everything seemed to be blowing out," said Anne.

Upon meeting her, Mary invited her to come to Canada with them that summer and then also arranged to have Anne win fifty dollars to apply to the costs. Anne said, "I told Mary that I wanted the fifty dollars to go to someone else if I couldn't come up with the money to go, and all she did was look at me, smile, and say 'Anne, I want you to go home and pack your bags.'"

"That's what stands out for me," Anne said. "'Go home and pack your bags' and how inviting and welcoming and open armed she was. She didn't have to know me to love me."

Mary told her, as she did to so many others over the years, that they were going whether they could pay for the trip or not. In fact, Mary's rule was that everyone who wishes to go goes—after all, God needed them too and the ability to cover the cost of doing so was never a paramount consideration. And so, she lived in debt and gave it to God and trusted completely in Him and in all those on earth who He might use to help her to keep on doing the impossible.

*That was it—Don't worry! Just go pack your bags!*

Among the stories Anne told was a humorous one about a series of coincidences in which people kept mistaking her for Mary. Since, as she pointed out, she was twice the size of Mary and looked nothing like her, it was surprising. Still it happened three or four times as women at both a Eucharistic Congress and in Canada approached her and inquired if she was Mary Varick.

Outside of noting that she joked with Mary about it, she said that nothing else was made of it.

"Mary," she said, "was just like the captain of a ship, always the first to board and the last to disembark." But departing from Canada and waiting to board for the trip home that year, Anne kept being told that they were waiting for a special lift chair for her as they loaded everyone else. Finally, to Anne's surprise, even Mary was boarded and she alone remained outside in her chair. Concerned that she had been forgotten, she started to yell and yell to get someone's attention. But no one responded or attended to her. "I was afraid that they had really forgotten me, and I began to get scared, until I finally heard Mary's sweet voice from inside the bus. 'If you want to look like Mary Varick, it's time you started acting like her.'"

A well-executed practical joke, instilling near panic, was on her.

The next Anne Gerhardt story was, to me, especially illuminating and mind-blowing, because it directly involved a man I have long known, but who, to my then knowledge, had never been associated with Mary Varick. This proved to be a story that I could investigate and "fact check" and ultimately embellish.

Who knew? After all, who knew? I sure didn't!

For Anne told the story of Mary's immersion into New Jersey state politics, a story that was unknown to me, upon her learning that Connie LoPresti was going to lose her nursing home bed if she were to go Canada that particular year (likely '71 or '72). A clear prejudicial process issue was standing in her way. In Anne's telling the story, of course, it was as if Mary rode a white charger down to Trenton and steamrolled the New Jersey legislature into action and that her speaking before a senate contingent saved the day.

Indeed, there is some truth to that.

"Usually after a bill passes, the attention is upon the senators," Anne said, "but the attention there, after it passed, was all upon Mary."

Well in all likelihood, Mary spoke at a senate committee hearing, as private citizens never address the senate itself when it is in full session. And in all likelihood, her champion had to be my friend Carmen Orechio who was, for nearly forty years, the mayor of Nutley and long the Essex County New Jersey state senator or Newark senator.

Anne knew him as the senator from Essex County only, but in the "it's a small world after all" category, I just happened to know him as a friend, who I discovered, only in the wake of my own disability. But Anne's story revealed that this state senator, her friend and mine, had been a First Saturday volunteer out of Holy Family in Nutley as far back as forty to fifty years ago. And, yes, we're talking about that same, familiar Holy Family, the home of yesterday's Father Matt Pisaniello, the "retarded priest," and today's Monsignor Paul Bochicchio and the sacred ground upon which Mary Varick was informed of her beloved Bill's passing.

And only in the wake of all of this did Carmen Orechio, former president of the New Jersey state senate and one of the closest friends of my close friend, former Senator Anthony Scardino, learn that I was the nephew of Mary Varick, who, as it turned out, he revered.

Former Senator Orechio, a larger-than-life New Jersey political legend, confirmed his involvement in Anne's story and in his working with Mary to eliminate what was a terrible flaw. He didn't quite remember the details, but he did remember introducing a wide-ranging bill that altered nursing home procedures, a bill that Mary Varick had mothered. "My usual work with Mary involved getting some of the disabled to First Saturday gatherings, but I remember being very happy to help her with this," he said.

Carmen Orechio was long the president of the New Jersey state senate and the second highest public office holder in the state of New Jersey. I knew him through work that I long did in the Meadowlands and for the state itself, as a New Jersey state planning commissioner, an employment and training commissioner, and as the cochairman of a state literacy task force. And in the wake of my disability, periodically meeting with former Senators Orechio and Scardino for lunch remained one of the few, but very pleasant connections to a life that I had once lived.

So, we talked of his relationship with Mary, and the very next time we met for lunch, he came with both his ancient First Saturday pictures and his personally autographed copies of

Mary's books in tow. Given her notes, he was clearly loved and a part of her First Saturday family.

"Mary pointed out a grave injustice and we structured a bill to eliminate it, and when she came to Trenton, we treated her like the queen she was," said Carmen.

"In order for her to speak, her wheelchair was literally carried, as it could not fit down an extremely narrow aisle. So if any senator hadn't been paying attention, that certainly woke them up."

"Of course, they were about to hear from Mary, and when she did speak, you could have heard a pin drop in an environment where that was simply never the case. I think that we would have unanimously affirmed anything she wanted. In retrospect, I think that she should have used us more for she mesmerized my colleagues."

And, of course, I didn't know of this piece of his past or Mary's, until I heard Anne tell the story, on an old tape frozen in time and in memory. To me, the all of this is, therefore, on so many levels, just remarkable.

For long ago, while I was likely still in college, Mary Varick and her friend and my friend to be Carmen Orechio did away with a terrible Medicaid-driven procedural injustice. I didn't even meet Carmen until a decade or more after this deed was done, and now, after thirty years of knowing him, I learn all of this stuff. And it's just remarkable and we never know, if you know what I mean.

For I have, since I became sick myself in late 2005, been sustained in my own brokenness by a fleet of angels, and Carmen Orechio of Nutley is among them.

He and my "angel in Boston" are wholly responsible for the disabled van that transports me. In essence, I guess that I'm moved by the simple fact that Aunt Mary and I are bound by his goodness.

Anne Gerhardt's great love for Mary Varick literally oozes out of her. She speaks of her devotion to Mary, to the club, and to the newsletter that she edited for ages. "Mary effortlessly changed my life," she said, "and she shared the great faith that she had in the Blessed Mother with me, and it is she, after all, who produced the finest wines. Oh, what a pleasure and privilege it was to be her best friend."

For the record, Anne always used the term *best friend*. That's how she saw it.

Now, a brief detour in order to capture one special Anne Gerhardt moment!

In later years, I learned that Father Jacques Fortin, C.Ss.R., the youth director of Sainte-Anne-de-Beaupre, visited Bruno and Mary Pisaniello in order to conduct a series of *Saint Anne's Nights* in local parishes. He would speak of good Saint Anne and of the life at and the work of his beloved basilica in Beaupre and then invite those attending to join him in venerating the major relic of Saint Anne that he carried.

As Bruno rode in the front with Father Fortin, Mary would sit in the backseat beside this relic, as they traveled to different parishes. Mary will tell you how tangibly present the spirit of Saint Anne was to her. "Blessed," she said, "it was as if I could feel her sitting beside me. It was as if she reached out and held my hand as I prayed."

Let the record show that this wasn't a thank-you for Mary Pisaniello's having swept those steps, as it happened well more than a decade before she took that broom to the mammoth stairways that lead to Sainte-Anne's Basilica.

Our friend Anne Gerhardt was failing and in the hospital, when this contingent of Father Fortin, Bruno, Mary, and the relic of Saint Anne surprised her with a visit. Anne was filled with joy, and while happy to see Mary and Bruno and Father, it was, noted Mary Pisaniello, the presence of Saint Anne herself, which accompanied that relic, that made all the difference for Anne Gerhardt and lifted her so.

Before she even knew that we were carrying the relic, she felt as if Saint Anne herself had entered her room, profoundly moving her.

By the way, I need to digress from this six-pronged conversation in order to relate and share another quick story that my sister Joan told me about *Connie LoPresti*, the benefactress of the legislative effort to straighten out the nursing homes and get her to Canada.

For it was, for Connie, long and simply, about the importance of getting to Canada.

My good sister Joan was, as it unsurprisingly turned out, with Connie when she underwent an emergency and massive radical mastectomy.

It was six weeks before Canada, and as her eyes opened in recovery, the very first words she mouthed to Joan were, "I hope this doesn't mean that I can't get to Canada."

She did, by the way, get there.

And talking to Maryanne Adriance not long ago, I learned, quite surprisingly, that although Connie never had two nickels to rub together, she never failed to pay for her own trip over the years, and since Monsignor Paul's good friends helped defray her funeral expenses, the little money she had left went to her First Saturday Club.

For if there was anything left in her meager estate, it was to go to the one redemptive force in her life, the Our Lady of Fatima First Saturday Club!

And so it came to be that Connie LoPresti, in her last earthly action, sent two other people on what was always to her a life-sustaining pilgrimage to the beloved Canadian shrines!

*Frances D'Amato,* who seemed so gentle that a breath might have blown her over, exhibited the humility that one might have expected of Saint Francis, of whom she spoke. The same might also be said of *Anne Toth.* For while Frances is Catholic and Anne Protestant, that could well be the only salient distinction separating these two gentle, humble, kind, and purpose-driven ladies.

Their personal humility speaks to the fact that they got far fewer sound bites than their friends. Anne, Howie, and Flossie were determined to be heard at every opportunity, and Frances and Anne were inclined to let them. They were not the types to fight for the mike. So outside of the "What they felt about Mary" question, Frances managed only to get two quick stories in and Anne but one.

Frances's first was about her relentless effort to simply sign up for the 1967 pilgrimage to Fatima, Lourdes, and Rome. "I called and called until I finally got Mary's son Jimmy, but he told me that I was too late and that it was all full. I didn't want to take no for an answer, however, until I talked to Mary herself. When I finally got to her, I was relieved to hear that they had gotten a second plane and so I signed up."

She then implied that having simply survived that fateful journey with her new *First Saturday* family, this disorganized, confused, but always-smiling bunch was somehow destined to become her family forever.

Beyond that, she spoke of the beauty of having the pope in their midst in Rome and of how stunning and remarkable it was to see the pope himself on his knees, talking to and praying with Neil Gulliksen on his stretcher. "That was," she said, "among the most moving things I have ever seen. I broke down and cried."

Frances D'Amato's first First Saturday Club experience was the '67 pilgrimage to Europe, while Anne Toth's was the '65 New York World's Fair, two mad-capped First Saturday adventures or experiences. "I recall that they kept squeezing more people in when it seemed that doing so was impossible," she said. "It was disorganized and crowded, and nobody seemed to know what was going to happen next, she noted, and everybody seemed perfectly fine with that. The only thing that really seemed to matter was getting to worship together."

"Nothing else mattered."

It's impossible to pass by these two without a comment or two. First, the clear madness of what both were introduced to did not dissuade either. The madness rather served to draw them in. For both found a group that had its priorities in order!

The focus was upon God, upon the worship, and upon the service and not upon the things of the world that we typically lose ourselves fretting over.

Second, it interests me that Mary Varick met Frances D'Amato upon speaking to her Saint Francis Society gathering at Saint Francis Hospital in Jersey City. It was after all, Saint Francis of Assisi who insisted that Jesus's greatest gift to us was neither in the crucifixion nor even in the resurrection, but rather in his very willingness to become as fully human as we.

There is to this writer, therefore, something interesting about the connotation of "Oh-so fully human" and Mary Varick's "oh-so disorganized" club and pilgrimages.

Both Frances and Anne looked dysfunction in the eye and said, "Fine with me."

To the witness of these six, let me quickly add the witness of others in a handful of letters to Mary.

Cookie writes in July of 1966 that, "I thank you with all my heart for everything you have done for me. I don't mean materially but in a way no one can measure. It's the thoughts and maybe only the few words you say that can bring more happiness and better understanding."

In March of 1967, Mrs. Helen Yowell writes, "There is no describing the living faith that grows in your particular corner of God's world. I shall cherish the memories I gathered there as long as I live."

In July of 1977, Carol Bolger wrote, "The experiences and emotions I felt while on the pilgrimage with you have left an indelible and beautiful memory in my mind and in my heart. I have witnessed Christ's healing power working through you as you touch so deeply and so beautifully all those you come in contact with."

In October of 1974, Sister Mary Baptist wrote, "Our prayer for you will be that our dear Lord and His blessed Mother will send into your life and the lives of all of your loved ones the same joy and happiness you constantly bring into the lives of others."

Upon reading *Not Without Tears*, Mary Dazi of Ontario wrote, "I cannot express the joy, contentment, and above all my feelings of gratitude to God for the many graces and blessings, spiritual and material, which you have bestowed upon me."

In March of 1976, Bishop Fulton J. Sheen wrote, "Because I have known you for some time, the book was not only made up of print but also of flesh and blood…Everyone who has ever known you has been inspired by your identification with the Suffering Christ who is on the cross until the end of the world in persons like your good self."

And so it goes—on and on and on!

Punctuating this brief but impactful chapter—where we explored the love that the six "faithful," devoted members of Mary's First Saturday Club family had for her, along with the impact that she had on their lives—with the content of a eulogy for Mary that was shared elsewhere upon the very day of her own funeral seems appropriate.

In Wauregan, Connecticut, there is one of the many First Saturday ministries that were outgrowths of Mary and Bill Varick's *Our Lady of Fatima First Saturday Club*. One of its spiritual leaders was Deacon Eduardo Dogue, a close friend of Mary Varick, who spent years with her, both programmatically and personally—so close that he also spent years bringing in the New Year at Mary's New Year's extravaganzas, where the New Year was always ushered in with a midnight celebration of the Eucharist.

The leader of this particular First Saturday contingent was, unsurprisingly, another friend of Mary, Father Pat Martin.

As you know, the day of Mary Varick's funeral was a First Saturday, and were it not for Mary's going home to God, it may well have been the first time Mary's group ever failed to celebrate a First Saturday together. Mary's illness and suffering, scheduling problems, and confusion had conspired together to leave them directing club members to go to mass in their own parishes. (Today, this practice has become periodically customary. While it is not common, it is done.) Through the grace of God, Mary herself, however, determined that this would not happen in July of 1989 by bringing the body and soul of her beloved First Saturday family together with her to celebrate the Eucharist at her own Mass of Resurrection.

With apologies to Father Pat Martin, I take the liberty of condensing and necessarily paraphrasing the content of his loving tribute to Mary Varick. In doing so, I will be wholly true to his intents and purposes.

Father Pat Martin spoke to his thriving First Saturday family on the day of Mary's resurrection. He told them that Mary Varick was their mentor and that she lived in each and every one of them, in the heart of their club, and in the soul of their ministry and mission.

He said that, "Mary Varick will be with us forever."

He told them that Mary had rejected chemo and that she was fully prepared to die and ready to go home to God. "How could this woman of God not be?" he asked.

"She was of God and she was here for our one hundredth anniversary First Saturday Mass, and she was here for our retreats and our workshops, providing direct and indirect support always. Her spirit also is in the Madonna House at Our Lady of the Cape in Canada, where we stay each summer, which she helped build with the proceeds from her books. All that we do together is an outgrowth of her ministry," he said.

"Finally," he added, "when we visited with Mary and her family and friends last evening, we were kindly provided with enough of her mass cards which depict the *Smiling Christ* along with a *Smiling Mary*, who smiled through her sufferings and sacrificed all for her own."

"To be sure, we come together always and devote ourselves to our Blessed Mother Mary who lovingly brings us closer to God, but it was Mary Varick who will ever be the mother of our First Saturday Club."

How do we measure this?

How do we measure what was done for the six and what they, in turn, did for others?

How do we measure the impact upon one, much less thousands or tens of thousands, or what it means to be the mother of any organization that brings the faithful together to better serve the people of God?

How do we measure the impact of words said and prayers prayed and a lifetime of Eucharists and rosaries and Stations of the Cross?

How do we measure the goodness and the good works?

What's the value of even one moment shared by Mary and Billie as the walls of this earth fell in upon the former?

The truth is that we can't even begin to measure or calculate such things. But the greater truth is that neither should we care about doing so.

There are interests and tribunals that demand specifics, hard facts, and details, but God, I believe, does not share their concerns.

Some insist on quantifying miracles to define worth, but it is our contention that the smallest of miracles that are effected daily are as valued as any and neither need be quantified.

If the miracle of the gift of each new day is accepted and the miracle of the boundless love that is there to drive our lives is manifested in one's life, one is a "king of kings or queen of queens for that."

Remember, it is not a number's game to God.

It is all of one to Him. For as we have been told, to have saved even one is to have saved the entire world!

By that measure, Mary Varick saved the world with an almost reckless abandon, again and again and again.

Sure, for those who care, Mary has her documented physical miracle and my bundle of them, and there are others attributed to her intercession in letters forwarded to the archdiocese and countless others waiting to be discovered, but there are literally no end to them in the good works and energy and prayers and love that she never stopped paying forward.

Her very life was a love affair with her God.

And somehow, I think that the love alone, just the love, is something that God Himself does have a way of measuring.

## Chapter 4 Placeholders

- Then in speaking about Mary's reflections upon the Stations of the Cross, Howie nearly began to cry, and he seemed, at first, to be reaching out for words that he could not find—words that might do justice to Mary's words. But he collected himself and eventually said, "How lucky I was to have the opportunity to hear Mary do the stations and how sorry I feel for those who never get the opportunity to do so."

- She said, "My poor Bill—that good man simply couldn't get a moment's break or rest. First of all, he was hounded all the time and constantly bombarded with 'Bill this' and 'Bill that,' but what was worse for him is that he roomed with Mary, of course, who lived in a constant whirlwind. Now, Mary thrived on—even loved—the energy in that whirlwind, but Bill needed a break from it every now and then and my room became his haven."

- And oh, the way Flossie said it ("*She made us feel like people*"), suggesting intricacies and tributaries that could well carry us beyond the initial depths and wonder—and so fascinate reflective minds forever. So simple a phrase—so basic, and yet so stunningly profound at the same time! For God created us "To be His people" and yet a messenger from and of God is often needed "To bring out the people in us," which is an act of blessing and sanctification and redemption.

- "Mary pointed out a grave injustice and we structured a bill to eliminate it, and when she came to Trenton, we treated her like the queen she was," said Carmen. "In order for her to speak, her wheelchair was literally carried, as it could not fit down an extremely narrow aisle. So if any senator hadn't been paying attention, that certainly woke them up."

- It was disorganized and crowded, and nobody seemed to know what was going to happen next, she noted, and everybody seemed perfectly fine with that. The only thing that really seemed to matter was getting to worship together.

- "She was of God, and she was here for our one hundredth anniversary First Saturday Mass, and she was here for our retreats and our workshops, providing direct and indirect support always. Her spirit also is in the Madonna House at Our Lady of the Cape in Canada which she helped build with the proceeds from her books. All that we do together is an outgrowth of her ministry," he said.

# 5

# The Keepers of the Flame

The neisseria meningitidis took me, and after fifteen months of intense suffering and hospitalization and prayer and acceptance and conversion—after miles of surgeries and amputations and epiphanies, I returned home, broken but unbowed, faithful, reverent, and somehow determined to live on higher ground.

Right before that first summer back home with my Maggie and an array of my twelve, with no legs and no fingers and no well oiled joints, my sister Joan invited me to return to Canada, with the First Saturday family, from which I had long been inadvertently exiled.

It didn't take me long to accept, although I had all kinds of caregiving reservations at the time. Once I accepted her invitation, I realized that I would be going back for what was to be the first time in thirty odd years.

Once, a regular, fervent, and energized volunteer, this time, for the first time, I would be taking my place among the disabled.

Wheelchair bound, it was to be something altogether different.

Then too, it was to be the first time without my gregarious, smiling, and laughing Aunt Mary at the helm.

Since then, it has again become one of those annual events that simply cannot be missed.

Having reestablished myself as a familiar face, I have been blessed to become intimate with today's spiritual and temporal leaders of the Our Lady of Fatima First Saturday Club's annual disabled pilgrimage to Saint Joseph's Oratory in Montreal, Our Lady of the Cape in Three Rivers, Sainte-Anne-de-Beaupre, and selected shrines in the American northeast. Pilgrimage directors and advocates, both temporal and spiritual, they are a most faithful and hardy—and though they may shy away from the words *holy bunch*.

Oh, they are holy! How can they not be, in extending themselves to God as they do and as their pilgrimage does?

Extend love, extend faith, extend goodness, and you are, like it or not, among the holy.

Just for the record, holy isn't a destination or an end or something concrete, it is rather to be found in how one journeys and what they journey for. Fluid and evolving, it is the qualitative by-product and the purest affirmation of great love and great faith and simple and untainted goodness. It is that which comes in when living for others first.

It isn't rocket science, and there is nothing complicated about holy.

They may disagree and fail to communicate at times, and at other times, they might not be able to get out of their own ways, as much as they would like to. But they are ever devoted and richly purposeful, and although the term has never before been used, they are all apostles of Mary Varick. Understand, their faith is their own, their fidelity is their own, their communion with God and the saints is their own, but their mission, as to the business of which I write, remains Mary's.

They are the devotees and the keepers of the flame of Mary Varick's ministry.

It is they who keep her theology of suffering alive and active. They who continue to minister to her "inner circle," they who believe that our world and our church and our individual parish communities are the better in having the spirit of and the ministry of Mary Varick still alive in them today.

On an unusually, chilly, dreary, and rainy October First Saturday evening in 2011, I had arranged to meet Monsignor Paul Bochicchio, Father Kevin Carter, Joan Murray, Maryanne Adriance, and Mike Lenehan at Monsignor's Holy Family Parish Center in Nutley, New Jersey. I also had expected Father Frank Fano but lost him to a young priest's parish priorities, and Amy Lenehan but lost her to surgery and recuperation.

This unprecedented attempt to bring together what I refer to as the "keepers of the flame" of the Our Lady of Fatima First Saturday family leadership once promised to draw out all of its spiritual and temporal leaders at one and the same time—together.

But that we still managed to bring five of the seven together to reflect upon their unique experiences and journeys and moments with Mary Varick was more than enough for me, more than enough to satisfy or fulfill what I was after. And truly unprecedented in its own right, as this is a genuinely busy bunch.

All of the planning and anticipating aside, they were, interestingly, true doubters in each other, as most of these loving servants assumed that pulling this meeting off was nigh on impossible.

They knew each other that well and betted on the fact that their colleagues were all destined to come up with something a bit more pressing. Reflecting and looking back, I well understand, is not quite so important as doing. But it has its place, as we need the potency and the power and the wisdom that are buried in our memories and our stories, buried in the sinew and substance that brought us to where we are today—buried in the sinew and substance that made us who we are to begin with.

And, yes, of course, I had ample opportunity to pick them off one by one, but it was the interaction with and the feeding off of and upon one another that I was most interested in.

I wanted to watch them excite each other and bore into each other's souls and extract that something more that otherwise would not have been realized.

I wanted them to pick on each other, remind each other, and, yes, even brag about each other.

Together, I knew that they were destined, if given the chance, to do just that. The common denominator was their great love for Mary Varick and for this ragtag of a First Saturday family that she created. But more than the family, even, I believe it was their faith in the nuances of her theology, the richness of her relationship with Mary, our Mother, and her abiding devotion to the Eucharist.

So, yes, five of seven was more than enough to satisfy my search for what it was in all of them that made them want to stay the course for Mary!

To stay the course after all of these years!

I was after whatever it was about their monthly gatherings and this pilgrimage that made it such a perpetual instrument of grace, an instrument of grace that was uniquely known to and appreciated by them!

That our meeting was timed to bring us together there during Holy Family's annual feast was pure dumb luck. Despite the cool rains that fell, the great Italian food, the scent of the meatballs and the sausage and peppers, the sweet smell of the cannolis and zeppolis, the passing by of a smiling Anthony Pesci, one of Holy Family's remarkable young pilgrimage volunteers, and the pleasant pandemonium of Ferris wheels and Tilt-A-Whirls were all unexpected plusses.

Pesci, who can evoke more laughs per minute than anyone else on the trip, was, in fact, bonus enough, in and of himself.

Born long after Mary Varick went home to God, it is so easy to close the eyes and to imagine her laughing so heartily at Anthony and loving him. And Anthony too, don't forget, all of seventeen then and with the all of life before him, is also, in his own way, but another "apostle of Mary."

Monsignor Paul Bochicchio first loved Mary when he became a deacon and was assigned to Saint Lucy's in Newark, and he devoted so much energy and time to her ministry over the years that these two became joined at the hip, as it were. Twenty-five years after her death, he is remarkably continuing, in his priestly ministry, to keep faith with hers, and if there had ever been such a thing as a hall of fame for devotees of the Our Lady of Fatima's First Saturday Club, he undoubtedly would have been the first to be initiated—right beside Flossie.

He was, indeed, "Mary's priest among priests."

Then too, Father Kevin Carter was Mary's from the beginning. Presently, the pastor of Saint Margaret's parish in Little Ferry, New Jersey, he was first one of Monsignor Paul's "seekers" and an Our Lady of Mercy volunteer on First Saturday pilgrimages as far back as 1977. His devotion to his First Saturday ministry had long been credentialed before he was even ordained, just a short twenty-seven years ago.

Joan Murray was a pilgrimage regular when the pilgrimages to Canada were but in their infancy in the fifties and sixties. Devoted to her aunt and devoted to her ministry, Joan has, in the true spirit of loving others as herself, earned the reputation of never once having had a crossword with any other person in some fifty-eight years of pilgrimage and First Saturday experiences.

More than anyone else, she has lovingly immersed herself into the lives of and personally cared for so many members of the "inner circle." To Brooklyn, to Newark, to Queens, to South Jersey, she'd go to get them to the appointments, to be there during their surgeries, and to help them rise back up whenever they were down.

Everyone loves Joan, because she is, like Jesus, the very incarnation of love.

Today, she continues to serve as the codirector of the pilgrimage.

Her partner is Maryanne Adriance, who simply grew up in the trade as it were. Destined to have it handed to her by her grandmother, she has threatened "just one more year" for years on end, but, in the end, she could no more shirk this duty than the sun refuse to accept its duty to rise each morning.

It is in her blood and in her DNA!

So the two longstanding spiritual directors and the two temporal directors were going to come together to talk about their mutual and collective Mary Varick memories and epiphanies. They would be joined by one other, Mike Lenehan, who together with his wife Amy, then youth ministers of Saint Mary's parish in Colts Neck, New Jersey, had long worked to supply a young army of volunteers for the pilgrimage each summer. Mike's encounters with Mary in life were few, but memorable and built to last, so much so that he and Amy are among this special company, our torch bearers or "keepers of the flame."

And seven is enough, from a leadership standpoint, it seems, to keep both the faith and the flames burning brightly.

On the day we gathered, interestingly, the Our Lady Mother of the Church parish in Woodcliff Lake just happened to have hosted the Our Lady of Fatima First Saturday Club for a thirty-second consecutive year. And there, for all of those years, had been Bob Monahan, the parish's volunteer coordinator for this event. For the thirty-second year, he had done his thing to make the experience a holy and happy and fulfilling one for all whom attended.

Thirty-two years of giving and dedicating and volunteering.

Thirty-two years. Longevity! A well-worn path and relationship! And so I thought that there must be so many others out there, so many other faithful volunteers and servants and believers and "keepers of the flame," like Bob Monahan and like Larry Crawford from North Arlington who for twenty-five consecutive years transported our Connie LoPresti to and from all First Saturday events.

And devotees of the club might be interested in knowing that Spectrum for Living alone sent fifty-seven wheelchairs and fifty-seven volunteers to Woodcliff Lake that day, fifty-seven additional children of God, no matter their faiths or belief systems, fifty-seven members of "God's inner circle," fifty-seven capable of giving all the more in sacrifice, for good and for grace in prayer.

Yes, there were lines to be crossed and gaps to fill and work to de done and some needed to learn what the rosary was and is, but oh, what a day it was and oh, how proud Aunt Mary would have been. All prayers, wherever they come from and to whomsoever they are directed, are to be valued.

How she would have rejoiced in being invited to build upon what she would have looked upon as the great blessing and opportunity of this one and formidable First Saturday, where Joan Murray, Bob Monahan, and Spectrum for Living had conspired together.

Yes, conspired together, in a most special way, to shine the great light of the First Saturday family upon minions of others who might just discover that something else or that something more sorely needed in their own lives.

That something was what Mary Varick had expected it to give in the first place! The handiwork of Jesus Christ! The stuff of miracles! A thing called love! Or hope! Or faith!

# Monsignor Paul

"The first time that I actually met Mary was at her brother Skip's funeral mass at All Saints in Jersey City in 1967," said Monsignor Paul Bochicchio on that October First Saturday night in 2011, a cool and rainy one at that, fully forty-seven years after the fact.

Monsignor immediately proceeded to say that he really began to get to know her intimately when he served as a deacon at Saint Lucy's Church in Newark, the same Saint Lucy's that literally bordered Mary's Colonnade Apartment home in Newark, the same Saint Lucy's where she almost daily frequented the Eucharist.

But while he moved right past the mention of that chance meeting at Father Francis "Skip" Cassidy's funeral, I couldn't help but stop to dwell upon the fact that it was ever so much more than a mere chance passing, but rather a bearing witness to the old verity that, "The Lord giveth and the Lord taketh away."

Skip was the fourth of Mary's five brothers.

Vibrant and passionate and loving and outgoing and energetic, to be in his company was to be swept up by a veritable whirlwind of laughter or joy or wonder or wisdom. Skip was always in overdrive, and whether it was a song or a tale about his young seminarians or the orphans he visited in Vailsburg or a book he had just read or a sweet elderly Italian lady who worked in the dining room at Seton Hall's President's Hall, he would, with an unbridled passion and enthusiasm, invite you into the heart of his world and his intense love of people.

Skip would stand up on his seat and scream "bravo" and "encore" when Judy Garland performed, and he would clear the buffet in our dining room so that he could stand upon it and perform the latest Broadway *song-and-dance* routine that he had learned for my mom, and he would stand upon rock outcroppings at Crater Lake and say the Mass so beautifully that many would be swept away by tears.

Everything about Skip or Father Francis was high octane.

So his all-too-early death at the age of thirty-six, interestingly at roughly the very same age that Mary Varick would have died, were it not for the miracle at Beaupre and the intervention of Good Saint Anne, was brutal for many. It was a great loss for those he served, for his community at Seton Hall University, for his church, and, most certainly, for his family, who loved him mightily.

Just as it was for all of his siblings, it was a loss that pierced Mary Varick's heart.

And yet unbeknownst to her at the time, at the very day of his Mass of Resurrection, she meets a young man, a young seminarian, who was going to grow and to become her "priest among priests," a priest who would come to minister to her and to her First Saturday family in a most profound way, and to serve her pilgrimage journeys in the most extraordinary of ways.

She did not know it then, in that demanding May of 1967, when she lost a rare and loving priest and brother, but there was to be a new brother and another rare and loving priest who was going to enter her life and change it and serve it and color it brightly.

Another beautiful young priest who was going to fill the void left by the great loss of Skip or Father Francis Cassidy!

And he was to come to be the most faithful of all possible servants and friends.

Yes, little did she know as that mile-long procession of cars wormed its way across the Meadowlands, from the beautiful, gothic All Saints Church at the corner of Communipaw and Pacific Avenues in the Lafayette section of Jersey City to Holy Cross Cemetery on Ridge Road in North Arlington, as she mourned her Skip, that God had already introduced her to one who would, indeed, "restoreth her soul."

When asked about this in late 2011, it had been forty-four years since Monsignor Paul Bochicchio first met Mary Varick, whom he was to serve for the next twenty-two years of her life and whose ministry he was then to continue to serve for the twenty-five years since she had gone home to God.

Now well into the forty-seventh year, the beat goes on and on and on.

While a deacon, Saint Lucy's, his then parish, hosted an Our Lady of Fatima First Saturday Club gathering for the first time. He well remembered it as being particularly special, in that the youth of the parish, one that was largely comprised of very poor people, put on a show for the disabled, a show that he recalled drew far more laughter than anything else.

He defensively added that some of the material was actually supposed to be humorous.

Once ordained and assigned to the Our Lady of Mercy parish in the Greenville section of Jersey City, his involvement with both Mary and The First Saturday Club moved into higher gear. "I became increasingly more involved with Mary at Our Lady of Mercy," he said. "There, I involved the parish in first hosting the First Saturday Club, and there, I then became one of the spiritual directors and eventually the spiritual director of the disabled summer pilgrimage to Canada, and there, I also began to help support existing First Saturday fund-raising events before beginning to sponsor events of our own. Both my parish and I had bought in hook, line, and sinker."

Mary, of course, he noted, grew to become one of his closest confidants and friends.

Out of the typical CYO contingent or the classic Parish Youth Group, he formed an entity there known as the "seekers."

Steeled by retreats and regular meetings, Father Paul believed it important to reinforce their spiritual development with an activism for good and for social progress. "One of the ready and waiting possibilities," he said, "was to immerse them into the First Saturday Club family by not only having them take on responsibility for hosting the club when they visited the parish but also by inviting the 'seekers' to participate directly in the summer pilgrimage experience and to assist the disabled in every possible way—from cleaning, washing, and dressing them to feeding them, to accompanying them, and to simply spending time with them."

"While Mary and I both knew that it wasn't going to be all wine and roses and that teenage pranks and nuisance and trouble were going to come with the package," he said, "we went forward with it and my 'seekers' and the youth of all future parishes of mine, as well as other parishes, forever became part of the disabled pilgrimages to the holy shrines of Quebec."

"The marriage of these two forces," he added, "became a rich blessing for both."

He explained how committed to the initiative Mary was and how she took on forces at some of the shrines that may have initially looked upon the initiative negatively. "Mary," he said, "loved my teenagers with the very same verve with which she loved her Jesus. Oh, how she would stand up for them. Seeing only the good in them, as she did, the good was inevitably and exactly what she got."

"You couldn't help but be struck by her belief in young people," he said. "She had enormous patience and an abiding understanding and insight, and she wasn't at all afraid of becoming personally involved when circumstances warranted." Without going into the details, he recalled the hand-holding that she did with one of his "seekers" back in the late seventies who was emotionally devastated by his parents' separation and divorce.

Thinking of her and the teenagers, he also couldn't help but recall when the Our Lady of Fatima First Saturday Club was banned from the Auberge at Sainte-Anne-de-Beaupre.

It was a price paid for too much youthful mischief and clowning around and late-night noise, in a place where pilgrims, in search of holiness and prayer, were supposed to be able to quietly rest. Confident that God too appreciated laughter and joy and good humor and good fun as much as the human species that he created, Mary Varick strongly believed that there were times for both praying hard and playing hard and that volunteers, who gave of themselves for others, were entitled to let off a little steam, even if that meant being banned from the Auberge for a number of years.

He also could personally recall Mary commenting that she was absolutely certain that, "Saint Anne's arms were going to be just as open and just as welcoming to us," despite the fact that we were staying at a secular motel.

Monsignor laughed when he said, "Mary was never one to let reality get in the way. She was always pushing the limits, sometimes to her regret."

What had him laughing was her taking on a tour guide in Rome who insisted that they could not take the wheelchairs down to the Tivoli Gardens. "'It is not possible,' the guide patiently explained and insisted." "But when it came to her 'inner circle,' he recalled, Mary had blinders on, as to the fact that nothing was impossible."

So Mary's own volunteers would get the wheelchairs down to the Tivoli Gardens, Mary insisted.

The truth was that doing so was insane and that it more than taxed the brawn and the goodness and the limits of her poor volunteers, all of whom were red-faced and shaken to have gotten them there—and none of whom enjoyed even a moment of being there, for dread and fear of the trip back up that awful hill. That fear was also manifested by the disabled who were just as uncomfortable, if not more uncomfortable, than those who were to push them back up a literal mountain.

Oh, how Mary regretted her "nothing is impossible" dictum that time, for even she looked upon what had been done to her typically unflappable volunteers as inexcusable.

She was not afraid to admit that she had pushed too far.

On another occasion, he recalled her battling the nuns at the cloisters by Sainte-Anne's over acquiring permission to bring her disabled into their adoration chapel. Permission was denied and Mary simply looked so sad.

Not angry, just sad!

Monsignor pointed out that it is among his most profound memories of Mary, for she looked upon the nun who denied them entry and said, "This is not about us. It is about something far greater than us. It is that you have denied those who carry the cross for Jesus."

Oh, what a stinging and powerful, but beautiful and emotionally driven and spiritually laden rebuke.

Oh, the power of her, "You have denied those who carry the cross for Jesus."

That was, of course, a quintessential component of the theology of suffering that she developed, a theology that we knowingly mention, again and again in this work, because of its unique importance. Emphasis is not redundancy, and each time, we offer a new link or yet another factor or thought or context to consider.

It was, as you already know, a theology that brought the suffering disabled into an intimate relationship with Jesus Christ, where they would both metaphorically and genuinely help Him carry the cross and lift high the burdens, a theology that would allow them to offer up their own suffering in sacrifice, for the procreation of goodness and grace and love, a theology that suggested that their physical inability was more than compensated for by a higher and greater spiritual ability, in that they had more time to pray and more time to give to God. It was a heartfelt and ultimately simple, and maybe even irrefutable, theology that placed her "inner circle" in the epicenter of God's plan.

The seed of this theology was planted by her own parents who taught her how special she was to God and how blessed she was to be disabled. Then armed with the miracle at Beaupre and the birth and growth of her First Saturday family, her unique theology of suffering and affliction naturally took shape.

In prayer and in reflection, it was a gift given to her by God and a gift that she was then free to give to all who joined her First Saturday family and her "inner circle."

Interestingly, Monsignor Paul noted that as it was their feast, when Our Lady of Sorrows was on prominent display, greeting all who entered Holy Family—Our Lady of Sorrows, pictured as an apparition, with arms extended outward, as if in acceptance of her suffering Christ. She is not, in her great love, pictured as rejecting the suffering of Jesus, but rather pictured accepting it on behalf of all of us, who are in need of reclamation and resurrection.

It was in that spirit that Mary Varick urged us all, in our daily comings and goings, to never resort to feeling sorry for ourselves.

Affliction and suffering and sorrow were neither to be mourned nor rejected, but rather embraced, lovingly embraced and ultimately, in wisdom, celebrated.

Yes, she urged us all to "never feel sorry for ourselves" and to accept our trials and misfortunes and challenges as the sum and substance of our own Calvary that must be enjoined with Christ's.

Give it to God. Give it all to God!

Switching gears, he laughed to think of what became of Our Lady of Mercy's one-thousand-dollar donation in January of 1977, a contribution that he quietly presented to Mary. But she took it and the wheels inside her turned, and she instinctively grabbed the microphone to publicly thank Monsignor, but not merely for the donation, but for rather making their trip to Russia later that year a reality.

"In our hearts, we were looking to help her reduce existing debt, but she immediately turned it into the catalyst for adding even greater debt," he said. "Impulsively, she felt and summarily announced, so as to immediately commit to it, suggesting that our gift had turned the talk and the hope and the tide of Russia into a reality."

Then he recalled Lee Marillo's phenomenal fund-raising efforts on behalf of Russia, her chairing the banquet, and her pushing not one, but two car raffles, both of which were remarkably won by the same person. Imagine that, the same guy won two new cars. "Everyone prayed that he'd donate one back to the club or, at least, make a significant donation, but he took his First Saturday club winnings and never looked back. Some took a chance, as it was, for chance's sake only, caring nothing at all for the club or its mission," he said.

One can only feel sorry for someone who is invited to a table like he was and yet refuses to take notice or to participate or to give or to serve. Invited to help others carry the cross, but without the ears to hear or the eyes to see or the hands to touch.

The body may well have been mightily fed, but the soul cried out for lack of nourishment.

Before leaving to say mass, Monsignor said that he had enjoyed many special and poignant moments with Mary over the years, but that their last conversation may well have been the most special of all. On the day before she died at Saint Michael's Hospital in Newark, which was but a few football fields away from the Colonnade and their beloved Saint Lucy's where the love of the other first fed them both, he was able to steal a few private minutes with his suffering and dying Mary.

Mary, he said, was looking back, questioning herself, wondering about all the havoc she may have caused for people. "Was it my vision or was it the Holy Spirit's?" she asked. "I know that it was all motivated by faith, and I was certainly impulsive, but I can't help but believe that it was all guided by the Holy Spirit."

Then Mary turned the tables and looked at her friend, who would in a few days be eulogizing her at the very church that made them one, and said, "You are the same as me and we are cut from the same mold, so trust your impulses, please, for the Holy Spirit is so alive in you."

The last thing she did was to give him a bit of advice and to remind him, what he likely already knew, that they were, indeed, one. The last thing she did was to thank him for his friendship and fierce loyalty and to bless him for being both a rock and a shield and a candle in the wind.

# Father Kevin

Father Kevin Carter is a passionate New York Giants and New York Mets fan, who, as established earlier, both takes a lot of grief from Monsignor Bochicchio and returns the favor with great passion.

So his mentor has this habit of teasing him for his propensity to check the scores on his cell phone or iPad regularly. So much so that he did a skit at a recent annual pilgrimage "*No Talent* Talent Show," where he himself played a highly distracted Father Kevin, who was completely caught up in the push-pull of a ball game! Compelled to check his cell phone for updates, he kept excusing himself to the confessor who was with him for reconciliation. He would mindlessly spout, "Yes, yes, yes," or "God forgives you" or "No, no, no," to each, until it reached a point, where, completely absorbed in the game, he paid no attention whatsoever to the penitents, mindlessly brushing all who came to him off.

Makes for good fun and Monsignor poured his heart into the part, and Father Kevin laughed at this bold attempt to humiliate in good fun.

He had been one of Monsignor's original Our Lady of Mercy "seekers" who joined forces with Mary Varick and her First Saturday Club and its pilgrimages to Canada.

Only his first trip wasn't to Canada, it was to Russia.

He likes to say that he was "transported from Saint Peter's in Jersey City to Saint Petersburg in Russia in what was a life-altering and earth-shattering trip."

Yes, he had, as an impressionable and young teenager, met Mary before—first, as a guest of Father Paul, at a dinner at the Westmont Country Club in Essex County celebrating the twentieth anniversary of the Our Lady of Fatima First Saturday Club. That is the dinner where her brother, Father John Cassidy, brought the house down by making fun of what it meant to be a friend or a family member of Mary's, who, of course, was so hard pressed to make demands of anyone.

After the dinner, he got to know her a bit better, in a more up close and personal or intimate setting when she came to visit Father Paul's "seekers" at Our Lady of Mercy. "I remember being completely mesmerized by her, taken by her, and maybe even transformed by her," said Father Kevin. "I knew that a holy woman had come into my life, and from that point forward, simply spending time with her was very important to me. The best time of day on the pilgrimages, for me, was always late at night, when we'd get to sit in her room and talk with her. Those are my most special memories."

The son of a working mom and a Jersey City policeman, just keeping him in Saint Peter's Prep stretched the budget, so getting a passport and dreaming of Russia and the Vatican and Lourdes was mind-boggling. "It was all so over the top to me," he said, "something that would never have been considered, were it not for Mary, because my parents were sold on her and not necessarily on the trip."

"Memories of Our Lady of Lourdes in Saint Petersburg and the Sistine Chapel and the grotto at Lourdes are never to be forgotten," he explained, "but the greater gift was getting closer to Mary and basking in the grace that she seemed to so freely dispense."

"Upon returning from Russia in the early summer of 1977, the annual pilgrimage to Canada still beckoned, and while it was time for me to earn some dollars and get back in the good graces of my father," Father Kevin recollected, "Mary herself said that she needed me with them in Canada. There was no way that was going to happen, until she personally ran interference with my dad. She personally asked him for me, and as we well know, people had this hard time saying no to Mary Varick."

He pointed out that Mary's return from Russia also was met by the death of her Billie, what was an incomprehensible loss. She had to be strong for her son-in-law, Don, and her grandchildren, Don, Mike, Maryanne, and Peggy. She had to reach through the harsh pain that enveloped her, a mother's pain, to be a source of light and life for those who mourned so great a loss.

There also was the natural guilt that came with not being with Billie while on the pilgrimage, something that Mother Teresa had helped her resolve.

With all of that swirling around Mary between Russia and Canada in 1977, Father Kevin suggested that he looks back on it all with a measure of astonishment. For she took time out to assure his presence in Canada and to make his presence an issue in the first place! "I have no doubt," he said, "but that her singling me out there and God's singling me out for a vocation to his priesthood are connected."

He suggested that the one purposefully preceded the other and that Mary Varick played a mighty role in nurturing his vocation.

So off to the great shrines of Canada, he went.

Unlike Europe, there had been no expectations on his part, but he noted that he was even more moved by the Cape and Sainte-Anne-de-Beaupre than he had been by Lourdes and Rome. He suggested that it had everything to do with the fact that Canada and these holy shrines were this group's home turf. They just belonged there.

"The real growth, the actual sanctifying happened in Canada," he said. Suggesting that Russia and Europe were more about sightseeing and Canada was more about getting close to God. "Canada is always about getting close to God," he affirmed.

Focusing hard upon his coming together with Mary Varick and his, in a very real way, belonging to her, there were two thoughts that he most wanted to clarify.

The first was that he strongly believed that it would be wrong to look upon or to try to label the membership of the First Saturday Club with a "holy" brush. "Oh, the club, indeed, had its saints and many who strove to be so," he said, "but so many others were anything but saints. It also had its sinners and people with grave flaws and limitations." He explained that most did better, for having been amidst Mary and the club, but some did not and there were some associated tragedies on the periphery.

"On the last night of the Russian trip, in Paris, we had to make last-minute adjustments to separate the club's beloved and gentle Freddie Vanderhoof from a volunteer who swore he was going to kill him," Father Kevin said. "Now that volunteer was a great guy when sober, but he also was an alcoholic, who became violent and delusional when under the influence."

The disabled too were not immune from sin or deceit or jealousy or anger, he pointed out. "Now don't get me wrong," he said, "for Mary was beautiful and her First Saturday Club was a force for good and for grace and for God and the overwhelming majority of those involved, indeed, were holy, but that doesn't mean that it needs to be idealized or misrepresented. Like all forces for good and for grace, it was tempered by the things of the earth."

The second point that he wanted to stress, in a completely positive vein, was that his social association with Mary, on the pilgrimages especially, was a most prominent nurturing force for his vocation. "In Canada, I would talk to Mary every night," he said, "and walk the grounds with Father Paul by day, pondering the profound 'what to do with my life' questions." In that he liked girls too much, he fought it hard, he noted, and initially entered college as an accounting major.

"At that time, I remember promising Mary that I was doing this so as to get rich and resolve all of her financial worries."

"I think," he said, "that I delivered something far greater than riches for her in the end." For in 1982, Kevin Carter gave up the ghost and the girls and the doubts and entered the seminary.

On his first Canadian pilgrimage, as a priest, he shared a particularly memorable moment with Mary. "We were at Our Lady of the Cape, amidst the pandemonium of settling in," he said. "Suddenly, she just grabs me by the arm and pulls me toward her. 'Here, Father Noel, here, this is one of those brats that you didn't want running around here. You see what becomes of those brats?'" For the record, Kevin was wearing his collar and Father Noel was then the director of the shrine, and he and Mary, indeed, had history.

Father Kevin shook his head and said, "Now twenty-seven years a priest, I have kept faith with Mary, and I am forever grateful for the grace and blessing that she was in my life. This is a part of me, the pilgrimage and the First Saturday, her legacy, and so, for as long as it's there, I'll be there—as long as I am able. And I will remain devoted to and grateful for it."

# Mike Lenehan

Mike and Amy Lenehan were the youth ministers at Saint Mary's in Colts Neck, New Jersey. Acolytes of Monsignor Paul's, Mike actually met Amy on one of his retreats and that was, roughly speaking, where their life together began. But Mike's original ties to Monsignor went back to the days that he taught at Roselle Catholic High school in the mid-eighties. He believes that he was first recruited to join the pilgrimage as a volunteer in 1984.

He first met Mary Varick on that trip, along with Paul Russell, a quadriplegic in his early thirties, who had an irrepressible sense of humor. How often he would yell, "It's a miracle. I can see, I can see."

"I was taken and moved," said Mike, "by the way both Mary and Paul took their disabilities and suffering and turned the tears into laughter."

"Mary had such a unique and special smile," he explained, "a smile that automatically relieved the tension or angst and even worry of anybody in her presence, and she had eyes that just seemed to look right inside you. Eyes that pierced the heart and soul."

Interestingly, Mike added that while he met both Mary and Paul in Canada, they both spoke at Roselle Catholic, at Father Bochicchio's invitation, as well that same year. "They were everything we're taught to value made manifest when they spoke, like grace and goodness and faith and love," he said. "That was the takeaway from their presentations to our class."

"As to her 'inner circle,' Mary clearly believed that not only did they carry the cross for Jesus," he said, "but that they were a living portal to Him."

As to Mary Varick, he noted that the more he got to know her and to know of her family and her community and of her many connections, what amazed him was how present she seemed to be to each and every one.

She seemed to give each exactly what they needed, when there simply wasn't the time with which to do so. "There was this belonging and this connectedness to all involved in her First Saturday and this capacity to do great things for God that so inspired people," he said. "You couldn't help but marvel at just how much she seemed capable of giving."

"The closer I got to her and to those she served, the more moved I became and the more she taught me," Mike said. "Mary clearly impacted and influenced my life and the direction that it took. Through her and her people, my strengths were maximized, and both I and Amy discovered how to better give of our own loaves and fishes. She wasn't about looking at or accepting life as it is, but rather about working, actively working, to make it what it can or should be."

Particularly close to some of the disabled today, Mike and Amy remain wholly invested in the Our Lady of Fatima First Saturday family.

"Mary Varick," Mike concluded, "won me over to her cause more than twenty-seven years ago when I was a teenager. And Amy and I feel as if we are still standing with her today."

# Maryanne Adriance

As Maryanne Adriance began to speak of her grandmother, Mary Varick, it was as if you felt her presence, because her devotion and love for her was so warm and palpable and tangible.

She talked and those who listened could not help but think, as I did—how great was this love?

First, she spoke of her intense joy and of her rich faith and of her contention that there is always meaning, in even the smallest of things, as well as the greatest of things.

Freely, openly, and willingly, she placed her own burdens and struggles and crosses on the table, because they were so often checked by her grandmother. "She was," Maryanne said, "always my anchor in faith, and when I wanted to die, I thought largely of what it would do to her, of what it would do to the one who was the guiding force for good in my life, the one who loved me unconditionally."

She explained that when she lost her mom (Billie), only Mary spoke to her about her mom and so kept her alive for her. While everyone else kept their distance, "My grandmother's great faith enabled me to embrace my mother's death," said Maryanne. "Yes, my mom suffered greatly, but my grandmother said that God never wished to hurt her in life and would never have hurt her in death."

Because of Maryanne's own suffering and the tragic, shattering sexual abuse that she had known, an abuse that she so courageously put on the table, it led her to look for and to become closest to those in Mary's "inner circle" who also had suffered from neglect or abuse.

She noted Patty Dix and Barbara Pinti who both had experienced extraordinary trials in life and Connie LoPresti who had in her youth suffered from sexual abuse.

On what Maryanne believes may have been their last Canadian pilgrimage together, and there had been so many of them, her grandmother did lay it on the line for her. As it happened, while at Our Lady of the Cape, Mary asked her to go to lunch with her at the Penn Masse Restaurant. "She wore that familiar smile of hers as she told me, 'You know that you're the one who is going to have to take this over,'" said Maryanne. In keeping with her style, she didn't ask, but rather assumed and insisted.

She quickly repeated the same statement as if it may not have registered. "Yes, you know that you're the one who is going to have to take this over for me," she repeated and smiled that knowing smile of hers.

"I know that my response was something to the effect that it was her promise, but not mine."

"Oh, her smile and laugh and propensity to assume," noted Maryanne, "could frustrate. But that was my grandmother. I clearly said no while she just smiled and laughed and look at me now. She leaves me laughing at myself."

Her love, her love, her great love, that was the long and short of it for Maryanne.

A grandmother's love that was intense and constant and complete. Unconditional and rich!

That's what Mary Varick was to Maryanne Adriance.

When she visited her for the last time, shortly before she went home to God, at Saint Michael's, Maryanne had to push her way through a crowd. Upon approaching her, she made some self-deprecating "Do you remember me?" kind of comment, to which Mary responded, "Oh, my angel, my angel, I would never forget who you are."

# Joan Murray

Joan Murray, wife, mother of five, and grandmother of ten, is some kind of loving piece of work for this earth. She is my sister and I know, and you can take this to the bank.

She is the real deal, and if there are truly angels walking this earth to do God's bidding and to make a difference, she is most certainly among them.

She will never say such things, but I can and I do so without any hesitation or reservation.

My sister Joan is an angel among us. She works with Maryanne Adriance, as the codirector of the annual pilgrimage today, but she has been associated with the pilgrimage and the First Saturday family for well over fifty-five years.

It has been part of the literal fabric of her life.

As siblings, we have memories of the last minute calls coming from Aunt Mary, inviting Joan to go to Canada. Many of us would have our shots later on, but we were all *pikers* compared to Joan.

"I fell in love with Canada and with the shrines and with Aunt Mary's 'inner circle' when I was a young girl, and while there was a sustained gap during *my 'building a family' years*, it has been a lifelong love affair," said Joan.

Again, as siblings, we have memories of her gentle treatment of those among the disabled who fell in love with her over the years. And why wouldn't they?

Joan grew so involved and enfolded herself in the work, so much so that in those early years of exploring what God wanted for her, she spent a couple of years with the Oblates of Mary Immaculate (OMI) who oversee Our Lady of the Cape. She even spent a summer working with them at the Cape.

Among her hard-earned First Saturday credits, she is among but a handful of veterans of the 1967 European pilgrimage who remain. She reimmersed herself into the First Saturday family when her children grew, and she kept the Canadian pilgrimage alive one year when it appeared that it might be sacrificed to the Guadalupe pilgrimage. She has, time and time again, become a primary caregiver for members of the "inner circle," and her great and transparent love of folks like Connie LoPresti and Freddie Vanderhoof and Mary Jane Burns and Cecile, most notably, come to mind.

Any number of the "inner circle" have spent their Christmases and Easters with Joan and her family.

Visiting constantly and loving fervently, she took the lead for them always.

"Aunt Mary," said Joan, "had a tremendous influence on my life as have the many members of her 'inner circle' whom I have been blessed to love and to be loved by. I have had a lifetime love affair with the First Saturday Club, with its pilgrims, and with its leaders.

"I have, faithfully and lovingly, been invited into the fabric of their lives," Joan said, "and I have tried, as Mother Teresa has asked us, to do the small things with great love, when I can. What a blessing it is for me to do so."

For all of these "keepers of the flame" for Mary Varick, there is this irrepressible attachment and devotion to her.

And so too, to her life's cause and work!

Sometimes, with tears in their eyes, and with great love, and with wisdom, and with commitment, they reflected upon that which attaches them to her and to her suffering "inner circle" and to each and every pilgrim who looks to enrich their lives and their relationship with God.

As such, they are exactly where they are supposed to be on the continuum of life, knowing that every single moment of it is pregnant with the opportunity to learn and to grow and to serve and to love just a little bit more.

To love just a little bit harder!

These five did look back and they did reflect and they were sometimes saddened, but, far more often than not, they smiled and laughed in the remembering and in the telling.

What they shared was a great love story, one rooted in constancy and belief and faith.

Each joined her and her "inner circle" in carrying the cross for a suffering Christ.

Magnificently!

## Chapter 5 Placeholders

- But oh, what a day it was and oh, how proud Aunt Mary would have been. How she would have rejoiced in being invited to build upon what she would have looked upon as the great blessing and opportunity of this one First Saturday, where Joan Murray, Bob Monahan, and Spectrum for Living had conspired together.

- Yet little did she know as that mile-long procession of cars wormed its way over the Meadowlands, from the beautiful, gothic All Saints Church at the corner of Communipaw and Pacific Avenues in Jersey City to Holy Cross Cemetery on Ridge Road in North Arlington, as she mourned her Skip, that God had already introduced her to one who would, indeed, "restoreth her soul."

- Monsignor pointed out that it is among his most profound memories of Mary, for she looked upon the nun who denied them entry and said, "This is not about us. It is about something far greater than us. It is that you have denied those who carry the cross for Jesus."

- That was, of course, a quintessential component of the theology of suffering that she developed, a theology that brought the suffering disabled into an intimate relationship with Jesus Christ, where they would both metaphorically and genuinely help Him carry the cross and lift high the burdens. It was a theology that would allow them to offer up their own suffering in sacrifice, for the procreation of goodness and grace and love, a theology that suggested that their physical inability was more than compensated for by a higher and greater spiritual ability, in that they had more time to pray and more to give to God. It was a heartfelt and ultimately simple, and maybe even irrefutable, theology that placed her "inner circle" in the epicenter of God's plan.

- Affliction and suffering and sorrow were neither to be mourned nor rejected, but rather embraced, lovingly embraced, and, in wisdom, even celebrated.

- Yes, she urged us all to "never feel sorry for ourselves" and to accept our trials and misfortunes and challenges as the sum and substance of our own Calvary that must be enjoined with Christ's.

- "Was it my vision or was it the Holy Spirit's?" she asked? "I know that it was all motivated by faith, and I was certainly impulsive, but I can't help but believe that it was all guided by the Holy Spirit."

- Then Mary turned the tables and looked at her friend, who would in a few days be eulogizing her at the very church that made them one, and said, "You are the same as me and we are cut from the same mold, so trust your impulses, please, for the Holy Spirit is so alive in you."

- "I remember being completely mesmerized by her, taken by her, and maybe even transformed by her," said Father Kevin. "I knew that a holy woman had come into my life and from that point forward, simply spending time with her was very important to me. The best time of day on the pilgrimages, for me, was always late at night, when we'd get to sit in her room and talk with her. Those are my most special memories."

- "Mary clearly impacted and influenced my life and the direction that it took. Through her and her people, my strengths were maximized, and both I and Amy discovered how to better give of our own loaves and fishes. She wasn't about looking at or accepting life as it is, but rather about working, actively working, to make it what it can or should be."

- "Aunt Mary," said Joan, "had a tremendous influence on my life as have the many members of her 'inner circle' whom I have been blessed to love and to be loved by. I have had a lifetime love affair with the First Saturday Club, with its pilgrims, and with its leaders.

- "I have, faithfully and lovingly, been invited into the fabric of their lives," Joan said, "and I have tried, as Mother Theresa has asked us, to do the small things with great love, when I can. What a blessing it is for me to do so."

# 6

# An Hour, a Half Hour, a Life

Two live interviews with Mary Varick had been saved, archived by Mary Pisaniello, and kindly sent to me for review. The setting of both interviews intrigued for different reasons and, of course, the interviews themselves—well there truly were no words to do them justice—but those that crossed my mind, upon viewing both of these tapes, largely had to do with just how fortunate I was to be able to view them.

The moment that I put them on, I was just blown away, for there was my extraordinary Aunt Mary, in the flesh again, alive and vibrant and so full of life. And oh, that remarkable, rich smile of hers and the gleam and the mist in those sweet eyes and the laughter that was so hearty for every laugh took her whole body away with it and the literal and palpable love that just seemed to ooze out of her.

Like Santa, she had a body that *shook when she laughed*, and like the mystics, she had eyes that were tangible portals to the mystery and the wonder of the heart and soul—your heart and soul and those of anyone and everyone else in her presence.

As I watched her begin to do her thing, I was reminded of how truly larger than life she was.

I had forgotten just how formidable a presence she had. Of course, I well remember how articulate and moving and inspirational she was and as to the free and easy, "this is how I breathe" extension of her devotion and faithfulness and love, there was nothing that surprised. But to be embraced by it all again, to be touched by it again was truly a knock-down, drag-out emotional experience.

The first of the two tapes, a one-hour-long production, was the then *Ave Maria Hour* which was actually a production of the Graymoor friars (or the Franciscan Friars of the Atonement) in Garrison, New York. From all appearances, the interview likely took place in the mid-1980s, maybe four to five years before Mary went home to God.

There is little or no information to be garnered about the *Ave Maria Hour* at Graymoor today, and were it not for my cousin and Mary's son Jim, I would have been unable to identify it as a Graymoor production to begin with.

Institutional memory fades as new directors and new friars and brothers replace those who served before. Sadly, either no archives exist or they are being hidden from the world for the time being.

Upon viewing, I would have thought that it was an Our Lady of the Cape production, as the host was clearly its director and Mary's dear friend Father Jacques Rinfret.

Those who either viewed it or heard it could not have known that Mary Varick wrote her books for the benefit of the host's Madonna House when it was but a dream or of how often, this host, Father Jacques Rinfret, the then director of Our Lady of the Cape, visited her homes in Jersey City and Newark, New Jersey.

They could not have known how often they shared the Eucharist or how often they broke bread together or just how deeply they loved and revered each other.

They could not have known that he had written the forewords to all of her books.

They could not have known just how much their mutual adoration of and fidelity to Our Lady of the Cape and to our Holy Mother Mary served to fashion this production. Where the audience was to see two, they were really only one.

For Mary Varick and Father Jacques Rinfret were, indeed, one in spirit and purpose and mission.

They could not have known of the beautiful poem that was to become a song that Mary had written upon the occasion of the twenty-fifth anniversary of his priesthood.

But I happen to be among the lucky ones who have been captivated by the resounding spirituality of her "In Host Held High, What Do I See," and I am certainly privileged to know that Mary Varick, guest, and Father Jacques Rinfret, host, were ever so much more than that and ever so much more than your average kindred spirits!

They shared the same perspective, the same passion, the same faithfulness, and the same burning love for Mary, the Mother of God, and *her only begotten son*, all of which was at the very epicenter of both of their lives.

Never before having seen Father Rinfret without his priestly collar on, I also was struck by his relaxed and casual apparel, something that wouldn't have thrown Mary at all, for late-night conversations and hot coffee in the AM were familiar to them both. And while his questions may occasionally have betrayed intimacy, for he had long been intimate with the inside and out of Mary's story, he, for purposes of the show, intimated that he was only then unraveling the mysteries of her life.

Her life, of course, was no mystery whatsoever to him.

The audience was to be left with the impression that this host was diving in and pressing in order to get to know this guest and so share her story with his *Ave Maria Hour* audience.

The second interview was much shorter, as it was produced for a one-half-hour program for the Paterson Diocese in northeast New Jersey. The host was a Father Eugene Gorayeb, and while it was produced by an outfit in Paterson, New Jersey, he appeared to be neither a Newark nor Paterson Diocesan priest. And while my research methods were basic and even primitive, I failed, in my initial and feeble attempts, to learn anything more about him, beyond his dying in July of 1987, at the age of fifty, two years before Mary. Another Mary Pisaniello find, I then discovered that he had fallen to cancer. And given the address that accompanied the sympathy thank-you card that she came across, I finally learned that his family hailed from Brooklyn but that he served the Archdiocese of Newton in Massachusetts. There was no history of this TV program on any of the diocesan sites, and needless to say, he had wandered a long way from his home base. What brought him to Paterson forever remains a mystery. That is, at least, to me.

The only names of a Eugene Gorayeb unturned at all in my personal searches were in a recent Maine obituary, but he was a hardworking man who had never been a priest, and the other was found in a nineteenth-century genealogical table.

The setting of this second interview was in a hotel-like conference or meeting room, and, interestingly, it was produced before a live and all-women audience. The show itself was devoted to the subject of the *empowerment of women*, and I well guessed, before Father Gorayeb even asked his first question, that my Aunt Mary was very likely going to turn that topic on its head.

I assumed that her definition of "empowerment" might well be completely different than those concerned about the glass ceiling and a woman's right to do what she pleased with her own body.

This promised to be fun!

To our Mary, to be sure, real power was ultimately and always to be found in sacrifice, in suffering, and in grace.

Thought by thought, we will now do our best to first trace the stories and tales that Mary Varick shared with Father Rinfret, rambling as they themselves rambled that evening, and then expounding, embellishing, and reflecting upon the same as needs require.

Familiarity and the ease of their being together trumped any attempt to practically structure the interview.

So at ease with each other, they rambled as good friends generally do. In lockstep with each other, we will extract the common denominators and central themes that give us Mary Varick in her own words as revealed on the *Ave Maria Hour*.

Later in this work, we will, of course, hear her own words again in a *Stations of the Cross* reflection of hers that could well stun the listener and span the years.

This is Mary, at ease and humble and happy, presenting her own story. It is as free and open and honest as Mary at 2:00 a.m. in her bedroom at the Madonna House.

Asked to describe herself by Father Rinfret, this victim of polio, cancer, diabetes, and countless other ailments said that it was impossible to thank God, "For all of the happiness extended to me, as I am the most blessed woman who has ever lived."

*"The most blessed woman who has ever lived."* If that isn't the most endearing prescription for living well and living abundantly, it certainly has to be the one that comes the closest.

She began by going to gratitude, a prevailing and formidable gratitude. An appreciation and a gratitude that enveloped every single aspect of her life! Can you even begin to imagine the idea of looking upon yourself as the most blessed woman or person who ever lived!

And while she will proceed to tell us why, we interject at the outset, to suggest that it had everything to do with being, so tangibly and so consciously, loved by God.

Profoundly and personally loved by God!

For in loving God, she was keenly aware of the fact that whatever one gave to God was returned in great abundance.

The blessing of that love and the happiness that consequently filled her life gave way to this fervent, unabashed, and pronounced gratitude, all of which was a by-product of her first being intimate with God—all of which was a by-product of the wonder of her personal relationship with Him.

She loved Jesus so much so that she could not go a day without embracing Him in the Eucharist, and she literally spent her days with His Mother, Mary, in prayer and in thought and in devotion.

As to that gratitude, she would proceed to tell Father Rinfret that she was grateful for her parents and her family and her life's cross and her Bill and her First Saturday Family—for each and every member of it—and, of course, most especially, for God's great love.

"There are," she said, "the gifts that were passed by both my mom and dad, who taught me that God must love me so much, because He had chosen me to help Him carry His cross."

Oh, what reverence she displayed for her parents, who lived their faith and so devotedly passed it on to her. And to be with Jesus, by His side, and to help Him lift the cross in suffering, why that was singled out, by her parents, as the most special of all possible gifts. Her disability wasn't the by-product of being cast aside or made less than...but rather and only of being uniquely blessed and having been chosen by God to be particularly close to Him!

While she would later coin the term *God's inner circle*, it was her parents who well introduced the concept of it to her.

So taken was she by that notion—a notion that was taught and not merely casually expressed—that she told Father Rinfret,

"I would, as a child, look at the healthy kids and think, 'You are not as lucky as I am,' and when I'd see someone else who was like me, I'd think, 'Do you know how special you are and how much God loves you?'"

Now understand, she both comprehended and bought into this most high-minded theological concept as a young child, and she so accepted this concept of suffering as gift and blessing, in that it brought her into intimate communion with Jesus.

"I wanted," she added, "to hug anyone handicapped, like me, because they too were, with me, walking on the road to Calvary."

As a mere child, she thought such things and it amazes.

As a child, she knew what it was to be walking on the road to Calvary.

She had legs that didn't permit her to play as other children did, and yet she claimed that, "I lived in a world that I couldn't believe was mine, a world where God so loved and so blessed His suffering afflicted."

As she further explained, "God writes in crooked lines" (I love this line), and while you and I might well accept that to be true after lives of study, prayer, and reflection, that Mary Varick understood that to be true as a child truly amazes.

For God, as Mary suggested, does, indeed, write in crooked lines.

In effect, and as a child again, Mary also was saying that, "It hurts and I suffer and it doesn't seem fair because I can't do as others do, yet it's wonderful, because I share in Christ's suffering and I help Him carry the cross."

In thinking so and living so, she would tell Father Rinfret, "I am uniquely blessed and privileged." Ultimately and most importantly, suffering was, to her, the most profound manifestation of God's love for her, as the love and the cross that she carried with Him were enjoined as one.

*As a child*—again and again and again, we remind you—as a child, she embraced this theology of suffering, one that is only embraced by the mystics and the poets after lifetimes of searching. Mary said that she was honored to be able to sacrifice herself for the redemption of the world as God, through Jesus Christ, had asked her to do.

And, yes, she embarked on that mission in her youth, so grateful for the grace showered upon her by a loving God, and yet we struggle to comprehend and to understand how it is that a young child could possibly appreciate the intricacies and nuances of the mystery of grace.

Yet Mary, physically and spiritually, knew what it was to be raised up by grace at the most tender of ages.

Unlike most children, she was not burdened by ego or jealousy. She honestly believed that she had it all.

She did and that is the first miracle in her life.

She accepted and she smiled and she embraced her brokenness and proclaimed, "Thank you, my sweet Jesus."

The first miracle was not at Sainte-Anne-de-Beaupre as we have always maintained.

The first miracle wasn't physically manifested there.

It was rather this miracle of faith in that she smiled and said, "Thanks for this pain and this suffering and for inviting me into the heart and the defining mystery of your love as a child."

The miracle is that she bought into what was destined to become her concept of "God's inner circle" at the age of five or six or seven. Her polio, for all purposes and at the earliest of stages, was deemed by her to be a sacred invitation from God.

And there is, make no mistake about it, in the all of this, a profound awakening for a child.

And if unbridled acceptance and profound understanding and an almost mystical maturity at such an age are not miraculous, then I don't know what is.

Next, she spoke of her dad and of his hope to one day take her to the Lourdes of North America or Sainte-Anne-de-Beaupre. She spoke of his "Someday, I'll take you there" of his earnest desire to fulfill a dream, a dream that was not to be in his abbreviated and all-too-short life.

And then Father Rinfret took a quantum leap forward (I think, for the record, that he must have had a laundry list of "I must get to" topics on hand, and he wasn't necessarily worried about smooth transitions). Not in this comfortable telling! So he jumped to one of the watershed moments or epic movements in Mary's life—to the cancer she contracted in 1951, the bone cancer that had been ravaging her body and that had effectively condemned her to death.

It interests me that he so casually jumped from what I have described as the first miracle in her life to what was going to bring them directly to the pronounced or very public and acknowledged physical miracle in her life.

Inadvertently, he also had, chronologically speaking, bypassed all of the great and wild "growing a family" years, and we would be remiss, if we failed to note that Mary Varick considered the birth of each of her children, Billie, Jim, Barbara, and Mary, to be among the profoundest of miracles of her life as well.

Bringing children into the world and growing a family was something that she, in her youth, never allowed herself to either envision or even to imagine.

She did not anticipate that which was the norm or normal being applied to her.

As important and vital as those years, indeed, were, Father Rinfret had only so much time, and this was about his Our Lady of the Cape and certainly not all of the trouble that Jimmy caused or Barbara's dates or Billie's cheerleading or Mary's goodness and silver dollars or running up the bill at Klapco's Grocery Store around the corner.

No, he took the conversation to the bone cancer that prompted the sum and substance of the "pilgrim's journey" that would define what was to be her second life—what was to be another fulfilling and extraordinary thirty-eight years!

There, with her beloved Bill and her four children and their mountain of debt, she had been told that all of the treatments and radiation experiments had failed and that they had regrettably only to wait for the inevitable, which would surely come in a matter of months.

Yes, death in a matter of months, not years, was the prognosis.

"I determined," she told her dear friend, Father Rinfret, "that the time had come for me to finally get to Sainte-Anne-de–Beaupre, and I talked to my dear Bill and Mom about it and they talked to my brother and everyone thought that either it or I was crazy, and my doctor said, 'Absolutely not.'"

"'It is ridiculous,' he argued. 'She will not survive the trip.'"

Mary also noted how very sick she was and also how sick their financial condition was, as they were on the verge of losing their home. For the record, the reader should already know by now that there is nothing ordinary about delving into the finances of Bill and Mary Varick.

For in doing so, one will inevitably and invariably find that "being on the verge of utter and complete disaster" never deterred them and that there would be many pilgrimages to come that would be accompanied by what became that all too familiar "being on the verge of financial catastrophe."

No problem, for they, as you well know, always went forward on faith alone. And that, they had in abundance!

Remember, they mortgaged the 241 Pacific Avenue home in Jersey City for the '67 trip to Europe, and poor Mary and Bruno mortgaged their beautiful Belvidere home for the '77 junket to Russia, Rome, and Lourdes. And lest you forget, when it came to her First Saturday family and its needs, Mary Varick, without the slightest hint of apology, personally turned begging into an art form.

In fact, they actually had to borrow one hundred dollars in order to make this trip in the heat of the summer of 1951. They also had to borrow a car. These obstacles, notwithstanding, the three intrepid pilgrims, Mary, Bill, and Mary's brother, Buddy, set off for Quebec, long before the National Highway Act had managed to build any semblance of the interstate highway system that was soon to be on the drawing board.

They would, in effect, be making the trip largely on byways, rather than highways.

"I was so very sick," Mary explained to Father Rinfret, "and I tried my best to rest on a makeshift bed on the back seat, but my condition required us to stop all too frequently and so, our progress was slow. It was hot, and I often needed to lie on the grass by the side of the road to catch my breath. Early on, I well remember my poor brother, Bud, wanting to turn back because we were making such little headway. But I kept promising to do better the next hour or the next day."

Turning back, she explained, was out of the question, as if she had a personal appointment with Saint Anne and could not possibly disappoint.

She was, she said, passionately driven, as if by angels.

It would take them three long days to get there, but get there, they most assuredly did.

"This happened a very long time ago, but I still find it so very hard to talk about," she said. "I was in my wheelchair at the foot of the beautiful statue of Saint Anne, carved from that one single piece of oak. I carried a lit candle in my hand for the procession, and it was during the benediction when my world turned upside down and my earthly destiny was redirected. In a daze, I heard someone crying loudly and praying, someone who was begging not to be perfectly cured, someone who still wanted to carry their cross, but someone who also longed to see her children grow."

In the spiritual intoxication and the glorious bewilderment of a transformative moment, she did not even realize that the voice crying out was her own voice!

Or that the prayer not to be perfectly cured was her own prayer!

Or that the deeply seeded and intense desire to see her children grow, while still carrying a cross, was her own desire!

Completely stunned and dazed, with tears streaming down her face, with sweat on her brow, and with the once hot wax from the candle having melted all over her hand, she was not even conscious of lifting herself from the wheelchair, at a time when she absolutely lacked the strength or power to do so. There on her knees before, the beautiful statue of Saint Anne, the mother of Mary and the grandmother of our Savior, Jesus Christ, she returned to the world.

Outer body, to be sure, she was shaking, and the priests from the altar had rushed to her aid, and while no one yet knew what had occurred, one priest who was kind enough to suggest or who had the grace or the insight quietly and calmly suggested, "Maybe, you have not been fully cured, as you asked."

It was the "Maybe, you have not been fully cured" line that was new to me. I had often heard the story and read of the story, and maybe, I just missed it in the past, but "Maybe, you have not been fully cured,' whether old or new, was new to me.

Has any saint ever deemed themselves worthy? The likelihood is that they did not, no matter how worthy, no matter the greatness of their love, no matter the gifts received or the gifts given, no matter the all of what was inexplicably "larger than life" about them.

God alone was aware of what happened to Mary, this servant of His, for Mary's humility, despite the new vibrancy and step in her, precluded her from basking in the light of what seemed like, felt like, and looked like a miracle. She would not lay claim until outside and objective sources weighed in.

This happened on July 17, 1951, but interestingly, Mary said that it was September 17 during this taping. For my purposes, this does not warrant a historical review, for July 17 was, indeed, the date of the official celebration of the sixtieth anniversary of Mary's miracle at Beaupre in 2011.

Hah, hah, with the kind help of Mary Pisaniello again, the mystery of Mary's *faux pas* has been solved. She informed me that September 17 was Mary's daughter Billie's birthday, her own Billie who carried the cross with a smiling grace. While she was talking of the astounding physical miracle at Beaupre, Billie's birth was ever the first miracle to her. Sometimes where there is apparent confusion, there also is perfect harmony and symmetry.

Mary told Father Rinfret how wonderful she felt on the ride home and that there was nothing that could dampen her uplifted spirits on the return journey, as all of life seemed to be renewing itself. Still, their borrowed and beaten vehicle broke down as they headed south and they were stuck in Sherbrooke for a time.

But so what?

Even Bud and Bill were too caught up with the change in her to be dismayed by the nuisance of a mechanical problem.

Her sickness had delayed the trip up to Beaupre and so it took three days. They then spent three days with Saint Anne. And finally, Mary said, "The car's breaking down on the return trip was a preordained blessing, because had it not, it would not have taken us another three days to get home." Always the Trinity— the Trinity—Mary's love for the Trinity and her corresponding obsession with threes! And there it was, there had been three sets of three or nine days, as in a novena.

Fortunately, gratefully, tellingly, nine days had been devoted to her first wonderful journey to Sainte-Anne-de-Beaupre.

In commemoration of that first trip and in celebration of its nine days, all First Saturday Club pilgrimages, up until this very day, are scheduled for nine days, three times three, in honor of the Holy Trinity.

On the very first pilgrimage that she arranged in 1952, just one year after the miracle, Mary then said that they had made arrangements to visit Sainte-Anne's and Saint Joseph's Oratory in Montreal and again only learned of the existence of Our Lady of the Cape while en route later in 1953. Having been told by May Gnapp that it was halfway between the two shrines that they had planned to visit, their then caravan of misfit cars detoured and descended upon the Cape unannounced. Welcomed warmly by Father Reneau, he invited them to spend the night in the Pilgrim's House. "I immediately fell in love with the grounds," recalled Mary. "I fell in love with this place of peace and prayer, and we promised to return."

The rest is history as the Cape, forever a place of peace and prayer on the banks of the Saint Lawrence, has become a destination on every pilgrimage.

Father Rinfret then asked about the formation of the First Saturday Club itself, which Mary lovingly recalled as the handiwork of her beloved Bill, who told Mary that she couldn't just love them nine days a year and let them go. And so, the First Saturday, as Our Lady of Fatima had asked, would be singled out as a special day for prayer for peace in the world and consecrated with a mass, a rosary, and a social celebration for all in the group.

"Ever since," said Mary to Father Rinfret, "be it sunshine or shadow or be it blessings or crosses, we have in love celebrated the First Saturday of August at Our Lady of the Cape."

To the First Saturday Club, the Cape, like Sainte-Anne-de-Beaupre, became another home away from home.

Twenty-five years after Mary's passing, her "sunshine or shadow, blessings or crosses" observation about the life of the August First Saturday and Our Lady of the Cape remains, we pray, as Dr. Seuss would say, "truer than true."

She proceeded to share the story of the battle fought to have mass said at Grand Central Station in New York, as a prelude to the 1959 pilgrimage by train.

A brilliant politician in her own right, Mary pleaded with both the public authorities in the city and the religious authorities in the chancery, and she tactically played them both off of one another and boxed them in. In doing so, she inevitably won the support of Cardinal Spellman, who would remain an ally of hers in the future.

"What I most remember about Grand Central Station," Mary said, "was the resounding and beautiful voices of the choir from the Immaculate Conception Seminary at Darlington. Oh, how their music filled the caverns of that old building with the spirit of God and His great love for us." On their way to the priesthood, both of Mary's two youngest brothers, the talented Skip and Jack, just happened to be in that very choir and Jack was its director.

Mary would come to rely on Cardinal Spellman again, when planning the famous pilgrimage to Fatima, Lourdes, and Rome in 1967. He ordered Bill Fugazy, an early trip and tour planner, who had a close association with the New York Yankees, to get it done and to get her pilgrims from Fatima to Lourdes by plane. However difficult the journey and however sorry the planes, he did get it done, and all pilgrims, however fractured emotionally, did get there in one piece.

What Mary most wanted to voice in this interview, at this point, however, was her, "Sixty-seven wheelchairs, two stretchers, one bishop, and nine priests."

I know—nine priests, three sets of three, the Trinity and a novena. She wasn't a numerologist, but threes, in any form or fashion, never got by her.

With humor and laughter, she proceeded to tell one of those stories that best manifests her devotion to Father Rinfret's Cape. As it happened, Estelle Clavette, a nun and dear friend from Our Lady of the Cape, herself happened to be visiting Mary and Bill in Jersey City. The plan was for Mary to return with Estelle to Our Lady of the Cape for the purpose of recording her "Reflections on the Stations of the Cross" for an album that the Cape and the First Saturday Club, the coproducers would collectively market on behalf of the shrine.

On the morning that they were to fly to Quebec, Estelle and Mary, on her crutches, walked to the Eastern Rite Catholic church, Saint Mary's, which was on the corner to the right of her house, no more than twenty yards or a stone's throw from Mary's house. All Saints and Saint Mary's boxed the Cassidys and the Varicks in as it were. Estelle had never before been to an Eastern Rite service, so it had been well anticipated. Together, they enjoyed it, and the beauty of its liturgical nuances and all was well until Mary slipped on the way out and severely damaged her leg (as it happened, it was badly broken), but there was no way that she was going to threaten the trip.

So like a little child, she slipped back into her wheelchair and determined to hide the injury from all beyond Estelle, whom she had sworn to secrecy. Her plan was to smile over and through the throbbing pain and sneak away before anyone realized.

"Back at the house," said Mary, "we were first going to have breakfast with Bill before departing for the airport. And lo and behold, what does Bill say but, 'Mary, I want to go with you, so I'm going to call in sick and tell them that you broke your leg and need me for a few days.'" Estelle almost choked and spit out her crumb cake, as Mary quickly and gently reminded Bill that they couldn't afford his being docked any pay at the time.

Later that night, in close proximity to her beloved Our Lady of the Cape at the hospital in Trois-Rivieres, however, Mary contritely called Bill to tell him that she had, indeed, broken her leg, just as he had amazingly prophesized. She admitted that she would have refrained from even telling him at the time were it not for her need to get the hospitalization number.

Conversation between the two of these kindred spirits then turned to what Mary suggested was "the joy of serving so many people over the years, who had no idea how very much God loved them." So blessed to serve her First Saturday family, she spoke of the countless lives that had been changed and maybe saved and of the more than twenty First Saturday family weddings!

Thinking of the lives turned over, she said, with bright blue and misty eyes and heartfelt passion, "There is a place in this world for suffering. There must be Simons and Veronicas. We must look to sacrifice everyday if we are to change this world."

Upon which Father Rinfret spoke of the wonder of her preaching the *Way of the Cross*, which led her to again herald the mysterious power of human suffering. "Yes," she said, "suffering is a gift, but what a terrible test it is to watch your oldest and 'oh-so beautiful' child die."

Tearfully and beautifully, Mary then recited a poem that ended with these words of theological affirmation, "Love must pay a price—suffering is just the kiss of Christ."

Briefly touching upon her *Catholic Woman of the Year* award from the National Catholic War Veterans, she noted that it was Bill and not she who truly deserved it. And finally before a rushed goodnight, she quickly spoke of an ancient Christmas Eve, when only a little girl, a Christmas Eve on which the heavy snows prevented her from being able to go to mass. Her consolation was that she would have the honor of placing the small statue of the Baby Jesus into the stable at midnight. "I so clearly recall," she said, "holding Him that evening and telling Him how very much I loved Him."

And so she did, every moment of every day

*Why the cross and suffering?*

*The actions surrounding Jesus's taking up the cross and dying upon it is the greatest manifestation of love, and there is simply nowhere else to experience a love as great or as meaningful as it.*

*Because upon the cross hangs the purest and the most complete Love.*

*So real life has everything to do with the Cross of Christ!*

*Jesus's sacrifice is profoundly perfect because it encompasses all of the crosses, great and small, that shadow the human experience: there is cruel torture and harsh pain and denial and ignorance and betrayal—there is despair and abuse and humiliation and rejection—there is the illusion of failure and loneliness and emptiness and loss and death.*

*Yes, we are taught that Jesus's purpose was to die so that all of us can be raised to new life.*

*Our response to this, to Jesus's great love must always and can only be to love as well. "Love is repaid by love alone," wrote St. Therese of Lisieux. When we fully love, when we die to ourselves, we rise with and become one with Christ and embrace His work of redemption and salvation.*

*We become redeemers—all of us—just as we are destined to be!*

The time spent with Father Gorayeb was briefer and, to great degree, much more pointed and focused.

As to the *empowerment of women*, Mary Varick was quick to suggest that it, first and foremost, has everything to do with one's perception of power.

She was equally quick to turn the tables on their prospective dialogue when she said, "The greatest gift that God gave women is their humility," hardly what a liberated, "You've come a long way, baby" crowd might be looking for.

She suggested that humility is a most formidable of all powers.

"Beyond any imaginable limits," she said, "what our First Saturday friend Anne Gerhardt does with her prison ministry empowers her to be of service and of good—to be an instrument of reconciliation and change." Then too, she added that her fellow pilgrim Jeanette, who is blind and committed to a life on a stretcher, is as powerful a woman as a Joan of Arc.

"How do you bear it, Jeanette is asked, when you don't even know if it's day or night? How do you bear it when you are unable to move or to do?" said Mary. "But Jeanette responds, 'I fashion my own light, and God doesn't give me enough minutes in the day to do all that I should or can do. The first hour, I pray to save the lives of innocent babies and to stop abortion, and the next hour, I pray for vocations, and the next hour, I pray for all those who have been injured and recently disabled, who must learn to accept and embrace their suffering, and the fourth hour, I reserve for a cause that is uniquely my own. And it goes on and on and there is never enough time.'"

Jeanette, insisted Mary, was as empowered as any woman could hope to be, and yet, her power was entirely fashioned by her humility.

Father Gorayeb was struck and moved. How could he not be?

To dwell for even a moment on what an extremely disabled, suffering child of God like Jeanette did, in all likelihood, for all of her brothers and sisters on this earth, is just mind-boggling.

The love! The sacrifice! The grace! It all astounds.

As Mary and Father Gorayeb spoke of Jeanette, Mary seized the opportunity to mesh the beautiful and moving story of Jeanette's way of being with that of her entire First Saturday family, whom Mary so lovingly suggested, "Suffer for Christ and for peace in the world. That is who they are and that is what they do, my suffering and joyous First Saturday family."

Then the conversation moved to one of Mary Varick's greatest love stories.

And while we have already focused upon it, Mary's grappling with the tragic loss of her beautiful daughter, Billie, was so tenderly discussed here with Father Gorayeb.

"As Billie was growing sick and meeting the early manifestations of the multiple sclerosis, the disease was playing tricks with both her heart and her head," Mary said. "It is so difficult when you are going through tests and waiting for a diagnosis, a hopefully manageable diagnosis."

It's that period where you are praying, wondering, guessing, and, most certainly, hoping.

When the dire news of multiple sclerosis came in, back in those days when the significant others got the news first, Don Adriance, Billie's husband, asked for Mary's help in breaking the news to her.

Billie took it like a champ, and the next day, she and Mary talked again. Mary reported that Billie, with rare courage and faith, said, "Mom, thanks so very much. I was beginning to think that it was my mind. So don't you worry, I promise that I will carry the cross well. I will not disappoint you."

That is exactly what Billie did. Her MS moved rapidly and harshly and brutally forward, but with a constant smile and gentle nature and deep faith, she took its relentless punches.

The many, Mary witnesses and embraces, who join her in carrying the cross empower her to do what she does to serve the disabled, her "inner circle"—to do what she does in urging them to look upon their own suffering as a gift and to offer it up as a sacrifice—as grace—in the great service of others.

In truth, the one empowers the next and the next and the next. Each one gives strength and conviction and faith and love to the next one.

Mary Varick herself is a master motivator *and power broker.* Looking at his packed audience, with its many tearstained faces, Father Gorayeb looked at that audience while pointing at Mary and said, "This is one powerful woman" Indeed, she was! Indeed, she ever will be.

For Mary, power and humility were kindred forces. She enjoined these two again and again in the service of others—and not just on behalf of her "inner circle," but rather all she embraced in a full life.

I had, for instance, long heard about her journey to the Holy Land in December of 1967 and about the relationship that she forged with an impoverished group of young people. With them at Christmas in Bethlehem, it is my understanding that she used the insurance money left by her beloved Bill to buy them all Christmas presents. To a burgeoning young musician, she gave a guitar. An advocate for them, she apparently made enough noise on their behalf and contacted enough agencies to leave a mark.

Only in the pursuit of this effort did I learn more. For I came across a remarkable January 9, 1968 letter from a Rabbi Abraham Klausner to Mary concerning the project (or children) that had attracted her interest in Israel. He wrote, "If you would give me further detail of the children and their needs, I certainly will have one of the established medical or social institutions look into the matter." He then affirmed the great influence that they have in Israel and promised to follow through.

In short, Mary was heard and she effected change. Note how she used Bill's insurance money—in the giving of gifts—or in what was the story of her life, for she was gift personified.

Dwelling upon that insurance money, the use of which she believed would have pleased her Bill, one can't help but dwell upon the power that it takes to overcome grief. For Bill Varick was a great and formidable love, and his loss was incalculable.

To that end, I also came across the letter that Mary forwarded to the entire First Saturday family thanking them collectively for their expressions of sympathy. So we have the power and the humility and the tenderness of her own words.

"How terribly, terribly difficult it is for me to find the right words to share these bittersweet days with you...How could Bill have known then that his dream for God and each one of you would bloom and grow into the beautiful plans (Europe in '67) we are working on now? And how many of you know, in the strictest sense, that Bill gave his very life for this labor of love?... Oh, please do not misunderstand, for his goodness and love of us have surely earned him a wonderful place in heaven, and I am deeply and completely happy for him."

Bill's loss did not disarm her or leave her standing still, but rather and truly and forcefully only further empowered her to move forward and to take action. The European trip would become the *Bill Varick Memorial Pilgrimage* and in just months after Bill's passing, she, in a letter to then Archbishop Boland, challenged him and his very understanding of her disabled family. She urged him to plan a mass at the cathedral that would bring together the disabled from throughout the archdiocese to pray for peace.

Loss like suffering, she told Father Gorayeb, only empowered her, this gentle woman who insisted that humility is the greatest strength of women.

Surprise, surprise!

The winner was and is humility, the most powerful of all attributes.

## Chapter 6 Placeholders

- Now, understand, she both comprehended and bought into this most high-minded theological concept as a young child, and she so accepted this concept of suffering as gift and blessing, in that it brought her into intimate communion with Jesus.

- "I wanted," she added, "to hug anyone handicapped, like me, because they too were, with me, walking on the road to Calvary."

- "God writes in crooked lines."

- She did and that is the first miracle in her life. She accepted and she smiled and she embraced her broken-ness and proclaimed, "Thank you, my sweet Jesus."

- The first miracle was not at Sainte-Anne-de-Beaupre as we have always maintained.

- The first miracle wasn't physically manifested there.

- It was rather this miracle of faith in that she smiled and said, "Thanks for this pain and this suffering and for inviting me into the heart and the defining mystery of your love as a child."

- The miracle is that she bought into what was destined to become her concept of "God's inner circle" at the age of five or six or seven. Her polio, for all purposes and at the earliest of stages, was deemed by her to be a sacred invitation from God.

- Of course, practically speaking, she did not know that the deadly cancer had been ripped from her body until she got back to Jersey City and her doctor confirmed what had, indeed, been a miracle. And yet, she was aware of a mighty "change in her" from the moment the shaking and the daze gave way to normalcy. So sick on the journey up, health, in the immediate aftermath of that daze, had been restored to her.

- Thinking of the lives turned over, she said, with bright blue and misty eyes and heartfelt passion, "There is a place in this world for suffering. There must be Simons and Veronicas. We must look to sacrifice everyday if we are to change this world."

- Then too, she added that her fellow pilgrim Jeanette, who is blind and committed to a life on a stretcher is as powerful a woman as a Joan of Arc.

- "How do you bear it, Jeanette is asked, when you don't even know if it's day or night? How do you bear it when you are unable to move or to do," said Mary. "But Jeanette responds, 'I fashion my own light and God doesn't give me enough minutes in the day to do all that I should or can do.'"

# 7

# Calvary's Road

## Reflecting upon a Reflection

It may well have been the last time she did this at her beloved Our Lady of the Cape, making it all the more special and poignant. Last times matter, but a last time as it relates to this almost makes you want to bow down your head and cry. For there are some times when someone does something so well, so moving, and so inspiring that it truly makes a difference in this world.

Those moved and inspired, touched and maybe changed because of it, therefore, mourn the passing of the service, the prayer, or the gift almost as much as they do the life of the one who extended it.

As to making a difference, everyone who touched Mary Varick, however briefly, would no doubt confirm the fact that she, indeed, was a difference maker.

So just to think that this may have been her last time made this time particularly meaningful and especially powerful!

It was a last time doing something that she especially loved to do upon the beautiful grounds of Our Lady of the Cape, where the cool breezes blow in off the mighty and picturesque Saint Lawrence to temper the often harsh July or August humidity and to raise up the hopes and hearts of those who brought their prayers to its sacred ground in search of grace.

This time, like so many times before, Mary Varick was there upon the grounds of her beloved Cape on just such a day with her First Saturday pilgrims in tow as well as the strays that she invariably attracted, those who just happened to be walking the grounds who freely joined this woman whose words brought the statues that they were humbling themselves before to life.

Mary Varick often shared this powerful heart song of hers, as she reflected upon each of the fourteen Stations of the Cross.

Earlier, Howie Daniels said the size of the crowd following Mary on the grounds usually doubled or tripled before she was done, as her reflections reverberated over the speaker system on the grounds, serving like a magnet that just pulled people in.

The *Stations* were one of her go to "to-do things," one of her acts of love, one of her gifts, one of her regular ways of so stretching herself spiritually that breath and prayer and grace became enjoined as one.

She did it so often that it was routine, but never ordinary.

No—never ever ordinary!

Born of rich devotion and great love, each and every time she did this, there was nothing ordinary about Mary's *stations*. Not a word said about hope or faith or love or Jesus's sacrifice or suffering was ordinary, and each expression and thought was a genuine by-product of her own ever-evolving and extraordinary love affair with the Lord.

Reflecting upon the Stations of the Cross had, over the years, indeed, resulted in the most beautiful of her heart songs. It was something that her pilgrims expected of her, something that they looked forward to, and something that they were invariably, year after year after year, raised up by.

Some people are born to write and others to lead and others to act or to sing or to explore the imponderable secrets of the earth, but Mary Varick, most certainly was, among other things, born to move you to tears while inviting you to walk along the road to Calvary with Jesus and with her.

Now we can't be absolutely certain that this was the last time she lifted up a crowd while walking these stations, but we can reasonably assume so—or, at the very least, reasonably assume that it was the last time she did so with her own inner circle, her beloved disabled. It was clearly the summer of 1988, and Mary, as hard as it is to believe now, went home to God early in the summer or June of 1989.

Getting to see this film took some time and effort.

Gratefully shared by Hank and Mary Colling, it was recorded on some kind of tape that must have been in vogue for, at least, a month or so. As we monthly enhance our technological toys and bells and whistles today, such regular improvements have become both the pleasure and bane of our existence. No product can go more than a few months without a new array of earth-shattering upgrades.

This recording device was certainly indistinguishable to anyone at first, but I was appreciatively able to lean on the family videographers, and every family should have them, my daughter Rose and her Kira, and they managed not only to capture the fuzz that was left there but also to digitally remaster and do all that other good stuff.

A few lines are lost and that hurts, but they are, fortunately, few and far between.

The background music to which it is set is extraordinarily moving and powerful. And I was shocked, when I first watched the recording, to discover that my son Billy, who was helping me set up the recording, immediately recognized the piece as Max Richter's "Autumn Music."

Surprised, I asked him how on earth he knew that and when he was introduced to it, and he simply said that while he knows little of Max Richter, he had a friend who often listened to a recording of his and that this is the kind of piece that so moves the soul that once heard, it is never forgotten.

The title of it also proved to be all the more appropriate as I listened and listened, again and again, to the words and thoughts of Mary Varick, for much of what she shared was autumnal in both meaning and spirit. She spoke often of ends and finality and the metaphorical colorful and dry leaves that fall in autumn before winter's cleansing. She spoke often of our inevitable encounter with death and of our letting go of this life so as to embrace the fullness of the life to come.

Such thoughts, of course, are not so strange upon such a journey, for Jesus, after all, did die upon the cross and Calvary and finality have ever been synonymous.

And while she clearly did not allow her prayers to become about her alone, anyone reading between the lines would realize that she was clearly letting the Good Lord know that she was ready whenever He was.

Again recognizing that it may well have been her *last hurrah*, we'll now turn directly to this particular reflection upon her stations.

She looked tired, truly tired and weary, but her patented smile and bright and wistful eyes were, as ever, magnificent and inviting. It was, however, almost as if each *station* seemed to take just a little bit more out of her, as if each drained her and took its toll. Because she didn't just reflect or comment, she rather lived the experience with Jesus!

She saw it, felt it, and embraced it in the same manner as did the Son of God's own Mother Mary.

She was not on the outside looking in, but rather on the inside looking out.

She was truly living it, both emotionally and physically.

There was nothing about this that was ethereal or removed or distant to Mary Varick. This was close, in the face, personal.

His cross and her cross were enjoined on Calvary. The stations were her own life's affirmation, her acceptance of her lot in life, her atonement, and her portal to redemption, salvation, and Jubilee.

Only out of the suffering, after all, could there ever be joy, joy, joy!

Anything out of the past moves me, but something like this moves me all the more. It wasn't just my remarkable aunt's holiness, for she was most certainly holy and nor was it her heartfelt words alone. It also was the spectacular setting on the inviting grounds of the Cape that I knew oh-so well, grounds upon which, you breathe in grace and blessings as well as air. There also were the faces of so many beautiful children in the crowd, children who have now long been fully grown themselves and have encountered their own life's struggles and crosses.

Knowing that and knowing even a bit about the hands that life has dealt them as they grew only added to what I witnessed on this tape. For all of us, over time, have tolls exacted.

Then too, there were the faces of those whom Mary liked to call her "Veronicas and Simons," many of whom have, I know, passed through their own heaven's gates, and even, I must add, the face of an ever so youthful and teenage like Father Kevin Carter.

He said the mass but he looked like he was twelve.

Oh, the sweet movement of life and time and spirit, for we were oh-so much younger then, but oh-so much richer and fuller now.

At the *first station*, Mary said that, "It is for the love of you, Jesus, that we come here to travel Calvary's road once again." She noted that for some in the crowd, it might be their first time while there were others who had shared this journey many times. For still others, she poignantly noted, it could well be their last time.

I was immediately struck by the thought that she was addressing herself when she noted her "For some, it could well be their last time." Sure, Jerry was right there as was her Mary and her Bruno and her beautiful grandchildren and her faithful brother and minions of ever faithful companions. But her beloved Bill had long gone home, as had her brothers, Skip and James and Buddy, and her mom had, in recent years, finally joined her dad. Her own beautiful daughter Billie had suffered gracefully, as had oh-so many of her pilgrims over the years, on their own Calvary roads and their own "bound for heaven" or "bound for glory" journeys.

She had served and suffered for a long time, and she mightily identified with Calvary and these stations, and there was no doubt that she was ready whenever the Good Lord was. But then too, she also was prepared to continue serving for as long as needs be.

It was, for her, always and ever, about His will.

For God's will be done!

She still madly loved each and every one of the loved and lost in her life. She had shed a lifetime of tears for them, vessels, as they were, in and through whom, she had discovered the glory and wonder and might of her Jesus. Each and every one was mysteriously embodied in the Eucharist that she so revered, in the Eucharist that daily sustained her. To die, she knew, was to die in the Body of the Eucharist to which she had always been wholly and entirely devoted, in the Body of the Eucharist to which she belonged.

Oh, the miracle of her faith.

Where Mary lived, there was no such thing as doubt.

She then said, "You were, in innocence, my sweet Jesus, condemned to death, and wonderfully, for us, you offered no objection." As we say in a familiar prayer, you freely accepted. You were willing to give your all, to give your last.

"Yet with the slightest provocation," she said, "we cry out, 'Why? Why? Why me, Lord? What did I do to deserve this?' We complain and we cry."

Yet to live, to fully live, we so easily forget also is to embrace the cross and the suffering and our own Calvary. What is sweet is only realized when we know what it is to taste the bitter in life as well.

"Not my will but yours," cried out Mary Varick. "Help us earn the grace to say not my will but your will be done."

At the *second station*, her transitions were off as she rambled a bit, but each and every thought, in and of itself, hit the mark.

It is at this station where Jesus is forced by the Roman guards to take up his cross. "When I hear this, I always become indignant," Mary said, "but then I realize that you picked it up willingly for the love of us. You loved us so that you willingly did the unimaginable and picked up the cross for us."

She then suggested that we all need to follow suit and to pick up our own crosses and to carry them, wherever they need take us, in our own lives. "Without complaint, we must do this and all for you, my sweet Jesus," she said.

"How can we not," she warmly asked, "be willing to pick up the cross for He who so willingly and lovingly carried it for us?"

"What a wonderful lesson, what a powerful example," she added, for it is in Him that we are mercifully saved.

She then asked Jesus to help us to emulate Him, to help us to share more, to help us to make every moment a prayer, and to help us to travel the roads in life that are less traveled, the roads that are not easy.

Yes, she asked quite a lot of herself and of all those in her presence in the flash of a moment's passing. The quick retort from those listening in the bleachers might be, of course, "easy for you to say." But truth be told, as hard as it may be, to live as Mary suggested is the portal to salvation.

Only in the sacrifice, the suffering, and the service is there true redemption and finally—finally—joy.

So if we heed the lesson revealed to us in the *second station*, if we learn to carry our own crosses for love of Him, as her "inner circle" does, and if we sacrifice willingly and lovingly, we will come to live a life uncommon—a life uncommon that is, of course, devoid of Jesus's perfection and likely devoid of Mary's willingness and earnestness as well, but certainly a life that will result in our finding ourselves walking along the right path—in a life lived on "The Way."

For to live as Mary did is to be right with the universe. After all, she powerfully concludes this reflection with, "Because of you, dear Jesus, I love everyone."

To love everyone, she said.

Everyone! She said everyone.

Jesus did, Mary did, but this loving everyone deal likely remains but a goal for most of us—an always tangible and always inviting and "to be resolved somewhere along the road to Calvary" goal.

Clearly, to Mary, understanding Calvary and the meaning of life itself was intricately bound.

At the *third station*, Jesus falls for the first time.

Mary suggested that, "The blood dripping from the thorns on his head and the lashes on his back began to take their toll, as did the torture and the sneers from the crowd and the weight of the cross." Mary makes a pointed effort to clearly explain that He will fall three times and that the level of pain and the level of suffering will rise accordingly.

In essence, the pain that we, his people over the all of the centuries, inflict will increasingly rise.

Unimaginably so.

With each fall, the price exacted by the human race that He saves will be greater and greater still. She suggests that He confronted our lesser and more innocent sins during the first fall. "It may even have been those sins that we were not even aware of at the time—cheating on that spelling test or stealing that candy bar or lying to one's parents for the first time about something inconsequential. Hurting you, still hurting you, still bringing you down, but lesser!"

"Oh-so much lesser," she said.

"We didn't even realize, dear Jesus, that we were hurting you. We did not realize the wrong that we were doing and the pain that we were causing you. We took it so lightly. We did not understand. We were foolish," said Mary.

She then spoke about the most critical life's lesson that we must learn—what is not to offend and not to hurt and not to inflict suffering upon others—upon those we love—and thus upon the loving God to whom we are mystically and spiritually enjoined. After all, in hurting Jesus, we inflicted pain upon our own life's source. Life to life, soul to soul, spirit to spirit! Inexplicably convoluted but incontrovertibly true.

We are, after all, you and I and all those you pass and see and those strangers six thousand miles away, one body. Enjoined together, we are responsible for one another.

We are our brothers and sisters' keepers.

Mary's last words in this reflection were a lament. "Oh, the time it took us," she nearly cried, "to learn not to offend."

At the *fourth station*, it really gets interesting, and Mary throws a curve ball at me, deflating a closely held assumption. For having been privileged to hear her reflect upon the stations in an earlier lifetime and having listened to her own recording, I had assumed that Mary brought Jesus's own Mother Mary more and more into her reflections as time wore on and as she herself internalized the unique suffering of a mother who loses a beloved child.

For as our Blessed Mother did with her Jesus, Mary Varick did with her Billie!

Like Jesus, Billie suffered mightily. Like Jesus, she carried a cross, a cross that she promised her mom she would carry well.

It was a promise fulfilled.

In earlier reflections, it was my contention that all of her thinking went straight to the heart of Jesus—that it was aimed, directed, targeted to Jesus. Where we might all well suggest that it belongs! But it also was my contention that she diverted more and more commentary in later years to the Mother who suffered alongside Him, to the Mother who bled with and spiritually died with Him.

But I was wrong, because Mary, our Blessed Mother, was most assuredly in the heart of her thinking, if not necessarily always in the heart of her commentary, from the very beginning.

I now know this!

Because Mary herself told me so.

Right here! In this recording!

"Do you remember my first time, Jesus?" she asks as she begins this reflection. "Do you remember the first time I did this?"

Not a time and not any old time and not one time, but the very first time.

The very first time!

Answering her own "Do you remember?" she tellingly said, "I told you then that I thought that your Mother suffered even more than you. I did. I told you that, just as I thought that my own cross in life had been heavier to bear for my mom."

Yes, she had the verve to tell Jesus that His Mother suffered even more.

She then went on to suggest that her own cross in life, all of the affliction, all of the suffering, and all of the pain paled in comparison to the cross she had to carry when she watched the intense suffering of her Billie, whose multiple sclerosis was fast tracked, harsh, and exceedingly brutal. To watch as every bodily function shut down and Billie's life ebbed away was for a Mother—was for Mary—as difficult as anything humanly possible.

She suggested that our Blessed Mother Mary felt every lash, every fall, every pounding nail, every cry for relief, every "to die would be preferable" thought, and ever so much more.

"My cross for my beautiful little child who could no longer walk was far greater than my own, just as I know that my mom's was for me and just as I surmise Mary's must have been for you, my sweet Jesus," she said.

She spoke of the perspective that is garnered as one position or place in life gives way to another and another.

You experience, you grow, and you learn to see and to understand life better as one vantage point gives way to another, as one window closes and another one opens. As for Mary Varick, she had been asked to live through "innumerable ports of suffering" and to embrace every kind of pain and tragedy and loss—and to keep on keeping on, no matter how burdened or how humbled.

She then reminded Jesus of the time her suffering mom (Agnes Cassidy) and suffering daughter (Billie Varick Adriance), and she sat before Him right at this station. (Mary here referenced the same 1976 pilgrimage that meant so much to her, the one where her greatest gift—the pilgrimage itself—was embraced by so many in the family.) "There we were," she said, "three generations in two wheelchairs and a stretcher, mother, daughter, and grand-daughter. There we were, three generations offering you our love from our individual chairs and crosses. Since you have called the other two home to you, I stand before you with a heavy heart, certain only of my love for you."

At the *fifth station*, Simon was made to help Jesus carry his cross.

Interestingly, Mary was so fond of saying that, "We need our Simons and Veronicas."

We need people in our lives who serve and fulfill the purposes and roles that Simon and Veronica fulfilled on Good Friday.

We need them always and not just on Good Fridays or Canadian pilgrimages.

"How many times, Jesus, have I talked to you about Simon, poor Simon, who we feel sorry for, because the soldiers made him do it and he did not know you," she said. "Simon, poor Simon, was confused and scared by the guards, but still, he had the privilege, unique in all of history, of helping you bear the weight and bear the burden of your climb up to Golgotha."

"For which, we are forever grateful to him."

While Simon was at first, and probably understandably, reluctant, it is noted that his natural compassion took hold, as he grew more and more concerned with relieving the pressure and burden on a suffering Jesus.

Then Mary did what she loved doing, what she could not help but do every time at this station and that is to draw the tender comparison between Simon of Cyrene (in what is now Libya) and Mary's own First Saturday Club Simons, all of whom willingly extend their hearts and their hands.

"Our wonderful Simons here," Mary said, "help you, Jesus, in helping us. They give up their vacations for love of you, Lord—my willing Simons who no one forces to be here and who so willingly give of themselves." Mary related all that they do from feeding and cleaning and clothing her "inner circle" to pushing their chairs to spending time with them and, most especially, to loving them.

"Without our joyful Simons," Mary noted, "there would be no one to care for her 'inner circle' and there could be no pilgrimage. Neither the grace nor the wonder nor the bounty of the pilgrimage experience would so bless and enlarge their lives as it does."

Yes, there must be Simons.

After all, "Whatever you do for the least of these," Jesus said, "you do also for me."

We must be Simons!

Then too, as we discover at the *sixth station*, "There also must be Veronicas!"

According to the legend, Veronica was a pious woman from Jerusalem who encountered Jesus on the Vio de Larosa on His way to Calvary. Deeply moved by His suffering and looking into His face pouring with sweat and blood, she wiped it with her veil—and found His portrait miraculously imprinted on the cloth when she took it back.

The secularists acknowledge that the white, almost-transparent veil measures about 6.5-by-9.5 inches and bears the dark-red features of a bearded man with long hair and open eyes.

The face on the veil is that of a younger man who has suffered greatly. He looks tired. The marks of blows that have struck him are clear: bruises and other scars on the forehead, clotted blood on his nose, one pupil slightly dilated. Yet, in spite of the evident signs of suffering and pain, the look is that of a serene man who is at peace with himself and his circumstances, of a man who is enduring his suffering with patience and purpose.

Sounds very much like Jesus to me!

"How you must have loved that wonderful, brave Veronica," Mary said. "In the heart and midst of a vicious crowd, who were hungry for crucifixion and blood, she showed you compassion."

Veronica extended herself in service to Jesus as she spiritually bled with Him.

Having held up her Simons just before, Mary now held up her Veronicas—"My beautiful Veronicas, who like your Veronica, wipe the brows of these, the least of your servants, my Veronicas who daily take care of so many of the unseen, gentle things."

In doing it for the least of these, for the broken, the infirm, and the lost, of course, they did it also for Jesus.

So Mary closes by saying, "When the time for our Veronicas comes to go home to you, I am sure, Jesus, that they'll find their image on your heart when they pass." Their image on the Lord's heart and a life fulfilled.

Blessed be the Veronicas!

We must be Veronicas!

At the *seventh station*, Jesus falls for the second time.

"We are older," Mary said. "And the things we do hurt you so much more. We are conscious and we are aware of what we do. Our sins are more painful. You have taken many more steps and this fall hurts terribly."

"Every First Saturday," she continued, "my so good and loving group gathers to pray for peace in the world, yet husbands and wives among us fight and so do parents and children and sisters and brothers and so do neighbors and friends. We are less than we should be. We fail to live as you intend us to live, and we hurt you."

"Each of us," she noted, "needs to be the one who throws the pebble into the stream or river or lake that creates the ripple that then creates the wave of change—and understanding and decency. We are destined and most certainly called to be the best that we can be."

"All for thee, Lord Jesus, in little ways, we need," she added, "to close our lashing tongues, to have the strength to think twice, and the decency to choose kindness."

"Through the pain of the second fall,' she concluded, "please help us to see through your eyes and to reach out for peace, while shutting out anger and eliminating violence."

Simply put, what we do to His creation and what we do to one another, we do to our God—just think about the magnitude of that, just think of what we do to a God who responds to us with only love and forgiveness.

With love and forgiveness always!

At the *eighth station*, Jesus encounters the wonderful women of Jerusalem whose compassion and empathy forever instructs us as to how we ought to live and love.

Mary said, "Oh, Jesus, those who love you so much must weep a little, but not for you as you said. We must weep for others and extend ourselves to others." Those with the gift of true faith recognize that faith is the greatest gift that they have to share.

She goes on to explain that we take this responsibility to "help others find you" too lightly. "You teach us how," added Mary, "but we so easily forget how to share, how to give, and how to love."

We witness the depth of feeling, the empathy, and the goodness for which these women are immortalized, but Mary explains that in turning it back to them as Jesus does, He is suggesting that the tears and the sorrow must not and cannot be ends, in and of themselves. They must be turned into forces for change, forces that will both uphold and redeem others. The emotion and compassion are of no value if they lie dormant, so they must be channeled into sources of energy and action and transformation.

Like these women, we are asked to extend our faith, to extend our love, and to redeem the world. Something, remarkably, that we together can do!

And so too, we, you and I and the stranger down the street, must be the sanctified women of Jerusalem!

"Weep not for me, but for all who suffer and wander in the wilderness!"

At the *ninth station*, Jesus falls for the third time.

"The suffering was so great that it would have been easier for Jesus to lie there and die. This was the most terrible fall of all and the pain was excruciating, yet you struggled to get up to fulfill your promises," said Mary.

"The price exacted here, by Jesus, was in payment for our most grievous sins," she explained. "We are a country that was built upon faith, a country whose motto is 'In God We Trust,' a country of freedom and justice, and yet we kill innocent babies and we pollute this beautiful earth and we exalt indecency and we nurture the power to destroy all of creation."

Such she submitted are our greatest offenses, the offenses that Jesus internalizes as he falls for the third time, the offenses that we must all consciously work to eliminate.

There could be no greater burden for "He who is love" to carry, what were our greatest sins, the collective sins of a society preoccupied with power and greed and selfishness.

As it was a presidential election year, Mary prayed, "Please, dear Father, give us leaders who will do right and put people in power who will do your will."

We can and we must do better for ourselves and for our country and, most especially, for our God.

At the *tenth station*, Jesus is stripped of his garments.

This, Mary suggested, is a station that holds out special meaning for her First Saturday family, her "inner circle," and her Canadian pilgrims.

Here, Jesus was so denigrated and humiliated. He is publicly scorned and laughed at by those for whom he would ask for forgiveness.

Yes, at every turn, no matter the situation, Jesus responds only with forgiveness and love, responds in a way that demands that we too, somehow—some way, do the extraordinary and the remarkable and the seemingly impossible like He.

"My 'inner circle' lives in their chairs and carries their afflictions and goes in and out of hospitals where they are poked and jabbed and prodded. They lose their dignity, as they too are necessarily, in their suffering, humiliated," Mary said.

Her "inner circle" lives the tenth station with Jesus, and there, Mary suggests, they truly atone for all of us.

"Accept the suffering of your 'inner circle' in atonement for the sins committed against you," Mary pleads.

Yes, bit by bit by bit, day after day, in oh-so many ways, the dignity of the disabled gets stripped away. Like Jesus, their humiliation is but another sacrifice extended to win grace for us all.

Humiliation is transformed and becomes a most special gift.

At the *eleventh station* where Jesus is nailed to the cross, Mary appears for moments to be lost, right there upon Golgotha, with her suffering Jesus. She places herself in the station.

Again, within and not from without!

Her love is so palpable, and her emotions are so rich that I can only watch and think that she is literally living this.

This is not a mere remembrance or prayer or story for my aunt. It is a living, cold, harsh, and so bitter reality.

She feels the station and lives the station and does not merely relate the memory of it, as she seems to be present in it. She suffers too.

Physically suffers. Tangibly suffers.

So much so that this *station*, above all others, appears to drain her the most.

Her words come slowly and sadly.

"I think so often of this moment on Calvary's road," she said, "and some say the Roman soldiers did it and others say the Jews did it, but the truth is that we all had a hand in it and that we are, each and every one of us, responsible."

"In the still of the night," she went on, "when I can't sleep, I hear the pounding of those nails two thousand years ago. My poor old heart longs to pull back that mallet and to free you from the agony, but all I can do is beg you to take our love and forgive us for what we did to pound in those nails."

Your love! Our love! The great, great, mind-boggling love that was Calvary and that is Our Lord!

The love of the cross.

The love of a crucified Christ.

At the *twelfth station*, Jesus is crucified and one might assume that this, the death of Christ, would draw great attention from her.

But it is almost as if she cannot linger there and so she says but a few words.

She recalls that John and Mary, our Blessed Mother, and Mary Magdalene are there, and she mentions the image of the body that is pressed against the wood and she reminds us that He did this to redeem the world—to redeem you and me.

Then she just makes a bee line to her "inner circle" and with poignant conviction says, "Love must pay a price—at last, I know that suffering is just the kiss of Christ."

That, by the way, was the last line of a poem that she often recited. Suffering, pain, sacrifice, death, etc., are all but the "kiss of Christ."

To pick up our own crosses, she notes, is to embrace "the ashened figure pinioned against the wood, He who is our love divine."

On the tape, a few lines here are lost but what follows will likely suffice. She said, "Jesus upon the cross was the greatest gift. In the cross, His suffering and our suffering are enjoined as one 'where love must pay its price.'"

I would add only the wonder and the magnificence and the promise of "This day thou shalt be with me in paradise."

There are days when it is but the thought of those words alone that enables me to breathe or to move or to act.

(At this station, the Mass was then said and the Eucharist received.)

At the *thirteenth station*, Jesus is taken down from the cross.

The image of the *Pieta* here crosses my mind as Mary says, "Jesus, this would be such a sad moment for us were we not aware of the happy ending and of your coming resurrection. Were this not so, this would be unbearable. It would have been more than we could take if you did not love us so."

Having just received his Body and Blood in the Eucharist, she notes that all she can think of or focus upon now is the resurrection and Easter Sunday.

He is taken down from the cross and Mary is happy. So something has been literally lifted from her, as if weights and burdens have been removed. I think it is simply because the suffering and agony are over.

For Mary, the act is consummated and there is no more agony, so it is already time, already okay, to let the joy in.

"Since we have you in our hearts," she says, "how can we be sad? We can only strive to be worthy."

Finally, at the *fourteenth station*, Jesus is laid in the tomb.

On the grounds of Our Lady of the Cape, there is a replica of a tomb at this station that pilgrims can enter and visit.

Mary called everyone's attention to it, noting that some may never have seen it before, so she urged them to enter it afterward. "What happens," she explains, "is that you enter and walk through a dark chamber and then, immediately thereafter, exit into today's bright sunshine. That is exactly what death is like, a brief passage through darkness to the wonder of God's own love and brightness."

"That is all death is for those who have Jesus in their lives."

"I often dwell now," she added, "upon the moment of my death, and I pray that my last words on earth will be my very first in eternity."

Those words were, "I love you, Jesus."

And there you have it, the alpha and the omega of her life—"I love you, Jesus."

Again, this was the last time she did this at Our Lady of Cape where she had so often done it before. Decades of practice and thought, a literal lifetime of reflections culminated in the above.

It was her final blessing, her benediction, her remarkably loving way of raising up her greatest love. Maybe, just maybe, it was her magnum opus.

And so she said, "Enough."

Because we have, in the above and its simplicity and clarity, captured Mary Varick and her Calvary roads—captured her great love for the Eucharist, for God, for her family, and her First Saturday family and her "inner circle" and all the Veronicas and Simons surrounding her and the magnificent bounty of all God's creation.

At every single station of the Stations of the Cross, she was telling us exactly "where the love is" that is destined to be the salvation of this world.

There could have been no "joyful and triumphant" were it not for Calvary's road, no "someone in the great somewhere," no chance for "peace on earth."

A final thought.

We have noted the fact that flocks of people generally descended upon Mary at the beginning and end of everything and anything. Always and everywhere, people crowded her to get a piece of her magic.

But not here—not at the end of these stations! It was as if everyone there intuitively knew that she needed a moment alone to exhale and to breathe.

Tired when she began, she was now exhausted.

Completely drained, she needed a few moments alone with the Lord.

So there she sat in her chair with a white sweater on, hands loosely clasped in prayer, misty eyed, with just the faint trace of a smile beneath a serene countenance.

Within and not without, she had, indeed, lived the stations with Jesus. She had bled and suffered with Him and found release only when it, as He had said, was consummated.

And oh, then the joy and that irrepressible smile.

---

## Chapter 7 Placeholders

- Some people are born to write and others to lead and others to act or to sing or to explore the imponderable secrets of the earth, but Mary Varick, most certainly was, among other things, born to move you to tears while inviting you to walk along the road to Calvary with Jesus and with her.

- His cross and her cross were enjoined on Calvary. The stations were her own life's affirmation, her acceptance of her lot in life, her atonement, and her portal to redemption, salvation, and jubilee.

- Only out of the suffering, after all, could there ever be joy, joy, joy!

- I was immediately struck by the thought that she was addressing herself when she noted her, "For some, it could be their last time." Sure, Jerry was right there as was her Mary and her Bruno and her beautiful grandchildren and her faithful brother and minions of ever faithful companions. But her beloved Bill had long gone home, as had her brothers, Skip and James and Buddy, and her mom had, in recent years, finally joined her dad. Her own beautiful daughter Billie had suffered gracefully, as had oh-so many of her pilgrims over the years, on their own Calvary roads and their own "bound for heaven" journeys.

- Yes, she asked quite a lot of herself and of us in the flash of a moment's passing. The quick retort from those listening in the bleachers is, of course, "easy for you to say." But truth be told, as hard as it may be, to live as Mary suggests is the portal to salvation.

- Only in the sacrifice, the suffering, and the service is there true redemption and finally—finally—joy.

- "Do you remember my first time, Jesus?" she asks as she begins this reflection. "Do you remember the first time I did this?"

- Not a time and not any old time and not one time, but the very first time!

- Answering her own "Do you remember?" she tellingly said, "I told you then that I thought that your Mother suffered even more than you. I did. I told you that, just as I thought that my own cross in life had been heavier to bear for my mom."

- "How you must have loved that wonderful, brave Veronica," Mary said. "In the heart and midst of a vicious crowd, who were hungry for crucifixion and blood, she showed you compassion."

- He is suggesting that the tears and the sorrow must not and cannot be ends, in and of themselves. They must be turned into forces for change, forces that will both uphold and redeem others. The emotion and compassion are of no value if they lie dormant, so they must be channeled into sources of energy and action and transformation.

- "In the still of the night," she went on, "when I can't sleep, I hear the pounding of those nails two thousand years ago. My poor old heart longs to pull back that mallet and to free you from the agony, but all I can do is beg you to take our love and forgive us for what we did to pound in those nails."

- And there you have it, the alpha and the omega of her life—"I love you, Jesus."

- After all, it was the last time she did this at Our Lady of Cape where she had so often done it before. Decades of practice and thought, a literal lifetime of reflections culminated in the above.

It was her final blessing, her benediction, her remarkably loving way of raising up her greatest love. Maybe, just maybe, it was her magnum opus.

# 8

# The Nexus of and Witness to
# Sixty-One Years

Upon returning from the annual First Saturday Club Canadian pilgrimage in the early August of 2012, my mind was preoccupied and running over with thoughts that pertain to this work, to Mary Varick's story and legacy.

Our annual journey to the great shrines of Canada in the heart of the summer of 2012 was, as always, bountiful and blessed. But we were once again confronted with that all-too-familiar and annual problem of adjusting to the real world in its wake.

What Mary Varick long ago called "our vacation with God," a week of prayer and reflection, in the company of beautiful and purposeful people, had, as always, filled our cups and hearts and souls with the great love of God. On the sacred and holy ground of Saint Joseph's Oratory in Montreal, Sainte-Anne-de-Beaupre, and Our Lady of the Cape in Three Rivers, we had once again freely opened ourselves up, and the great and sustaining grace of God had, as usual, poured into the nooks and crannies of our being.

It just happens.

Every pilgrimage, it just happens.

Yes, every summer and every time, it happens.

Worthy or not, we are there made full of grace.

Celebrating the sixty-first anniversary of the miracle and cure of Mary Varick's terminal bone cancer at Sainte-Anne-de-Beaupre and the sixtieth anniversary of her Canadian pilgrimage through which she long honored the living instruments of God who had so warmly and lovingly intervened on her behalf, our Blessed Mother and good Saint Anne, we, happy pilgrims, followed in the wake of the thousands who had gone before us. We followed in the wake of our parents and aunts and uncles and cousins and friends and "Simons and Veronicas," past the ancestral pilgrims who walked before us, most of whom, given the passage of time, have long since gone home to God.

In Canada at these beautiful shrines and along these old and familiar paths, we walk among their spirits. Their presence is so rich and so palpable there that it is as if they almost physically lift us up.

There is a rich history that we have, in this work, longed to capture the essence of. Mary's history, of course, but also that of her mission and ministry. To that end, we have been focused upon both The Our Lady of Fatima First Saturday Club and upon its Canadian pilgrimages, because it is in those two entities and in their history where we discover the heart and soul of Mary Varick's purpose. Mary and Bill Varick formed the First Saturday Club that took on the welcome and very meaningful task of bringing her beloved disabled or "inner circle" together on a monthly basis and not merely annually on the great journey to Canada.

Today's First Saturdays are ably administered by Mary Varick's niece Joan Murray and the pilgrimages by both Joan and Mary's granddaughter Maryanne Adriance. They are supported by the great hearts and fertile minds of long-serving spiritual directors Monsignor Paul Bochicchio, Father Kevin Carter, and Father Frank Fano, Newark Archdiocesan priests.

In 2012, Maryanne was lost to other major obligations, but the other four noted above were there to lead us once again. They were heartily assisted by Mike and Amy Lenehan, Saint Mary's then youth ministers; Cathy Buchanan; and Brother Luke Gilchrist, CFC, and others helping Joan nurse pilgrims in need included Dr. Flor Alto, Louise Plentus, Maureen Tierney, and Johanna D'Albenzio.

Those in wheelchairs included Bob Gilleck, Mary Jane Burns, Peter Grzyb, Vione Peloquin, Sister Anna DiCarli, and myself, while those cancelling at the last minute because of health complications, who remained with us in prayer and spirit only, included Hank Colling, Sandi Gautreau, Anne Evans, and Rose Ronda. Later on Christmas Eve of that same year, our great and extraordinary friend Hank, ever a son of the First Saturday family who had a burning love for Mary Varick, peacefully went home to God. The wonderful young volunteers from Saint Mary's in Colts Neck, Holy Family in Nutley, and other parishes in Bergen County—our 2012 class of "Simons and Veronicas"— included Ricky Jewell, Anthony Pesci, Phil Lam, Reuben Pereira, Kaitlyn Lenehan, Chris Duffy, Lizzy Mirasola, Jess Soolin, Mike Buchanan, Alexa Watchorn, Brooke Murray, Joelle Filippi, Jackie Kueken, Paul Smagula, and others.

All of the above "Simons and Veronicas" and their service more than earned a mention here.

While blessed with a tremendous, loving, and faithful band of brothers and sisters, we remained ever conscious of Mary Varick's great legacy and of the fact that there were as many as thirty-seven wheelchairs or more on single "disabled pilgrimages" in the past. As such, our desire and need to serve more and more people in the years ahead remains paramount. To that end, there will be extensive outreach to parishes in the future. And while it is not a numbers game, it is and always will be about service and our determination to grow more intimate with our God through the handiwork of that service—and so, the more served, the better.

We will never forget the elderly gentleman who collapsed in the hallway at the Auberge at Sainte-Anne's on the Tuesday afternoon of our stay. In all likelihood, he went home to God as Ricky Jewell was applying CPR and our Joanie was relentlessly blowing breath into and trying so hard to breathe for him. Oh, how they fought to revive him and to save his life, and while they did restore some color to his gray face and while he resumed breathing for a brief time, his well-worn heart simply refused to cooperate.

To our knowledge, it never did beat again.

It was understood that he went home to God well before the paramedics and authorities even arrived on the scene and well before the many desperately running around finally located a priest. Father David Purcell, a gentle Redemptorist, who had joined us for the Stations of the Cross on the grounds just moments before, was located and he came to the Auberge as did our own Father Frank Fano shortly thereafter, but neither was permitted to approach or pray by the side of the fallen, as the professionals had arrived and the emergency protocols did not allow or permit the same.

This seemed very strange, for he was certainly in a place where the company of a priest would, more than likely or no doubt, have been much preferred by him.

The public authorities did him, I fear, a grave injustice. They must rethink how they do what they do in the hope of saving a life, while at the same time allowing those they serve to move on to the life to come with grace, as they would like to, when their time comes.

To deny any minister of faith access to the dying, when dying is prospectively imminent, is absurd and very, very wrong. The picture of Father Purcell idly leaning against the wall with the multitude of us who had been struck by this obvious life-and-death situation, while the paramedics did their thing, is burnt into my memory.

As a priest of God, that certainly was not what he had signed up for. He had signed up to burn in use for Christ and to bring all possible to Him. But our culture reviles death so much and rails against it so mightily, I fear, that it goes so far as to push the priest aside, when it is prayer and spiritual comfort that is needed and not necessarily heroic efforts.

As we did not know this man at all, there was little or nothing for us to do, but pray.

He appeared to be a friend of two distraught, non-English-speaking French-Canadian women who were able to convey only that they had planned on meeting him there and that he had a pacemaker.

In the aftermath, as we all grappled with watching a man of faith die in our midst, we could surmise only that for whatever reason, he had come to visit Good Saint Anne and Blessed Mother Mary, the Mother of God on holy ground, and that it is certainly not a bad thing to die among such extraordinary friends and in such good company.

I wanted to, at least, know his name so that I could pray for him and not an "oh-so distant" anonymous and cold victim. So I inquired at the desk and learned that his name was Claude Bare and that he hailed from the borough of Saint Agapit which is just south of Quebec City, so I imagined that he well could have been a frequent visitor to Sainte-Anne's, as he lived within easy hailing distance of her beautiful basilica. I imagined that Sainte-Anne's could very well have been home to him. I imagined that it was we and not he who were the strangers.

On Thursday at Our Lady of the Cape, Father Kevin surprised me by asking if I'd like to offer reflections at our traditional Friday morning *Stations of the Cross* by the riverside, which always preceded mass at the twelfth station right upon the grounds.

This was my Aunt Mary Varick's turf; this was one of her go to to-do things in Canada every year. The *Stations of the Cross* and *Calvary's road*, as manifested just before in chapter 7, were her special province. There on those spectacular grounds upon the banks of the Saint Lawrence, I can still picture the sun radiating through the branches of the trees, shimmering above her as her great love of Jesus and her profound understanding of the stations invariably brought people to tears. Our own group of pilgrims, as noted before, would grow in size as all there, upon those grounds, were pulled in by the sheer power and resonance and eloquence of Mary's words, words that enlightened minds and lifted souls and freed spirits.

Oh yes, I was aware of her *Stations of the Cross* legacy and of the fact that the rector of Our Lady of the Cape itself wound up recording her, years ago, for the production of an album that was sold to help defray the cost of building the very Madonna House that we were staying in.

For nearly forty years, it was Mary who delivered the reflections at these stations and for the twenty plus years since her passing, one of our priests. Now, our priests were and are great—truly a cut above—and they too invariably do beautiful work, but they too, like everyone else on the planet, just don't quite measure up to Mary Varick.

And neither did I!

But I had a particular advantage, in that I had been growing especially close to my Aunt Mary while working on this work of love. So I felt her presence that morning. In truth, it's very easy, in that holy setting, to feel the spirits of those well loved and long gone. So the presence of the spirit of Mary Varick did not surprise on this particular August 3 morning. How could it have been otherwise? After all, Mary Varick and the *Stations of the Cross* had in life, on either the last Friday of July or the first Friday of August, long ago bonded together as one.

Oh, I was ready all right, but I absolutely believe that it was she who helped take everything that I said to higher ground.

She took my words and made moving music and, together, we walked *Calvary's road* and we spoke of the price paid at each fall, and when He was pinioned to the wood, we spoke of what it all has to do with our very lives today and with the wonderful "Simons and Veronicas" who were standing right before me still, Mary Varick's *Simons and Veronicas* still. We also spoke of the tears that Jesus instructed the women of Jerusalem to turn into active forces and instruments of spiritual transformation, and we looked to the crosses that we all must pick up and carry, in order to live meaningful and purposeful lives of humility. We added that the suffering was even harder for Mary who was intimately joined with her son in sacrifice, and we especially noted that there is, in the stations, a most remarkable prescription for living.

There, so powerfully and beautifully and hauntingly, in Jesus's great sacrifice on our behalf, we suggested that all lives must be about love and compassion and service and also about personal sacrifice and forgiveness and still even more love, the kind of deep and abiding love that hurts.

"We must," my Aunt Mary said very often, "help Jesus carry his cross."

"Oh, how privileged we are," she would cry out, "to be able to carry the cross for Christ." We are all, she insisted, invited to be *Simons and Veronicas*—invited to bear witness to and to live the passion of Christ in how we conduct ourselves in our every-day lives.

Like all of our pilgrimages, the days were bridged by morning and evening masses, by stations and rosaries and adoration, but also by walks on the grounds and great fun and laughter and by camaraderie and long conversations and by those sacred moments in which yesterday's memories manifested and by the occasional party and our now infamous *"No Talent* Talent Show." I had the pleasure of getting to know so many people better, of being helped by Ricky and Anthony and Brooke and Phil and Flor and Brother Luke and Mike and Kaitlyn, and most especially by my angel sister, Joan.

I fell in love, again and again in love, as I do each year, with so many of our band of brothers and sisters.

I also was delighted that my jokes in a skit mocking Monsignor Paul's directorship of the show were so well received. They included lines like, "The last musical advance or trend that Monsignor took notice of was the Gregorian chant," and "It is said that music is that which expresses the inexpressible, but in Monsignor's case, it is that which expresses the inexcusable." The priests always take the hard hits in our annual *"No Talent* Talent Show."

But I missed my fellow pilgrim and great friend Hank Colling, who had carried the cross with such grace for so long and who, so kindly, helped teach me to do the same when the world turned upside down on me. Not long after, I was to learn that terminal cancer had seized his long broken, but very beautiful body. Again, it finally claimed him on Christmas Eve in 2013, when he was, no doubt, welcomed home.

The priest on TV uttered the words, "Go in peace," and so he did.

I was shocked to learn that it had been twenty-five years for Father Frank and thirty-seven for Father Kevin, both of whom first came to Canada as children. Frank was only ten and Kevin sixteen. And it has been forty-five or more for Monsignor Paul and the lineage for some dates as far back as forty-eight and fifty-five years ago. As her younger brother Father John Cassidy used to say, "Once Mary hooked you, you were hooked for good."

But I was, during the course of this pilgrimage, especially inspired to make this book, *this story of Mary and of her witness on earth*, what it needs to be for you and others. There were things, I realized, that needed to be focused upon and/or crystallized in the beginning and in the end, things about Mary Varick that needed to be better highlighted and/or clarified. There were thoughts that came to me as I rolled through the grounds and beside her sacred haunts, thoughts that I had been searching for in order to bring this project home, thoughts that were there to be discovered in the nooks and crannies of Sainte-Anne-de-Beaupre and Our Lady of the Cape.

Yes, Mary Varick long ago went home to God, but her spirit so lingers there and I brushed up against her often.

There were thoughts about structure and simplicity and meaning—about why we write and about what is there for you to take away from this.

There are, in fact, *six primary notations* that I came away with. If I seem redundant in some cases, I apologize and submit that it is rather about emphasis. I will briefly highlight each, as we go about the business of tying a bow around this loving effort to bear witness to the story of—and to what I humbly and purposefully suggest—is the sanctity of Mary Varick.

# One of Our Own

Mary Varick is one of our own.

Catholic—whole and pure and simple—ever and always of God.

Now this first premise or notation could well be labeled as gratuitous or self-serving, but it is not intended to be so. It is straightforward and honest and from the depths of the soul. It has to do with Catholicism today and with its need to heal from within, as it has been institutionally fractured and disabled.

More importantly for us, it has to do with Mary's prospective role in that healing.

It has to do with a particular and long road to Golgotha that some are made to journey upon.

For years, the Catholic Church, which was the alpha and omega of Mary's life, has been reeling, and not just because of the tragic and great scandal but because all too many committed to serving God as leaders have lost their bearings and inflicted harm upon their own—egregiously and so unnecessarily. It has, at times, attacked its very best religious orders and nuns who work in the muck and mire in the trenches to truly do the Lord's work. When orders like the Sisters of Saint Joseph of Peace and great priests and servants of God, for instance, are made to look for protective cover from the shots coming from their own, something is amiss.

That the Church has allowed itself to become embroiled in controversies, often of its own making, deeply saddens those who have been served so well by the very religious provinces and individuals who have been wrongly challenged.

While this is no place to discuss details, some of this has sadly come home to touch our pilgrimage family itself and as it is ours, so too is it Mary's! Some who stand among the accused are absolutely innocent, and yet while lengthy processes play out, our Church, certainly in the Archdiocese of Newark and the Diocese of Metuchen, punish priests who stand by them and that very innocence, as it runs for cover at the mere hint of accusation. Justice and loyalty and friendship and love are all so inappropriately tossed, and the magnificent service of so many is just wantonly and callously disrupted.

We must remember that Jesus ever identified with the impoverished and the poor and the outcasts and the wrongly accused, and we must standby those who walk in His footsteps and serve the same, in goodness and in grace today. But sadly, the very openness and inclusiveness and proactiveness of religious orders who serve with great love and great faith have left them open to criticism, and that very criticism falls upon those who love them, as does a jagged-edged boulder settling into the pit of one's stomach.

It is, of course, our hope that our new Pope Francis and his great compassion and love will, in time, serve to check this discord and to restore the full integrity of our Church.

But the very fact that this has happened and that it continues to happen, and the very fact that it has touched Mary's First Saturday family are all the more reason for us to look to and to celebrate the life and service of Mary Varick herself, who served yet another contingent of outcasts—the disabled—with unbridled love. It is all the more reason to focus upon a member of the laity who was entirely holy and of God, upon one of the people's own whose life bridges today's controversial divides.

And, yes, my broken church should look to her and celebrate her life.

In Mary, the faithful can be powerfully reminded that holiness and sanctity are not the province of the religious alone, but rather of all of the faithful.

They will, in Mary, see an active goodness and grace that changed the world and that is capable of changing them. And shortly, you will hear the firsthand testimony of a most noteworthy handful who were, indeed, changed by and even saved by Mary.

I have saved the best for the end. Just like the wine at Cana, I have waited to take my best shot now—as the most poignant affirmations of the good effected by the gentle and suffering humanity and spirituality of Mary Varick will finally be shared.

Mary was just an ordinary woman who did so many extraordinary things, while carrying her beloved cross and loving her perfect God.

In her, so many may see themselves and look to ascend and to grow and to serve in their own lives.

*So the first premise is simply that today's broken and muddled and yet still vigilant communion of the faithful needs Mary Varick and her example and her very laity. It needs her great smile and her laugh and her wistful eyes and her passion. It needs her exuberance and her honesty and her extraordinary devotion to the Eucharist and her great goodness and her relentless desire and determination to help bring people closer to their God.*

*Why not a lay saint in whom we can all find fragments of ourselves? Why not a wife and a mother and a cripple? Why not a loving sister and daughter from the Lafayette section of Jersey City who battled polio and brightly rung in the New Year with friends and family and daily embraced the Eucharist, the sustenance of her life? Why not a kid who lumbered down Pacific Avenue on crutches on her way to All Saints Church and its tall steeples and its polished oak pews? Why not the one who couldn't play kick the can or kick ball? Why not Mary Varick or my Aunt Mary or Mother Teresa's friend or Bishop Peter Sutton's "ray of bright light"?*

*Why not let her help us to heal.*

# A Theology of Suffering

The second notation is to again affirm and sharply emphasize her very *theology of suffering*, a set of principled beliefs that have been discussed over and over again in this work, from the top down and the bottom up and the inside out.

In the interest of emphasis, always and every single time, and not redundancy, we relate this theology one last time.

Mary, a childhood victim of polio, was taught by her mom and dad that she was special and that her very affliction was, in actuality, a gift. Her affliction, they assured her, was an invitation by God to become closer to Him, because she was, in her illness, being given the time to think and to pray that those healthier children often lacked.

Most especially, in carrying her own cross well, she was being spiritually invited to help Jesus carry his own cross.

From the beginning, she is taught that affliction and suffering lead to more time for prayer, a closer intimacy with God, and the power, in carrying your own well, to help Jesus carry His cross. All that was negative about disability was turned on its heels, so as to be made positive.

In her youth, Mary said that whenever she saw another child with a disability, she wanted to reach out to them and say, "Do you know how lucky you are? Do you know how lucky you are to be carrying the cross for Christ!"

That was a powerful notion that she would never let go of, and it became the formative tissue of her sustaining *theology of suffering*—the idea that there was in disability an unbridled and overarching joy.

As Mary grew and matured, this invitation to prayer and to intimacy with God and to the higher invitation to help Christ carry His cross and her feelings about the all of this only expanded. She started to dwell more and more upon the attendant suffering rather than the mere disability. For the suffering that accompanied the disability was an active and living force—an energy if you will—and, as such, it could, in fact, become a sacrificial vessel or tool. The suffering could be offered up in sacrifice, and it could be freely given away to God, in order to become the formative tissue of transformational grace for the redemption of others!

Wow! Are you wrapping your arms around the wonder of this? Again and again and again, I have directed attention to this and if I have, in any way, failed to convey its wonder and power, then I have summarily failed.

Disability and the suffering generally attached to the same first gave one more time for prayer and for love and for intimacy with God, but later and invariably and powerfully, it invited one to sacrifice and to transform and to become an instrument of grace, and finally, it empowered one to become a redemptive force and to work, in and through Christ, to redeem others.

That bears repeating—it empowered one to become a redemptive force and to work, in and through Christ, to redeem others

Wow! The disabled, she insisted, were extended a mighty power, the power to transform and to redeem the world, the historic terrain of saints and kings and heroes.

Sure, there was pain to grapple with, but pain too was but a heralded instrument of grace and goodness that freely given to God, in sacrifice, helped to transform and to redeem. Once one invited God to be in the pain with them, after all, it was tempered or tamed and made more manageable than any pill, known to science, could possibly render it.

*Just consider the formula of this second of our six notations, the* theology of suffering—*out of their disability and/or suffering, one sacrifices all and grace, redemption, and inevitable joy are extracted. It is a spiritually transformative process in which the disabled and suffering invite God to be with them and to take their pain in exchange for grace and for goodness.*

Suffering, Mary believed, ultimately enabled the disabled, who she came to refer to as her "inner circle," to become true pilgrims who were privileged, always, to do God's work on earth.

It gave them the privilege of carrying the cross.

# Defining Mary

*To best describe Mary Varick, we look to our third notation which suggests that she was always on fire for Jesus Christ—on fire for God and for the Blessed Mother—on fire for the Holy Trinity and Sainte-Anne-de-Beaupre and Saint Joseph and her family and her pilgrims—on fire for the Eucharist which was her profoundest and greatest love.*

In the above, she found extraordinary happiness and so she smiled her very big smile, forever and always, upon the world. Her confinement to a wheel chair never precluded her from traveling in the express lanes, as she sought always to bring others home or closer to God and to holiness.

Forever a pilgrim, her life was a pilgrim's song.

She was a great friend of many bishops and monsignors and countless priests and nuns and of the most disabled and broken and lacking among us. The lowliest to her stood always on the same ground as the most lauded and esteemed. As a little girl, she never forgot the tremendous happiness that was hers when she was assigned the simple task of placing the small statue of the Baby Jesus into the stable as Christmas arrived. At midnight or at the exact same time that the pope heralded, "*Christus natus est*," or "Christ is born," from Saint Peter's in Rome, she placed Baby Jesus into the family creche.

In a very real way, that is how best to think of or to see Mary, as the child who never stopped finding great joy in placing or bringing Jesus into the lives and hearts and midst of people.

For truly, bringing Jesus to people was her life's work.

Into every home and every place and everywhere she roamed!

She smiled broadly, she spoke wistfully, and she invited all she encountered, in oh-so many ways, to join her in going home, to both salvation and to the sanctity to be nurtured within.

# Her Ministry

*As often explained within this work, Mary's ministry was largely comprised of both the* annual pilgrimages *to the great shrines of Quebec and to the administration of the* Our Lady of Fatima First Saturday Club. *Through both, she served her suffering disabled or her* "inner circle" *and the countless "Simons and Veronicas" who worked with her. Their mission was to help carry the cross for Christ, to carry the cross for redemption and peace and love.*

While the love and joy noted in "Defining Mary" enveloped every aspect or object of her life, her ministry was twofold. She created the *Our Lady of Fatima First Saturday Club*, first to bring her suffering disabled or "inner circle" together on a monthly basis to share mass, to pray the rosary, and to enjoy each other's company and socialize over a meal. Secondly, they were to be a force to regularly pray for peace in the world, but the truth is that they rather became a force for each other—a source of sustaining sustenance. In getting them out of their homes and their hospitals on a regular basis, another world and another family were created for them.

For many, this extended family or the First Saturday Family was the only family in their lives. Each month, another parish would host the club and extend both hospitality and joy. Largely through the efforts of Joan Murray and her great team from Saint Joseph's parish in Oradell, New Jersey, this faithful ministry continues to this very day.

The second aspect of her ministry revolved around the *annual pilgrimages* to the great shrines in the province of Quebec, Canada. Yes, there were the occasional junkets elsewhere, to Lourdes and Fatima and Rome and to Russia and the Holy Land and Guadalupe, but it was the shrines of Quebec that forever were at the heart of her mission and that were forever defined by her own pilgrims as the places that brought them peace and understanding and hope.

Her devotion to them and to what they brought to her pilgrims was sacred.

## The Shrines of Quebec or Home

For the all of her second life or the all of the second block of thirty-eight years that followed her July 17, 1951 miracle, Mary Varick led pilgrims to her homes away from home, to Saint Joseph's Oratory on the crest of Mount Royale, the highest promontory in Montreal; to Sainte-Anne-de-Beaupre, or her "heaven on a hillside" where she was cured of the cancer; and to Our Lady of The Cape, on the banks of the Saint Lawrence in Three Rivers. There would be, at least, one disabled pilgrimage each summer, during the week that bridged July and August, and during the heydays, she actually took as many as four journeys each year, from June through September.

The point to be noted here is that these three places, these three shrines, were the sacred and holy and perpetual ports of call. They were her homes away from home. They were accordingly mentioned again and again in this work, and there was a particular focus upon each of them in chapter 1. *The point is— notation 5—that you cannot get Mary Varick—that you will neither know nor understand her, unless you know these three ports of call to God for her—Saint Joseph's Oratory, Sainte-Anne-de-Beaupre, and Our Lady of the Cape, three shrines that were as much home to Mary Varick as were Jersey City and Newark, three shrines that were woven into and buried within the deepest recesses of her heart.*

Each, in its own right and own way, is a genuine slice of heaven. They invite you to reflection and to prayer and to peace and, most importantly to your God.

They invite you home.

# A Recognition and a Tribute

*The first component of the sixth and final notation is that no family is perfect and that neither was our First Saturday Family. The second was that it was predominantly comprised of people of good will and great faith, by people of goodness and grace.* Yet indeed, there were some who were sinfully human or who lived on society's edges. Organizations like this historically attract many victims of addiction and abuse, as did the First Saturday Club, along with its own small handful of the socially pathological. Most of these, through their involvement, however, were helped and driven to be become better or to heal. In doing better and in giving more, in transcending and rising and reaching higher, many who were troubled, indeed, ascended, but not all.

Even though, a nearly perfect woman gave her all!

Even though, she loved each and every one of them mightily!

Over the wide expanse of the years, of course, the overwhelming majority were truly a pilgrim people, people who were destined, in devotion and service, to lovingly serve and to become increasingly intimate with their God.

Some, in search of God, walk the Way of the El Camino de Santiago in the Pyrenees, some go to the Holy Land to explore the paths that Jesus walked, and still others go where they can be surrounded by the great Renaissance art of Rome, but those in Mary's First Saturday Club go to embrace the "inner circle" and to do good works. They go to Montreal and count the steps and wrap themselves up in the great goodness and profound humility of Saint Brother Andre and to the Scala Sancta or to the Immaculate Conception Chapel at Sainte-Anne-de-Beaupre, that "heaven on a hillside," and finally to the Rosary Bridge and the Old Chapel along the banks of the Saint Lawrence on the beautiful grounds of Our Lady of the Cape.

And those three are more than enough for anyone's lifetime.

The Archdiocese of Newark is today the repository of information, forwarded by some good souls who bore witness to Mary's holiness and by others who believe that it was through her intervention that miracles occurred or that favors were granted by God to them. The above was forwarded to the archdiocese, at the request of Father Kevin Carter, in the interest of advancing Mary's cause for sainthood.

All well and good, but only time will tell, and without advocacy from the faithful, achieving the same remains doubtful. But again, let me be clear, I do not write to simply advocate her cause.

*I write to bear witness to her story and to her holiness and to her extraordinary devotion,* and to do what I can to pay forward the grace and goodness that have been showered upon me in doing so. *I write to pay tribute to Mary, to thank her, and to share her with as many people as possible.* Through her example and faithfulness and service and goodness, it is my hope to touch and to advance and to inspire.

It remains my hope to give you Mary.

Through and in and by her story, I hoped to make some difference, for in touching Mary, as you will here, one cannot help but reach higher. It becomes as natural as breathing.

*I write because Mary still has gifts to give and not to advance a cause that I absolutely believe she has already won. Of course, the recognition of the church and the faithful would be wonderful, but humility and goodness and grace and holiness are not the products of glory or honor or even well-deserved recognition.*

*To be certain, there is no contest to win*

*They are their own prize, and Mary has them in abundance, and they are beyond contestation.*

*Again, it is this writer's opinion that she already is a saint,* which, we pray, may one day be acknowledged and proclaimed by the church that she was intimate with and ever faithful to. But, but, but! It need not be proclaimed in order for it to be, as all those, fortunate enough to be intimate with her, would loudly proclaim.

I received copies of much, but not all, of the material known to be in that archdiocesan record. The "not all" includes the written testimony of Mother Teresa, although we did find verification of what she wrote in a copy of a letter sent to Father Kevin Carter by the then bishop of Newark, Archbishop Theodore McCarrick, on February 12, 1992.

In it, he wrote, "I did get a note from Mother Teresa about our friend, Mary. I am glad that we sought it. It is testimony from another holy lady."

Handwritten from Mother Teresa, it was said to have read, "Mary Varick was a very holy person and she offered everything for the salvation and sanctification of priests." In his note, Archbishop McCarrick also suggested to Father Kevin that they needed to talk more to make sure that they "were doing everything to keep on track for Mary's cause."

When dissected, one realizes just how powerful a sentence Mother Teresa forwarded, in that she referred to our Mary as a "very holy person," a very holy person who did "everything." Now, it is no small thing to do everything or to give the all that one has to give or, in effect, to bleed oneself dry for a cause.

But that is exactly what everything is!

It is the giving all one can possibly give.

And what cause does Mother Teresa single out among the many possible choices? Why she suggests that Mary was, in her intimacy with the Eucharist and in her devotion to the Blessed Virgin Mary and Good Saint Anne and so many others, an active acolyte or advocate for "the salvation and sanctification of priests." Ever devoted to her "inner circle" and broken disabled, Mother Teresa knew Mary well enough to appreciate her overarching love for the priests who gave themselves—lock, stock, and barrel—to the Lord and to her.

Doing so, Mother Teresa believed only helped them perfect their own vocations. Doing so brought them closer to their God.

Yes, Mary loudly, boisterously, tearfully, joyfully invited them to embrace Jesus—to be Jesus.

*Priests, beginning with her two younger brothers Jack and Skip, were always at the very heart of her ministry. And note, suggests Mother Teresa, she wasn't just after their salvation, but rather the ultimate, their sanctification* and their standing among the holy saints. In giving her all to them, they gave their all to her own and grace abundantly flowed. Monsignor Paul is in his forty-fifth year of doing so and Father Kevin is in his thirty-sixth. Indeed, their mutual service and pursuit of sanctification and Mary's are forever entwined, as were their ministries.

The old First Saturday Club stationary comes to mind as I envision the names of the more than thirty priests and one bishop—Bishop Martin Stanton—whose names graced the letterhead, all of whom were touched and moved by Mary's fire and light.

On the Mother Teresa front, I very gratefully, with Mary Anne Adriance's help, received copies of a handful of short and highly personal notes that she sent to Mary Varick, her friend, notes which shed far greater light upon what she thought of her friend, Mary.

What is more, I also came across wonderful written testimony from Mary herself about her life with Mother Teresa. It was penned on the back or "flip side" of *First Saturday Club* stationary, in as informal a fashion as possible. Entitled "My Life with Mother Teresa"—not her friendship or her time or her encounters, but her life—it was a love story.

Mary describes her glowingly—"How does one even begin to talk of this tiny, less-than-one-hundred-pound gift of God's love? She is as gentle as a summer rain, as strong as a dynamo, and so close to Jesus that she exudes His love wherever she goes."

She met her, by chance, in 1971, at the twenty-fifth anniversary celebration of Sister Marie Bernard, a Franciscan Handmaid of Mary and faithful pilgrimage nurse. Kindred spirits, for years, thereafter, Mary and Jerry Sheehan would pick Mother Teresa up at the airport and help her run her errands when in New York City. When Jerry joked about her driving for a change, she said, "She would only drive them into eternity when they still had so much work to do for God."

Mary explained that when Mother's worldwide fame ascended, she became surrounded by volunteers and their transport services were no longer required.

Mary, however, would still be with her at all significant events, when at the United Nations, whenever members of her order took their vows, and when she spoke at events. They also would spend down time together.

Once Mary confessed that she felt awed and humbled to be in the presence of one who did such tremendous worldwide work for God. Mother Teresa's response was, *"Your work is just as precious to Jesus, Mary. Shelter and food can be provided for the homeless and hungry of the world, but the poverty one faces here is so much more painful. How many lonely, unwanted shut-ins are there in this land of plenty? Each time you bring your First Saturday family to mass, as you go from parish to parish, it becomes an eloquent sermon. Willing volunteers give of themselves to care for your severely handicapped members, who have learned to carry their crosses for Jesus, offering them to Him through Mary for peace in the world. Oh, what an eloquent sermon! Never underestimate your work, Mary. Never!"*

Wow!

How often, Mary noted, Mother Teresa's words kept her going when it all seemed too much for her.

While we have written of her last visit to Billie, Mary's first daughter, and of Mother Teresa's profound advice that it was "time to give Billie to Jesus and for Mary to go to Russia for God," the truth is that Mother Teresa visited Billie no less than three other times and, at least, twice upon her own suggestion. Upon one of the visits when Billie was first committed to a stretcher, but before she lost her voice, Mother took her in her arms and said, "Billie, I need you, for you are doing what I cannot do. When I grow weary and my work seems so heavy, I will remember you lying helpless and still. If you offer these long hard days for me and I offer my tired working days for you, together we become a perfect act of love for Jesus and both of our lives become precious and holy." Before her voice was stilled, Billie spoke often of the meaning that Mother Teresa had given her suffering. Mary records her saying, "Each day is valuable and worthwhile, Mom, when I live it for Mother Teresa."

Indeed, their lives were enjoined. Mary Varick and Mother Teresa shared rosary beads and bread and company and rides and masses and their devotion to the Eucharist and their great love.

They also shared and gave each other their service to others, one to the disabled and the other to the poorest of the poor.

As to the letters, the only one dated was sent in November of 1978. In it, Mother Teresa notes that she was so "happy" to get Mary's letter. She inquires about the family and suggests that she is praying for all, but most notably for her Theresa or namesake. At the time, Jerry Sheehan was a "brother" in her missionaries, so she also notes how glad she was to learn that Mary will be there to hear him take his vows. She adds that she will not be able to come over to "your side," the United States, that year, but that she will be with her and her two families in prayer and in spirit.

This tender letter also makes a moving observation clearly prompted by Mary's loss of Billie only a year earlier. Mother Teresa wrote,

> *You know God loves you with a very tender and delicate love. You have been His love and compassion, His Sunshine of Joy, His hope of eternal happiness to so many, many souls and it is only natural that in being so close to Jesus' heart, you must share the pain and the loneliness. You are all right, Mary—it is only the kiss of Jesus.*

Here, while profoundly holding Mary's own saintliness up, she also dialed directly into the very nexus of her "theology of suffering" in that the pain and sorrow and loneliness of loss and separation were referred to as but the "kiss of Jesus," the line that Mary herself referenced very often.

"You are all right, Mary—it is only the kiss of Christ."

Others might well have been blown away by the directness, rawness, and almost harsh honesty of that sentence, but not Mary. *That sentence was an affirmation of the very story of her life. That sentence was the culmination, the omega, and the wonder of her story.* In the pain and in the suffering, there was the greatest of loves, the love of Jesus who knew just what it was to bleed out for all of us.

I read that line and pictured my aunt at the altar, with her hands clasped in prayer, the moment before—just the precious moment before—she was to receive the Eucharist.

But in the moment immediately after I penned the line above, my daughter, Rose, called because she had to speak to someone about a breaking news story—the numbing December 14, 2012 mass murder of twenty young children and of twenty-six altogether in an elementary school in Newtown, Connecticut, children who were looking forward to Christmas.

Just to think that I was reflecting upon Mother Teresa's and Mary's "It is only the kiss of Christ" at the very moment this happened.

As my heart dropped and the "Oh my God, why?" reverberated within and my mind turned to the families of the slaughtered innocents, I again imagined my aunt, literally pictured her, at the altar and reflected upon the kiss of Christ and the unfinished work that we, as a society and a people, must do to be worthy of the love of God.

I imagined the cherubim and seraphim of Advent and the heralding cry of "*Christus natus est*" and Mary Varick and Mother Teresa and my Lord embracing those whose lives were just lost. As we are, in this moment, lost! Too soon, too soon for us! Too wrong for us! Too tragic for us! Too unfathomable for us and only the perfect love of a loving God can sustain us.

For we are otherwise lost!

*Were there no Bread of Life and no kiss of Christ, there could be no life or light in a world where such madness threatens to break us.*

*But it does not break us, because faith never succumbs to madness or even to mass-indifferent murder.*

*It does not break us because the promise of redemption is ours and the Bread of Life is there for us, in the Eucharist, and Christ's arms are ever and always open. No matter the darkness, there is always the light. "You are all right, Mary—it is only the kiss of Christ." As Billie suffered and as Mary and Teresa lived and died in the suffering of others and as these children were taken in a rapid and sudden and appalling fury and in that moment to come when our own bodies will break, there must be—there will be—the kiss of Christ.*

*There is always the kiss of Christ!*

*To be worthy is but to lay our selfish tendencies down and to give ourselves away in faith and in love.*

In light of today, our only response must be to go to faith and to love.

Mother Teresa did so always. Mary Varick did so always. In suffering and in tragedy and in humility and in our hopelessness, to God! "Yes, Mary, you are all right—it is only the cross of Christ.

Earlier, we wrote that Mother Teresa and Mary were kindred spirits, who knew and touched and embraced the soul of the other. That is so clearly affirmed in this most loving and moving expression of consolation.

It is, after all, all God's—and Mary well knew that. But there is more, Mother Teresa suggested in writing, "You are his, and He is yours, Mary."

Billie's pain, Mother Teresa proclaimed, was but "the kiss of Christ"; and there could be no greater testimony than to be looked upon by one who the entire world's faithful knew to be a saint, as the Lord's own "Sunshine of Joy" or "hope of eternal happiness."

Such words, so lovingly intoned and so positive, stun we who are among the fortunate to hear them.

Then, as to advice, Mother Teresa so simply noted, "So try to give them a big smile with great love." No one, after all, need do anything more than to do all that they do "with great love." Mother Teresa's famous mantra was "to do small things with great love." It was never the action, but rather the power of the emotion and intention. If powered by great love, the ends would out.

In a previous note, framed by a "My Dear Mary" and a "God Bless You" from what was obviously earlier in 1977, Mother Teresa writes specifically about the suffering of Billie. The writing here is more rushed, as the lettering is larger, and one imagines that it was likely penned shortly after her visit to see Billie with Mary in the late Spring of 1977, when Billie was most grievously ill and death unceremoniously stalked.

Here, she wrote, "*God is good to you even though your child is going through this again and again, sharing in Christ's own passion. Look up, Mary, and see only Jesus in your suffering child.*" We must, each and every one of us, pick up the cross and carry it, again and again, Mary Varick said time and time again.

We must give the pain away to God, she said again and again, and so transform the world through hard-earned, tear-scarred, and redeeming grace.

Likewise here, her gentlest of all possible friends poignantly, in the throes of raw and rugged emotion, reminded her of the same.

The fullness of life is manifested there in the devastating passion of Christ and there in the throes of death by multiple sclerosis.

In later years, there were a couple of simple, prayerful notes. In one, she wrote, "Jesus loves you, Mary. Love others as He loves you." Those words were written over a prayer card of Mother Teresa's that read,

> *Mary, Mother of Jesus, give me your heart, so beautiful, so pure, so immaculate, so full of love and humility that*

*I may be able to receive Jesus in the Bread of Life, love
Him as you loved Him, and serve him in the distressing
disguise of the Poorest of the Poor.*

Mother Teresa herself was pictured, in prayer, by the side of
the card. I was struck by the fact that *"Poorest of the Poor"* was
capitalized, as was the *"Bread of Life,"* the one juxtaposed to the
other, the one clearly and visually incorporated into the other—
Jesus into the *poorest of the poor* and those bleeding and destitute, in turn, into Him. And so it was with Mary Varick's broken,
lonely, and often forgotten disabled. Mary saw Jesus in her disabled "inner circle" and her disabled in Him, as did Mother Teresa
in her steadfast and perfect service to the *poorest of the Poor.*

To look at this note and the image of Mother Teresa is to be
captivated by the love emanating from it and to realize that it
represents one of the million or two or five or ten million or more
expressions of love in the life of one who referred to herself as
"just Teresa." It, like the others, is but a mere slice of the powerful
love that never stopped flowing from one of our age's universally
recognized saints, and it bears witness to that saint's recognition
of the very same kind of love that drove the life of our Mary.

*In how they lived and how they loved and how they served, they
were truly cut from the same cloth.*

The fourth note found among Mary's belongings poignantly
affirms the above, as Mother Teresa wrote, "God love you and
keep you in his Love for all the love you give." She asked Mary
how things were in the hope that all was well, and she asked
Mary to please pray for her and her people—her "poorest of the
poor" in whom she saw her Jesus.

Given the tenor of these notes, the familiarity, the mutual
understanding, the sense of belonging, and the very type of questions asked, one gets the impression that there were more and
that these two women of God had each other's backs. While
noted earlier, that is again why Mother Teresa, who rarely got to
the States more than once a year, if that, was there to visit with

Mary's dying daughter Billie no less than four times; there to visit with a dying Sue Anne Murray, Mary's great-niece and my sister Mary Anne and her husband Bill Murray's eight-year-old daughter; and there to be with a dying Mary herself at Saint Michael's Hospital in Newark in 1989, there to say good-bye to her friend and to raise her up to Jesus and to ask for her help, because she had earned the grace to go to God first.

In abject humility, Mother Teresa looked upon "Her Dear Mary" as more blessed than she, as a friend who had run the race and earned a victor's crown.

At the time he wrote his testimony on behalf of Mary, *Archbishop Peter Sutton's* flock was in the Archdiocese of Keewatin-Le Pas in the province of Manitoba, Canada. Having met Mary when he was a young priest who spent his summers at Our Lady of the Cape, he like so many priests who Mary met was pulled into her orbit, and a life-sustaining friendship evolved.

Again one hears Mother Teresa's voice, "for the salvation and sanctification of priests."

His testimony is personal and rich and very loving. I have carved out a few excerpts from it that best capture his intent, which was clearly to hold up Mary Varick as a holy woman, whose cause does not merely warrant, but rather demands consideration from the church.

*Yes, he uses the word* demands.

He refers to the *Monday Evening Prayer, Week 3 of the French Edition of the Liturgy of the Hours* where there is a verse that reads, *"It is through much suffering that we come to God's Kingdom." To that, he added, "This is my humble and intimate way of saying that if Mary isn't in God's heaven, I'm not too sure at all that I can put human terms to expressing what heaven is all about."*

In essence, he argued that if Mary is not raised up and blessed in heaven—that if she is not in the arms of the Lord—then he would not be able to speak of heaven, for nothing about what we do as people of faith would then make any sense. *Faith and love personified, as they were in Mary, must exact a loving response from God—can only exact a loving response from God. Of this, there is and can be no doubt, Archbishop Peter suggested.*

He went on to explain that the group of people he first met with Mary at Our Lady of the Cape, when he was a young priest, had been inspired by her and molded into *one faith-filled family.* "They were," he explained, "men and women who knew the suffering of the cross and the joy of the resurrection."

In writing of her, he could not help but think of all of them, of her "inner circle" who embraced her theology of suffering and her insistence that the answer lied in freely embracing one's trials and tribulations always for God's greater purposes and needs.

But his purpose in bearing witness to Mary was to "add his personal word of appreciation of and admiration for Mary's example" in his own life and for her long-suffering tribute to her God. "Her style of spirituality," he further noted, "was totally Trinitarian, never haughtily theological, but well punctuated with tears, both of pain and of joy."

Totally open and at peace in telling God to take her as she was, without shadow or pretense or pride, simple and humble, that is the Mary he wrote of. *"Among all of my acquaintances," he continued, "this woman of the cross, this joyful wheelchair-bound lady has surpassed any teaching I've had on the meaning of Jesus' passion and Jesus' love for the faltering followers of an unbounded hope in the Great Reward promised by Jesus to those who allow themselves to love and to love without counting the cost."*

*To Mother Teresa, she is a "Sunshine of Joy" and to Bishop Peter Sutton, always she is, "among all of his acquaintances, a witness to Jesus' passion and Jesus' love."* He wrote that and then drew the following picture:

"One of my most memorable experiences with Mary and her fellow pilgrims was to see her mother in a wheelchair, her daughter Billie on a stretcher, and Mary commenting on the fourth of the Stations of the Cross where Jesus meets his Mother. This scene and prayer have been etched in my mind, for indeed, He touched the sorrowful mothers there."

Earlier, we commented upon that same remarkable scene on the grounds of Our Lady of the Cape where three generations of suffering Mothers grieved and prayed together, in "faltering" faith for what well might have been Mother Teresa's "salvation and sanctification of priests." Out of themselves, selflessly, for their fellows, their community of faith, and their church.

He concluded his testimony with this,

> An intimate friend of Jesus, a woman of simple, passionate prayer; a woman with a tremendous sense of the divine providence in her life and the life of her family and the life of her friends…may Mary's memory lead us to a greater fidelity and may her prayer accompany those who loved her so dearly as she wheeled her way into our lives."

*And so to the* "Lord's Sunshine of Joy" *and* "witness to Jesus' passion and Jesus' love," *we add the profoundest of all possible titles—that of* "an intimate friend of Jesus."

*This is how the holy people in her life saw her.*

*This is exactly who and what she was, and it clarifies and moves and astounds.*

*Mary Varick was above all an intimate friend of Jesus.*

Previously and unsurprisingly, *Father Jacques Rinfret*, the once and longstanding pilgrimage director at Our Lady of the Cape and Mary's dear friend, the author of the forewords to all of her books, had submitted a five-plus-page narrative to the Newark Archdiocese, singing Mary's praises in a profound way in which only he could.

Beautifully and profoundly and lovingly, his words foreshadow those that Archbishop Peter Sutton so lovingly echoed. In fact, each echoes the other.

These humble priests of God so mightily loved her. Father Rinfret wrote,

> In all my life as a priest, I have never met a person who seemed so intimate with God. She talked about HIM as you would about your best friend. As I wrote in the "Foreword" to her second book, *Not Without Tears*: "This book leaves me with a memory of love that permeates each chapter, each line. I envy her the intimacy that she has reached with Our Divine Savior. And I know that one of the great graces that I will have to render account for at the end of my life will be to have known Mary Varick so well. One cannot come near a fire without feeling its warmth. As such, one cannot approach Mary Varick without feeling the warmth of her love for God. It is a precious grace to have known Mary.

As I continue to copy and listen to the words of these most intimate of recollections, by people who devoted their lives to the service of their God, I am consistently blown away by the sheer power of their witness or testimony…and I am ever reminded of Mother Teresa's *for the sanctification of priests*.

They loved Mary so because she and her intimacy with her Savior profoundly affected them and impacted them and made them stronger in their service, their faith, and their grace.

Yes, for the *sanctification of priests*, wrote Mother Teresa.

Father Rinfret diligently details what he referred to as the "unbelievable events of her life," events that required the strongest of faiths. He maintained that she took each and every hit, no matter how difficult or challenging, as but another occasion to speak both privately and publicly about the great love of God for us all.

*He wrote, "The heavy crosses that weigh on each of us (handicap)*
*have been placed there by Christ Himself, and the only element of*
*choice which is ours is whether we will sanctify our sufferings for the*
*love of God, or whether we will squander our chance for sainthood,*
*in useless complaints and discontent. One does not have to die to feel*
*God's nearness."*

In accepting and celebrating it all, Mary squandered nothing. She took it all and infinitely more!

He recalled, just as her grandson Michael did, that each and every day of her life revolved first around the celebration of the Mass and around the receipt of the Eucharist—always the Eucharist. He explained that this wasn't just at the Cape, "But also when I visited her at home, where I often remained over-night: the next morning, Mass was always the first item on the agenda." During private visits to the Cape, it was always, "When are you saying Mass?" Everything in the day revolved around the Mass.

Father Rinfret closed his testimony with the following:

> I remember one of our professors in Theology telling us "that the closer we get to God, the more stable we become." This I have noticed concerning Mary. In the twenty years that I have known her, she remained the same person—stable and constant. Her serenity was contagious and her "heroic life, personal holiness, and selfless dedica-tion to the honor and glory of God were a true example of catholic womanhood." May the Church one day recognize her as a Saint, as many people around here already believe she is.

While it is referenced earlier, I would be remiss if I failed to include the witness of the celebrated Bishop Sheen. Of Mary, he wrote, "Everyone who has ever known you has been inspired by your identification with the Suffering Christ who is on the Cross until the end of the world in persons like your good self."

Yes, her identification with the suffering Christ.

A fascinating letter also was submitted by a *Kathleen Miri of Jackson, New Jersey,* a friend and fellow parishioner of Mary's daughter Barbara. She secured a number of Mary's famous Mass cards where her magnificent smile was juxtaposed to the image of a smiling Jesus. They were, among others, secured for and utilized by close and dear friends of her sister Macie—*Meg and Joe Coltran.* Their young daughter Lauren had been diagnosed with neuroblastoma at the age of six months, upon which she was treated with chemotherapy for nearly ten months.

*When not quite a year and one-half, radical surgery was being planned at Sloane Kettering, as the tumor was growing on the inside of her spine and attaching to the heart. The planned surgery involved first removing vital organs before scraping the tumor. At the time of the surgery, Meg and Joe held Mary's card and repeatedly prayed over it, pleading with Mary, as one Mother to another, to help their little baby.*

The doctors then opened her up only to find that the tumor was gone—just gone. Their work was finished and she was, oh-so suddenly, declared cancer free.

*Yes, the tomb was empty and the tumor was gone!*

*Miri wrote, "I truly believe, in my heart, that it was Mary Varick who was responsible for this cure,"—as do the Coltrans.*

*Again, it must be noted that we struggle with miracles and have trouble accepting that which was an impossibility just the moment before. So it was with Mary Varick in 1951 and so it was with Mary's Lauren in 1990.* Suddenly, the cancers were gone, in and through Mary, by God alone, who is the source of all that is miraculous.

*Suzanne Gallagher* of Easton, Pennsylvania, submitted a very faithful letter with detailed and specific testimony relating her prayers to Mary to positive outcomes in moments of crisis. *She attests to Mary's direct intercession on behalf of her baby, Joseph, who survived a troubled pregnancy and then overcame multiple infec-*

*tions, internal problems, and blood disorders in a neonatal intensive care unit.*

*She wrote, "Mary Varick intervened for us. It isn't often that some-one as special and as holy as Mary Varick comes into one's life, and we feel very blessed to have her as our special friend in heaven."*

*As for me, I write this long after the doctors told my wife that I would never again be able to utter a cognitive thought.* And my heart never gave out on me as predicted and my kidneys alone came back to fully function for years after six months of complete renal failure.

And I alone seem to have survived what no one my age ever did before.

So many prayed to Mary on my behalf, and I have miracles galore of which to speak.

Truly I do and I am Mary Varick's own.

*But like her, after fifteen months of near-death battles and comas and amputations, I returned to the world wholly disabled and ready and willing to carry the cross, as Mary would have it. I returned ready to live her "theology of suffering" and to bask in its unique bless-ings and graces. After all, she would, most certainly, have told me that, "It is but the kiss of Christ."*

There were other letters submitted, faithfully insisting that Mary helped with everything from the taming of arthritis to acute back pain to the long-delayed procurement of disabil-ity payments.

For the Church's consideration, therefore, there are Mary's own miracle, as verified in the *Archives of Sainte-Anne-de-Beaupre,* Lauren's miracle, and the miracles that returned me to life, maybe for efforts like this, I sometimes think—maybe to be a witness to the sanctity of her life. And there is Baby Joseph, but especially, there are the words of three most holy people, Mother Teresa of Calcutta, Archbishop Peter Sutton of Keewatin-Le Pas, and Father Jacques Rinfret, first and foremost, of Our Lady of the Cape, all of whom are, to me, saints themselves.

For, oh, they were and are holy.

This may be a peculiar comparison, but it fits.

There is a scene in the movie *We Are Marshall* about a football program that is beginning to rebuild the season after a tragic plane crash took the lives of every coach and player on their team. There is a moving scene in a church where the new head coach suggests to one of his assistants that, for them, it is not about winning. Not at Marshall, which could well be the only team in the country for whom it is not about winning! "No," he said, "what matters is only that we suit up and take the field. What matters is only that we play the games."

And so it is today with Mary's ministries, after sixty-two years of striving and contriving!

Services might not be as grand or as well attended as they once were under Mary's tutelage, but people still suit up for the First Saturdays across the northern tier of New Jersey and they take the field, on pilgrimage, at the great shrines of Canada each summer. They honor Mary and her memory and her ministry, and they look to do even more with it in the future.

One day, it is hoped that it will again be all that it once was and more.

Much remains to build upon.

As Mary no doubt wills it, so do her faithful keepers of the flame!

A band of loving and relentless volunteers will never stop singing the same old songs. Pilgrims all sing a pilgrim's song on a pilgrim's journey.

Steeled by Mary Varick, they lift high the cross.

Today and tomorrow, they lift high the cross.

For sanctification, they lift high the cross.

*Gloria tibi, Domine!*

## Chapter 8 Placeholders

- "We must," my Aunt Mary said very often, "help Jesus carry his cross. Oh, how privileged we are to be able to carry the cross for Christ." We are all, she insisted, invited to be *Simons and Veronicas*—invited to bear witness to the passion of Christ in how we conduct ourselves in our everyday lives.

- But the very fact that this is happening is all the more reason for the Church to look to and to celebrate the life and service of Mary Varick, who served yet another contingent of outcasts—the disabled—with unbridled love. It is all the more reason to focus upon a member of the laity who was entirely holy and of God, upon one of the people's own whose life bridges today's controversial divides. In Mary, the faithful will be powerfully reminded that holiness and sanctity are not the province of the religious alone, but rather of all the faithful.

- Just consider the formula of this second of our six notations, the theology of suffering—out of their disability and/or suffering, one sacrifices all and grace, redemption, and inevitable joy are extracted. It is a spiritually transformative process in which the disabled and suffering invite God to be with them and to take their pain in exchange for grace and for goodness.

- The point is—notation 5—that you cannot get Mary Varick—that you will neither know nor understand her, unless you know these three ports of call to God for her— Saint Joseph's Oratory, Sainte-Anne-de-Beaupre, and Our Lady of the Cape, three shrines that were as much home to Mary Varick as were Jersey City and Newark, three shrines that were woven into and buried within the deepest recesses of her heart.

- Some, in search of God, walk the Way of the El Camino de Santiago in the Pyrenees, some go to the Holy Land to explore the paths that Jesus walked, and still others go where they can be surrounded by the great Renaissance art of Rome, but those in Mary's First Saturday Club go to embrace the "inner circle" and to do good works.

- I write because Mary still has gifts to give and not to advance a cause that I absolutely believe she has already won. Of course, the recognition of the church and the faithful would be wonderful, but humility and goodness and grace and holiness are not the products of glory or honor or well-deserved recognition. They are their own prize, and Mary has them in abundance.

- "You have been His love and compassion, His Sunshine of Joy, His hope of eternal happiness to so many, many souls, and it is only natural that in being so close to Jesus' heart, you must share the pain and the loneliness. You are all right, Mary—it is only the kiss of Jesus."—Mother Teresa to Mary

- Were there no Bread of Life and no kiss of Christ, there could be no life or light in a world where such madness threatens to break us.

- But it does not break us, because faith never succumbs to madness or even to mass-indifferent murder.

- It does not break us because the promise of redemption is ours, and the Bread of Life is there for us, in the Eucharist, and Christ's arms are ever and always open. No matter the darkness, there is always light. "You are all right, Mary—it is only the Cross of Christ. As Billie suffered and as Mary and Teresa lived and died in the suffering of others and as these children were taken in a rapid and sudden and appalling fury and in that moment to come when our own bodies will break, there must be—there will be—the kiss of Christ. To be worthy is but to lay our selfish tendencies down and to give ourselves away in faith and in love.

- "God is good to you even though your child is going through this again and again, sharing in Christ's own passion. Look up, Mary, and see only Jesus in your suffering child."—Mother Teresa to Mary

- In how they lived and how they loved and how they served, they were truly cut from the same cloth.

- "Among all of my acquaintances," he continued, "this woman of the cross, this joyful wheelchair-bound lady has surpassed any teaching I've had on the meaning of Jesus' passion and Jesus' love for the faltering followers of an unbounded hope in the Great Reward promised by Jesus to those who allow themselves to love and to love without counting the cost."—Bishop Peter Sutton on Mary

- And so to the "Lord's Sunshine of Joy" and "witness to Jesus' passion and Jesus' love," we add the profoundest of all possible titles—that of "an intimate friend of Jesus."

- This is how the holy people in her life saw her. This is exactly who and what she was and it clarifies and moves and astounds. "In all my life as a priest, I have never met a person who seemed so intimate with God. She talked about HIM as you would about your best friend. As I wrote in the "Foreword" to her second book, *Not Without Tears*: "This book leaves me with a memory of love that permeates each chapter, each line. I envy her the intimacy that she has reached with Our Divine Savior. And I know that one of the great graces that I will have to render account for at the end of my life will be to have known Mary Varick so well. One cannot come near a fire without feeling its warmth. As such, one cannot approach Mary Varick without feeling the warmth of her love for God. It is a precious grace to have known Mary."

• "The heavy crosses that weigh on each of us (handicap) have been placed there by Christ Himself, and the only element of choice which is ours is whether we will sanctify our sufferings for the love of God, or whether we will squander our chance for sainthood, in useless complaints and discontent. One does not have to die to feel God's nearness."—Father Jacques Rinfret on Mary

• Again, it must be noted that we struggle with miracles and have trouble accepting that which was an impossibility just the moment before. So it was with Mary Varick in 1951 and so it was with Mary's Lauren in 1990. Suddenly, the cancers were gone, in and through Mary, by God alone, who is the source of all that is miraculous.

# 9

# A Placeholder

There is no real ninth chapter, but you are not to consider yourself cheated, as this ninth chapter was only and ever intended to be a symbolic placeholder.

We needed nine because we wanted to pointedly and uniquely celebrate Mary Varick's devotion to the Trinity and to the number *3* and the number *9*, which is after all, to be exalted, because it is three times three.

God the Father and God the Son and God the Holy Spirit!

Mary and Bill made a nine-day novena to the Sacred Heart to ask what God wanted of and for them, and when they determined that it was marriage, they then began their life together on the June 4, Feast Day of the Sacred Heart.

They came of age when nine-day novenas to saints and to the Blessed Mother and to the Holy Trinity and more were commonplace. The ninth day or that third three was the rounded or squared culmination of great devotion.

So when it happened that Mary Varick journeyed with her cancer to Sainte-Anne-de-Beaupre in that remarkable summer of 1951, it took three days to get there, as she was sick and needed rest. Then, they spent three glorious days in the actual arms of Saint Anne and the Blessed Mother at the basilica when unbeknownst to all, her very world had been turned upside down or, we should rather say, right side up. Then finally, she, her Bill, and her brother Bud spent another three days making their way back home, as they had mechanical problems with the car. Fortuitously, the greatest journey in her life had been nine days in all.

Nine days it was to Beaupre and to miracles and to thirty-eight more years and to the crystallization of her *theology of suffering* and to the birth of The Our Lady of Fatima First Saturday Club.

Nine days to new beginnings and to rich purpose and to sanctity.

An extraordinary novena it had been and will forever be.

Her very life had been a novena.

Consequently, all pilgrimages of Mary Varick's would forever be targeted for nine days.

Just another series of novenas!

Nine days at the Cape along the Saint Lawrence and atop Mount Royal and on the trails atop her "heaven on a hillside."

And so we here, however briefly, by way of a placeholder, celebrate Mary's devotion to her beloved Trinity and to all things three and to three times three and to a novena and to all of her pilgrimages or nine-day vacations with God.

For hers was a life that had been a sustaining vacation with God.

# Afterword

It was Wednesday, July 29, 1987, and it was about two in the afternoon. We had just disembarked from the bus at the shrine of Notre Dame du Cap in Cap de la Madeleine (Our Lady of the Cape), and we were taking the luggage off and lifting or carrying our disabled brothers and sisters from the bus. Normally, I would be very active in that effort, as I had been since I started coming on this pilgrimage as a teenager ten years earlier. This year, however, I had something else to do. You see, having been ordained the previous November, this was my first time coming as a priest.

And while I would continue to happily contribute to the physical work of transporting the disabled on and off the buses for many years to come, I was excited to be meeting with Mary Varick and Father Noel, the director of the shrine. We were about to schedule our activities for the next few days. Monsignor Paul Bochicchio, then Father Paul, was not with us as he had accompanied the group on its trip to Israel earlier that summer.

Well, when Father Noel walked into Mary's room, she startled him, her daughter Mary Pisaniello, and myself by forcefully pointing at him and yelling, "See, see! This is one of those brats that you never wanted around here." You see, as director of the shrine, Father Noel had often expressed some frustration that the teenagers who came up with Mary's group often didn't measure up to his definition of pious pilgrims.

On the contrary, Mary Varick always saw the value of having young people on her pilgrimages—both for the benefit of those with disabilities as well as for themselves. She never gave up on the young people who she came in touch with. Whether they were of her own family or among the legions of often troubled teenagers who came to Canada over the years to help with the disabled. Even when they caused trouble or embarrassed her, she never lost faith in the youth in her life.

At the heart of the essence of Mary Varick is an intense and deep love of Jesus Christ. At the heart of this love is an appreciation of His Cross. You've read in these pages about her abiding theology of suffering. If one understands this, then one understands Catholicism, Mary Varick, and this book. We Catholics are often misperceived as having an unhealthy attraction to suffering, but that is far from the truth. We rather understand suffering, when it comes our way, to have great value. It enables the person of faith to participate in the cross of Jesus Christ.

Mary Varick lived this journey her whole life. Very blessed, she believed, that she had been granted, as she so often said, a place at the foot of the cross. Her suffering was used as means to serve Christ and his Church, by first radiating with great love her love for her God and secondly, by enabling others, including her First Saturday Family, to share the same journey.

Rich Fritzky is not only her storyteller but also the inheritor of her theology of suffering. Ironically, I first met Rich in the summer of 1977 on my very first pilgrimage to Canada with Mary and the First Saturday Club. I was only sixteen years old. We both were helping with the lifting and moving of the disabled. As the years evolved, I continued by going to Canada for most of these past thirty-seven years, the last twenty-eight as a cochaplain with Msgr. Bochicchio. Rich would on occasion join us, but marriage and a huge family took most of his time. However, the spirit of his Aunt Mary came upon him in a very special way when an illness significantly disabled him. It is this spirit that led Rich to write this book. In my opinion, there could be no worthier author.

Fr. Kevin Carter
Pastor, St. Margaret of Cortona, Little Ferry, NJ
Chaplain, Our Lady of Fatima First Saturday Club

# A Letter

June 1, 2014

Dear Richard,

Your cousin, Mary Pisaniello, brought me up to date regarding the manuscript that you have completed about the life and the sacred ministry of Mary Varick, for which you are seeking a publisher. I wish you the best of luck in that effort.

You already know of my great admiration for Mary and her intimacy with our Lord. I have always hoped that someone would attempt to capture and do justice to her service to the disabled and to God, as you have done with *A Pilgrim's Song*.

I was privileged to meet Mary and Bill and their pilgrim family or "God's inner circle" in 1961, the year that I was ordained to the priesthood. We became and remained close friends for the twenty-nine years between that promising summer of '61 and her death in that equally promising summer of '89.

Her life of suffering strengthened all of us, and I am delighted to know that many more might have the same grace showered upon them when *A Pilgrim's Song* is published. What a cross section of people were touched by Mary's life from her own family, to her pilgrimage family, to the young people who cared for the pilgrims who needed assistance, to the friends of all ages for whom the pilgrimages were a moving and purposeful experience, to her faithful "Simons and Veronicas." I think of the folks who went as far as Russia with her on behalf of a "suffering Christ" and of the many who remained faithful to their vocation of suffering because of Mary's example, love, and prayers.

I just want to suggest that this is a blessing worth repeating, so I am delighted to think that Mary's profound *theology of suffering* will again become familiar to many more friends and families of all ages in the days to come.

Thanks, Richard. I look forward to some good news real soon, as it will be so good reading from yet another author with a fresh perspective and some much-needed "good news," twenty-five years after our Mary Varick celebrated her own Mass of the Resurrection.

I want to assure you of my prayers and encouragement.

Yours has been a tough journey personally, and I wish you the best of blessings.

Sincerely in Our Risen Lord and Mary Immaculate,

+Peter OMI
Most Rev. Peter A. Sutton, OMI
Archbishop Emeritus of Keewatin-Le Pas (Canada)
460, 1st Street
Richelieu I QC
J3L 4B5 Canada

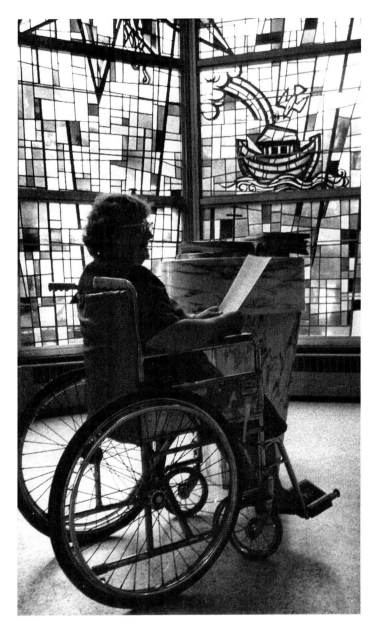

A silhouette of Mary Varick where she was most at
home besides the stained glass of a Church.

A small group photo of some of the early pilgrims in 1955 at the Cape. The group includes 3 of her children, Barbara and Mary immediately behind Mary and Jimmy with the black jacket and tie in the center, as well as the author's Grandfather and Aunt Helen Fritzky and Mary's Bill Varick in the rear. The author's Great Aunt Anna Fritzky also is pictured in the white dress on the right.

One of the earlier pilgrimages. Photo shot at the base of Saint Anne de Beaupre.

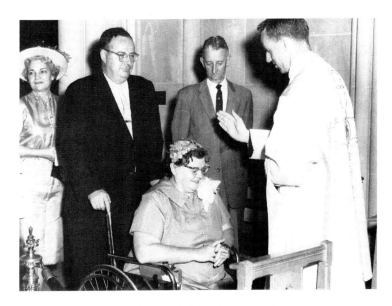

Father Francis Cassidy (or Skip), Mary's younger brother gives his first priestly blessing after his ordination in May of 1962. The 3 original pilgrims in 1951, Bud Cassidy and Mary and Bill Varick are the recipients.

One of the disabled being carried aboard when they regularly flew Trans Canada Airlines to Quebec City or Montreal.

In this 1963 photo, Mary is 2nd from the left in first row. Immediately behind her are the author's next door neighbors, Ed and Mary McDonald and immediately behind them are his Uncle Joe Cassidy and Freddie Vander Hoeven, a victim of cerebral palsy, whose smile and sweetness would warm the hearts of his fellow pilgrims for some 50 years, up until he passed in 2011. The inimitable and beautiful Flossie is pictured in the center

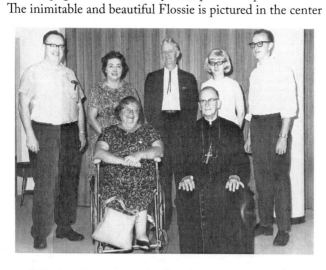

Mary with Bishop Stanton, an Auxiliary Bishop of the Archdiocese of Newark and one of her devoted pilgrims in front. Bud and Anne Cassidy, Bill Varick, Mary (Varick) Pisaniello, and Jim Varick (from l to r in rear)

Bill and Mary Varick with their friend, Brother Allie.

Bill and Mary at home in Jersey City display-
ing the image of their beloved Saint Anne.

This is the famous immediate family photograph at the Cape in 1976. It features the 3 suffering Mothers in the center, Billie (Varick) Adriance on the stretcher, the daughter and granddaughter, Agnes Cassidy, the grandmother, and Mary Varick, the mother in the wheel chairs.

Mary and Bill with their friend, Bishop Stanton.

Here is the group that went to Russia in 1977. Mary is 3rd from the right in front. And there in the center, in the Saint Peter's garb, next to Father Paul, is a young Kevin Carter, the volunteer who would become priest.

Then Barbara and Laura Pisaniello flank their Grandmother, Mary Varick. Mary Anne Adriance, today's Co-Director is imme-diately behind her Grandmother. Among those on her right and your left are Mary and Bruno Pisaniello, Joe and Dot Cassidy, and the author's parents, Rose and Frank Fritzky. Pictured on your right are Agnes (Cassidy) Duffy, Father Rinfret, Maureen (Cassidy) Newell, Mike Adriance, and Father Don Arel.

Father Don Arel and Father Jacques Rinfret with our ever smiling Mary.

Mass at the 12ᵗʰ Station (The Crucifixion) upon
the grounds of Our Lady of the Cape.

Father Jacques Rinfret gives out Communion.

This is the Immediate family group photo outside the Old Shrine at the Cape in either 87' or 88'. Pictured in front are the author's Mom, Rose Fritzky, Laura and Billie Pisaniello, Mary, Jerry Sheehan, Barbara Pisaniello, and Maryanne Adriance. In the rear are Mary and Bruno Pisaniello, Mike and Patty Adriance, Dot and Joe Cassidy, the author's father, Frank Fritzky, and Anne Cassidy.

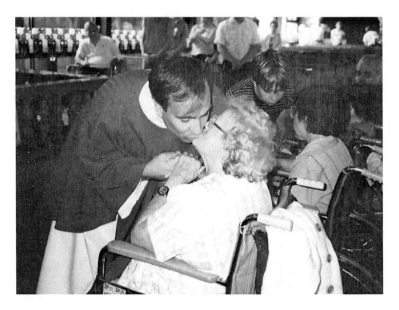

After mass in 1987, Father Kevin Carter greets Mary
in the Old Shrine at Our Lady of the Cape

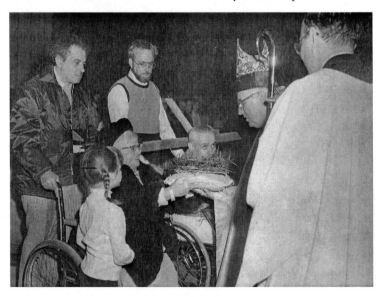

Mary and Howie Daniels present Offertory gifts to the Archbishop
of Newark. Behind them are Bruno Pisaniello and Jim Varick

A 1989 shot of Father Kevin Carter with Freddie Vander Hoeven, a victim of cerebral palsy who kept Mary's pilgrims laughing for more than 50 years.

This is the huge family group photo in front of the Basilica of St. Anne de Beaupre upon the 40th Anniversary of Mary's miracle in July of 1991. They are, in front, flanked by today's Monsignor Paul Bochiccio and Mike Adriance and his child. In between are all things Cassidy, Varick, Murray, Adriance, Duffy, Pisaniello, and more. The author's Mom, Rose Fritzky, is 4th from the left on the bottom

This, we believe, is the 50th Anniversary family group photo in the Immaculate Conception Chapel at Saint Anne de Beaupre.

Another special family photo in front of the altar in the Old Shrine at the Cape. Joan Murray, the author's sister and one of today's co-directors, is pictured (2nd from the right in the front row).

Hank Colling, the beloved friend who urged the author to write this story, is pictured here on the right before the main altar in the Basilica of Saint Anne de Beaupre.

Waiting to board the boat for a cruise down the Saint Lawrence River in 2006 are a number of the young "Simons & Veronicas" or volunteers. Pictured behind on the far left is Monsignor Paul Bochiccio.

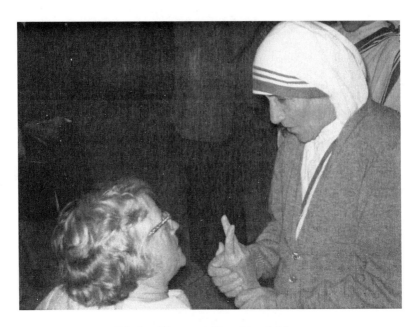

Mother Teresa and her friend, Mary

Worthy of another look.

And still another

The beautiful Flossie Oates

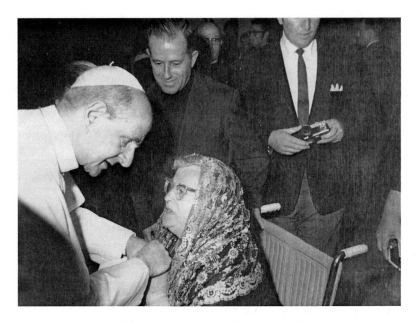

Pope Paul VI holding hands with our Mary.

Mary Varick and Jerry Sheehan with Pope
John Paul II at Saint Peter's Basilica.

In 2012, at Saint Joachim's, just north of Beaupre, Father Frank
Fano, 25 years a volunteer on the pilgrimages, says his first mass on
one. Father Kevin is to his right and Monsignor Paul to his left.

Rich Fritzky, the author pictured with a 2009
'Veronica', the beautiful Julian Franklin